APPROACHES TO ARCHAEOLOGY

To my mother and father

APPROACHES TO ARCHAEOLOGY

Peter J. Fowler

St. Martin's Press
New York

© 1977 Peter J. Fowler
All rights reserved. For information, write:
St. Martin's Press, Inc., 175 Fifth Avenue, New York, N.Y. 10010
Printed in Great Britain
Library of Congress Catalog Card Number: 77–81910

ISBN: 0-312-04665-0

First published in the United States of America in 1977

CONTENTS

ILLUSTRATIONS

Illustrations

Plates

FOREWORD

Stuart Piggott's *Approach to Archaeology* was published in 1959. It has not been surpassed since as an introduction for 'the beginner who wishes to know something about the foundations of a subject in which he has become vaguely interested, and especially to those early in their intellectual career at school or in the university'. Professor Piggott, accepting that his book needed bringing up to date, suggested two years ago that a new book written by someone else might be more appropriate than a revision of his work. Hence *Approaches to Archaeology* was commissioned by the publishers of *Approach to Archaeology* as a successor or sequel rather than a replacement, since the *Approach* has a permanent place in British archaeological literature. In view of this pedigree and the unlikelihood of the same publisher producing two 'classics' on the same topic within two decades, the commission, I would add, was accepted with considerable diffidence.

My *Approaches* makes no conscious attempt to copy or update the *Approach* except in its title which reflects the publishers' continuing interest. For practical purposes, rather have I taken account of Graham Webster's *Practical Archaeology* (2nd rev. ed. 1974) and Kenneth Hudson's *Industrial Archaeology* (3rd rev. ed. 1976), with which the present book forms a trilogy in the publishers' eyes. Though there are some areas of common interest between my *Approaches* and the other two, I have deliberately not covered most of their contents and in any case have not tried to be comprehensive.

In some respects, archaeology has changed a lot since 1959, as it happens my first year as a professional archaeologist. It is less approachable for one thing, yet commands if anything greater public interest and certainly more resources. It is more complex, yet its basic principles and popular appeal remain simple; it is less confident of its objectives and results but is intellectually as stimulating and technically more sophisticated. I hope these pages reflect the concerns, uncertainties and optimism of their time, as much as Piggott's *Approach* reflects the 1950s. Like him, I have tried to keep my *Approaches* straightforward, not least because I have had in mind the adult 'who has become vaguely interested' as well as the schoolboy and undergraduate. Nevertheless, this is a subjective essay in which I have tried to write at an introductory level about some of the principles, recent developments and present trends of archaeology and its practitioners, about the why rather than the how of a confused yet dynamic discipline. I confess to knowing less about this now, as my *Approaches* makes clear, than I did when the *Approach* made it all so clear to me seventeen years ago.

I acknowledge the tolerance of my 'Tuesday morning ladies' who suffered the labour pains of *Approaches* in the guise of a University Extra-Mural course in the Autumn term, 1975. The text was revised and updated six months later. It was written without direct help from anyone but clearly I owe an enormous general debt to all my tutors, whether they be nominally my students, colleagues, critics or friends. Mrs P. A. Lees and Mrs V. Camp prepared a virtually flawless typescript which my wife Elizabeth, in addition to coping as is the wifely lot at times of husbandly distraction, read and indexed. To all, and for my accommodating, academic base in the Department of Extra-Mural Studies, I am indeed grateful.

University of Bristol   *Friday, 13th August, 1976*

ABBREVIATIONS USED

Agric. Hist. Rev.	Agricultural History Review
Antiq. J.	Antiquaries Journal
Archaeol. J.	Archaeological Journal
Bull. Bristol Archaeol. Rsch. Gp.	Bulletin of the Bristol Archaeological Research Group
C.B.A.	Council for British Archaeology
Cornish Archaeol.	Cornish Archaeology
D.o.E.	Department of the Environment
Medieval Archaeol.	Medieval Archaeology
Proc. Devon Archaeol. Soc.	Proceedings of the Devonshire Archaeological Society
Proc. Prehist. Soc.	Proceedings of the Prehistoric Society
Proc. Soc. Antiq. Scot.	Proceedings of the Society of Antiquaries of Scotland
R.C.H.M.	Royal Commission on Historical Monuments
ROB	Berichten van de Rijksdienst voor het Oudheidkundig Bodemonderzoek
Somerset Archaeol. Natur. Hist.	(Proceedings of the) Somerset Archaeological and Natural History Society
Trans. Bristol Gloucestershire Archaeol. Soc.	Transactions of the Bristol and Gloucestershire Archaeological Society
Wilts. Archaeol. Natur. Hist. Mag.	Wiltshire Archaeological and Natural History Magazine

1
APPROACHING ARCHAEOLOGY

'... the past, though of its nature alterable, never had been altered' George Orwell, *1984* (1949)

The study, or knowledge, of man-made things is a strict definition of the word archaeology. Though much of the rest of this book will be devoted to discussing the inadequacy of this definition in modern terms, it is a useful starting point in approaching the subject because straight away it reminds us that archaeology itself has a history. It would be ridiculous to study the history of 'man-made things' without appreciating that the nature and objectives of that study have themselves changed through time; that our objectives now are different from those a century ago, indeed twenty and even ten years ago, and that present approaches to the past will be out-dated well within the working life-times of today's practising archaeologists. So there is no finality: the subject of archaeology, like the subject it studies, witnesses a continual process of change, for every age produces two archaeologies, one from itself to the future and one from the past to itself.

The variety of approaches

The variety of the archaeological approaches to the past needs to be stressed at the outset. Not so long ago a whole symposium was needed to explore the variety of *Approaches to History*.[1] Its contents listed Political History, Economic, Social, Universal and Local History, Historical Geography, The History of Art, The History of Science and, just squeezing in by virtue of a relationship with a particular sort of documentary evidence, Archaeology and Place-Names. This book is no symposium, but the present diversity of approaches to archaeology is suggested by a selection of some of the adjectives (or nouns used adjectively) in use today before the word

[1] H.P.R. Finberg (ed.), *Approaches to History* (1962).

13

'archaeology': prehistoric, Roman, Classical, medieval, post-medieval, historical, modern, current, contemporary; world, American, South Western, European, Near Eastern, Mediterranean, Old World; urban, rural, agrarian, settlement, church, marine, nautical, underwater, industrial; local, regional, landscape, practical, field, aerial; armchair; total; salvage, rescue, motorway, public, conservation, community, popular; amateur, professional; new, traditional, scientific, theoretical, environmental, experimental; and, in some ways my favourite for its ambiguity, social archaeology. There is then no shortage of approaches to archaeology. This plethora of specialisms within it really represents an explosion of interest and activity over the last 25 years and presumably says something about post-War society's attitude towards its past.

Attitudes to the past and its study

Attitudes to the study of the past have themselves changed and are changing still; and these also reflect attitudes to the past itself. The past, like the poor, is always with us, and a curiosity about it is a common characteristic of human societies. But an 'attitude' towards the past need not necessarily promote or even demand the study of the past in any disciplined sense: a society might well prefer simply to receive and perpetuate a traditional view of its past without further enquiry (Pl. I.1). In such a case we can recognise that the past, and the attitude towards it among the society which is its product, is primarily serving a social function irrespective of the historical accuracy of the version of the past that is being received. This point is well worth stressing at an early stage for it is a common, if often unconscious, assumption by students of the past that there is an unquestionable validity in seeking 'historical truth' or at least in producing more, and more accurate, information. In the interests of scholarship, perhaps this is so; socially it may not be desired or even be desirable at all. A traditional view of the past may well be a vital bond of social or political cohesion—communal cement,—which could easily be weakened by academic research. So although archaeology in Britain, for example, derives from the usually implicit premise that more is better, this basis involves an assumption which, theoretically there and actually elsewhere, can be questioned. The study of the past can apparently take place in the abstract as it were, just as a 'good thing' in itself; in fact, in that its practitioners are

I.I.1 'To receive and perpetuate a traditional view of its past', symbolised here by Boadicea ('resistance to foreigners'), Big Ben ('imperial greatness') and the Houses of Parliament ('our island democratic tradition'). The new light thrown on Boudicca, the British Empire and Parliamentary history by research and changing social attitudes since the heyday of Victorian culture matters little to the intellectually casual if genuinely responsive interest expressed every year by millions of visitors who see and, in many cases, accept past attitudes to the past fossilized in these structures. As 'monuments', they are also now archaeological evidence of a past culture.

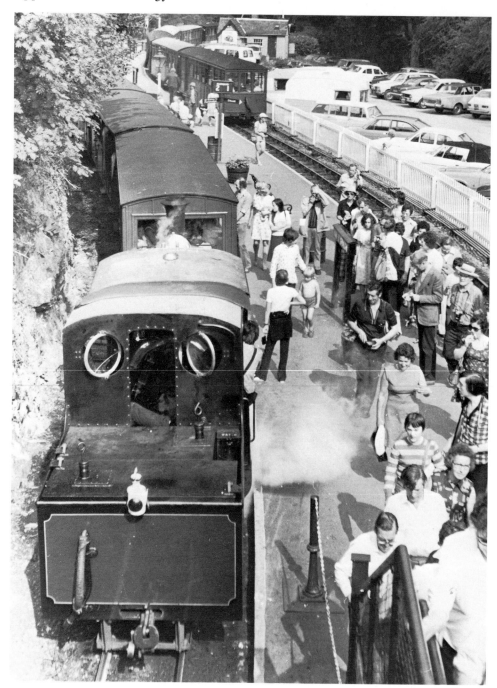

I.2 'The cult of steam-driven machinery . . .' Dduallt Station on the Ffestiniog Narrow Gauge Railway, Gwynfedd, Wales, September, 1975.

themselves products of society working in a social framework—and even ivory towers have to be supported,—that study is conditioned by social attitudes towards that past and towards its exploitation. In this context, the study of the past is a form of exploitation, of making use of something that is there intellectually as well as materially.

Societies' attitudes towards the past and the study of it are then a conditioning factor in the investigation of that past; and these attitudes change through time and space. That they do so can of course be in part the result of investigation itself, a phenomenon very clearly illustrated today. In America, for example, recent legislation (which presumably expresses society's wishes in some way) arising from the development of a general environmental concern is producing a profound effect on the rationale, organisation and methodology of archaeology itself.[2] Such legislation also in part reflects archaeology's achievements in the last two decades in influencing American society's attitudes towards its past. In this particular case, phrases like 'the rehabilitation of the Indian' may exaggerate but, in relation to the American Indians' past, they contain at least an element of reality in reflecting a complex relationship between political pressures, changing social attitudes and academic research.

Even if we do not fully understand why social attitudes to the past change, we can note these changes occurring in the past. Indeed, archaeology itself provides evidence of such changes in prehistoric and undocumented contexts. A simple illustration comes from Roman Britain where we see what can be interpreted as a social attitude towards the past (whatever it 'means') being expressed by the use of second millennium BC burial mounds both as depositories of the newly-dead and as sources of antiquities (an interesting but incidental point here is whether the latter exploitation was the result of accidental finds made during the former socially acceptable use). In Egypt in the second millennium BC itself an attitude, for whatever reason, towards the glories of the past is expressed by the later, smaller pyramids apparently aping the politically expedient and religiously sincere modes of royal burial long after the social and economic base to support the realities of such practices had changed. Perhaps similarly, we see today the cult of steam-driven machinery in many a volunteer-run railway line and traction-engine rally and it may be too superficial to dismiss the phenomenon merely as nostalgia in a society dominated by the internal combustion engine (Pl. I.2); while, for reasons we need not explore now, many a school text-book in use in Britain still projects the fragments of a shattered Victorian, Christian yet materialistic view of the imperial past hardly justified by other contemporary attitudes.

On the other hand, changes in social attitudes to the past can be influenced by philosophic concepts rather than arise from field research. Sir Isaiah Berlin, for example, has recently made us much more aware of Vico's contribution to the concept

---

[2] The seminal book is C.R. McGimsey, *Public Archaeology* (1972), followed by W.D. Lipe and A.J. Lindsay, Jr. (eds.), *Proceedings of the 1974 Cultural Resource Management Conference, Federal Center, Denver, Colorado* (Museum of Northern Arizona Technical Series no. 14, September, 1974). See also *Antiquity* 50 (1976), 230–2.

of the past in west European thought. Vico, an eighteenth century Neapolitan philosopher, taught that history is created in men's minds 'as a collective social experience extended through time'. As a reviewer remarked, our sense of historical perspective goes back no further than the eighteenth century—'the pastness of the past is a modern discovery'.[3]

We can also see that different values are attached to the past as attitudes towards it change. And indeed, while we can identify consensus attitudes among various societies at different times in the past, at any one time of course there are likely to be different views within any given society challenging the consensus, or socially accepted, attitude. This point sees a discussion of archaeology and history trembling on the edge of a philosophical abyss of fairly large dimensions, and we should perhaps withdraw in good, if empirical, order; but such a position makes the point that while the activities of historians and archaeologists may seem irrelevant normally, and expendable in times of economic or political stress, in as far as these activities are, in general and in the long term, an expression of society's attitudes towards its past, they both represent and should fulfil what appears to be a fairly basic social function. On the whole, society has a curiosity about its past although many individuals within a society may not only be uninterested but may positively regard themselves as untouched by the past (they are wrong, of course). Granted that, however, the social value of the past varies according to what society itself regards as its changing needs. Rome, for example, did not regard itself as in any way beholden to the preliterate barbarian past of those societies which it sought to encompass whereas, in the early medieval Europe which covered the areas formerly occupied by those barbarian societies, there was a quite conscious harking back, politically and legally, to Roman imperial precepts which had by then become part of Europe's cultural heritage. Similarly, in later medieval times, and again in the eighteenth and nineteenth centuries, educated European society looked to a Classical imperial past, now modelled to suit changed needs, first for intellectual refreshment and stimulation, then for inspiration in the fine arts and finally for political guidance and even moral justification during a new but brief phase of imperialistic activity. It was recently quite interesting to see how the same source, despite another century of research, was once again raided in the interests of promoting the case for Europe's off-shore island State participating in the completely different concept of internal continental economic union. Clearly the value of Rome to Europe has varied through time and with place, a point easily made by comparison of the writings and speeches of Hobbes, Gibbon, Mussolini and Heath. Though this is a common case to cite, it can be used to argue further that, if there is indeed such a direct connection as occasion demands between a society's past and the use made of it by that society or by an individual in the society, then there could be some relevance in the disciplined study of

[3] I. Berlin, *Vico and Herder: Two Studies in the History of Ideas* (1976), reviewed by J. Rosselli, *The Guardian*, 26 Feb. 1976.

that past. Immediate academic benefits apart, at the very least the results of such study offer a wider range of choice to the exploiters of the past.

Archaeology and History

One, albeit debatable, approach to archaeology, is then that its place is in the humanities and its role in the wide field of historical research. From this, it can be argued that its function is to complement, indeed to be subservient to, 'real' i.e. documentary, history. This argument was stated, for example, in 1723 as follows: 'The Main and Principal Helps to walk through the dark Recesses of Time, are the testimonies of unexceptionable RECORDS ... There are other Things, as ... Erections, Monuments, & Ruins: Aedifices & Inscriptions: The Appelations of Places ... which accord here and there little strinkling Lights ... which we ought likewise to scan ... and from them extract such Secondary Supplies and Assistances, as may help to fill up, and enlighten those obscure chasms and interlinary Spaces of Time, which interpose the brighter Stroaks, and more undeniable Certainties of RECORDS.'[4] The 1976 version of this viewpoint runs: '... a historian, whose discipline, mercifully, confines him to the consideration of record and literary evidence ... That the contributors to this book are not exactly the parthenogenetic offspring of Clio may be shown from several instances, and most revealingly by their regarding of archaeological finds ... as admissible evidence.'[5] Splendid prejudice, of course, splendidly expressed, but it undermines one's hope that history broadens the minds of at least its practitioners. Fortunately, there is no need to follow this particular hare much further since the work of W. G. Hoskins, M. W. Beresford, and Henry Loyn, to mention but three of the most eminent economic historians who have seen the archaeological light, shows it to be but a sugar mouse; and David Dymond has written a whole book on Archaeology and History, albeit without being entirely sympathetic to the former.[6] The argument can of course be reversed and needless to say an archaeologist has done so: in his inaugural lecture at the University of Southampton, Professor Cunliffe reviewed the complementary interests which could focus on one piece of landscape—geography, historical geography, economic geography, history, geomorphology, sociology,—and concluded 'But *all* of these points are of direct interest and significance to the archaeologist—they are an essential part of the study of man in his environment, which is the prime object of our discipline. In addition, the archaeologist projects his study back as far as possible into the past, well beyond the written record. Strictly, then, I suppose one could make the debatable point that *history* is one aspect of the more recent part of the archaeological record.'[7] The historical function of archaeology is clearly

---

[4] Quoted in R. Jessup, *Curiosities of British Archaeology* (1961), 183.
[5] Review article by E. Kerridge of *Studies of Field Systems in the British Isles* (1973), in *Agric. Hist. Rev.* 24 (1976), 49.
[6] D. Dymond, *Archaeology and History: a plea for reconciliation* (1974).
[7] B. W. Cunliffe, *The Past Tomorrow* (1970), 6.

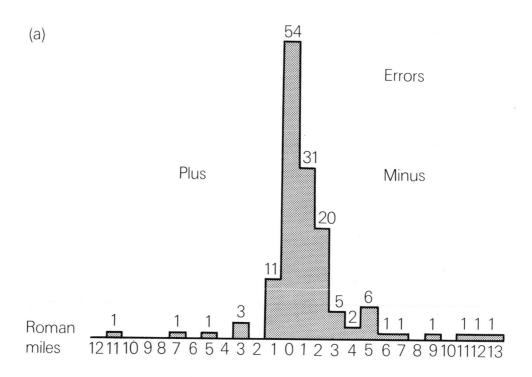

(a)

1.1 'The idea of archaeology . . . is firmly rooted in an historical context'. The figure illustrates two very different examples: (a) a histogram expresses the results of a textual analysis of the British Section of the Antonine Itinerary, a much-debated Roman 'route-book' of crucial importance to an understanding of the geography and topography of Roman Britain. The errors in the mileages of the surviving documentary evidence have significant implications for archaeological fieldwork e.g. in locating places mentioned, and in interpretation e.g. in naming sites found (*cf. Britannia* 6, 1975, 76–101); (b) The Iceni are known from contemporary documentary evidence as a late prehistoric tribe in E. Anglia. Archaeologically it is known that they produced a distinctive coinage in the century before the Roman conquest. This distribution map of where and in what form these known coins have been found also expresses a spatial relationship at the very least implying the general location of the Icenian territory.

(b)

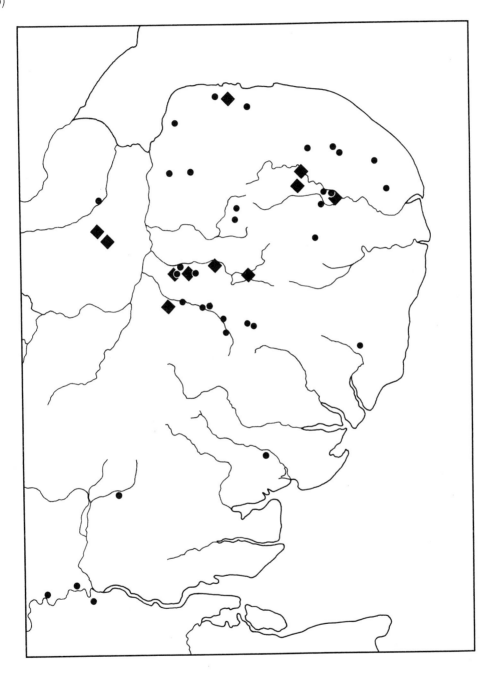

◆ Hoards   • Isolated finds

contentious but the point here is that, whether or not archaeology eventually finds a satisfactory academic niche, the idea of archaeology and its development in Europe is firmly rooted in an historical context (fig. 1.1). In America, the background is different (p. 104) and both there and elsewhere an alternative view of archaeology would now be argued in some quarters.

Archaeology in its own right

In simple terms, the argument is based on the premise that archaeological evidence has a validity in its own right, irrespective of its date and of the presence or otherwise of documentary evidence—such factors are irrelevant. It follows from such a premise that meaningful, relevant, useful, valid—whatever adjective is most appropriate,— deductions can be drawn from accurate observation of artefacts of any sort and date, and of the relationships between them and between them and their environment. An existing town, for example, can be examined and, irrespective of any documentary evidence about it, a perfectly valid body of information about it can be assembled relating to its total physical and environmental context; and such information can be interpreted quite legitimately to provide a 'model' of that town as a cultural expression through time. Whether that 'model' coincides or conflicts with documentary evidence does not affect the validity of the evidence or of the archaeologically-legitimate inferences drawn from it. '(If) archaeological data ... constitute a well–defined set within the general field of knowledge, then it follows that archaeology can be considered as a subject in its own right of comparable status to both history and anthropology ... archaeology is concerned with developing description and explanation of archaeological data in terms of itself. This does not exclude the possibility of calling in anthropological, or historical, or any other form of explanation as required, but it emphatically denies the right of any one of these to act as a controlling model.'[8] It is only fair to say that such an approach, though promoted with intellectual force, has not yet exactly swept the board amongst the British archaeological establishment, let alone amongst other students of the past.

Surely—and here I reflect an Arts-based approach just as the last quotation reflects the Cambridge Tripos,—the objective of archaeology, like history, is to try and understand past human behaviour. To achieve this, unlike history, it primarily studies material culture. The emphasis in its approach is therefore on surviving physical evidence and on the relationships between such evidence in space and time. Those relationships are themselves as much evidence as the material which is related. Furthermore, relationships between culture and environment are central to such a study and, in view of the ultimate objective, the archaeologist must, as the historian should, draw on all other sources of relevant and available evidence including the documentary. Nevertheless, as we shall discuss in Chapter 3, archaeology's distinctive

[8] D. Browne, *Principles and Practice in Modern Archaeology* (1975), 2.

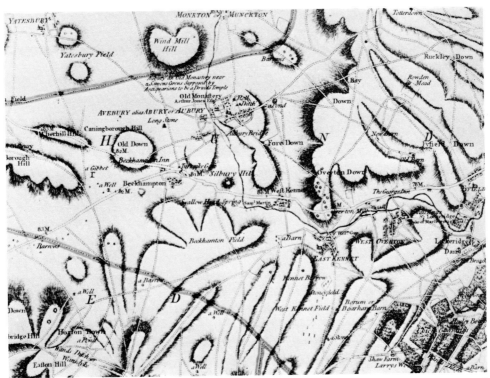

1.2 The Avebury area as depicted on Andrews' and Drury's *Map of Wiltshire* (1773), a good example of pre-Ordnance Survey cartography illustrating numerous field monuments and the general style in which the first O.S. maps were produced *c.*30 years later. The map, by representing features of its contemporary landscape in detail e.g. village morphology, and usually with great accuracy, is now a major source of information about land-use in the mid/late eighteenth century and, by careful extrapolation backwards, in earlier times too.

activity is excavation as a controlled and highly complex exercise in data-recovery. Its other functions in the field and indoors are essential but are held in common with other disciplines.

The development of archaeology

Once archaeology is accepted as being motivated by a wish to contribute to knowledge about the past, we can then discount as archaeological most of the pre-modern activity involving cultural material. The documented diggings into burial mounds, in medieval times for example, were certainly motivated by a desire for loot, not for the furtherance of Man's knowledge of mankind; it would seem reasonable to assume that undocumented but archaeologically attested digging into similar mounds in Roman times in Britain was similarly motivated. The idea that what we now call 'material culture', the physical, man-made remains surviving from the past, can be used as evidence about the past and thus have a value different from what it may or may not have in cash, curiosity or aesthetic terms, emerged in Europe out of the ferment of Renaissance ideas, finding its insular expression characteristically in the study of field monuments rather than in portable antiquities.[9] Camden, Aubrey and Stukeley visited known sites and found new ones, they described them, surveyed them and made a prospect of them (where we would now photograph them). Their attempts to give them meaning, to interpret them, were limited by the conceptual framework about the British past, the 'historical model' of that past, within which they were naturally thinking as educated men of their time (sixteenth to eighteenth centuries); and their interpretations now have little more than historiographical interest. Yet their observations and records, what modern mid-Atlantic jargon would now identify as 'field data', remain valuable in themselves as archaeological 'facts', additionally so since much of what they saw has since been destroyed. Furthermore, they have now, merely through the passage of time, acquired an extra dimension as primary documentary evidence bearing on aspects of historical research, e.g. later land-use history, social history, and the history of topographical art (fig. 1.2).

The interest and general level of competence in field archaeology declined in the later eighteenth and nineteenth centuries, being superceded by what has subsequently come to dominate archaeology: digging—or as we now prefer to call it, —excavation. In many regions of England, like Cornwall, Wessex, the Pennines and the Yorkshire Moors, the magnet was the many 'tumuli', the later prehistoric burial mounds so obviously surviving mainly on what was then marginal land. The objective was certainly 'finds', curios, preferably complete and, better still, aesthetically rather than monetarily valuable; but the hints of conceptual, and even technical, advance are present in the records of some of these activities.[10] The better practitioners like Colt Hoare (a considerable local historian apart from anything else), Bateman and Borlase were consciously seeking, not loot for personal profit, but evidence of their 'rude forefathers', dimly aware of the 'ancient times' existing before the Roman Conquest—and indeed before Caesar, for they were only too well aware of their Classical literary heritage. Their activities, the growing bulk of material accruing from the major land-use changes like urban expansion and railway construction in Victorian times, and intellectual stimuli from the work of people like Worsaae, Lyell and Darwin, moved the study of the past in the second half of the nineteenth century on to a very different level.

In the field, entirely due to the genius of one man, General Pitt-Rivers, the principles, technique and, to a remarkable degree, the objectives of modern excavation were developed, even though they were not followed until the second quarter of the twentieth century. And although the General's contribution is seen now primarily in

[9] P. Ashbee, 'Field Archaeology: its origins and development' in P.J. Fowler (ed.), *Archaeology and the Landscape* (1972), 38–74; *see generally* G. Daniel, *150 Years of Archaeology* (1975).
[10] P. Ashbee, *The Bronze Age Round Barrow in Britain* (1960).

terms of excavation, he also established very high standards of field surveying and mapping, again not immediately emulated. Indeed, the practice of non-excavational field archaeology waned, not least because the main pre-occupation of the developing discipline of archaeology was the artefacts now available in quantity and, in particular, the arrangement of them in a meaningful order. Typology was the order of the day. Field archaeology, though not excavation, began to re-assert itself about the turn of the century, interestingly as an archaeological expression of the development of a social conscience about 'Britain's heritage' which was seen elsewhere in the formation of, for example, the National Trust (1895) and the Society for the Promotion of Nature Reserves (1912). This form of activity continued on a minor but significant scale throughout the 1920s and 1930s, its particular exponents tending to be men from the professional middle class in southern England.[11] It was, however, in those decades that Wheeler took Pitt-Rivers' example in excavation and applied it in a coherent pro-gramme of major work across southern Britain, Brittany and, a little later, India and Pakistan.[12] The use of this now-powerful tool was primarily directed in his work and that of others to elucidating chronology, probably the main concern of at least prehistoric research in the first half of the century. In the 1950s and 1960s, following the seminal approach to and technical advances at Little Woodbury in the late 1930s,[13] emphasis began to shift to economic, cultural and social concerns, with a dawning realisation of what was literally at stake as the implication of archaeological air photography really began to affect thought and action. Equally if not more significant was the growing application of scientific techniques to archaeological material and problems, developing quickly under strong American influence into conscious attempts to rationalise a 'new' archaeology. About the same time—the late sixties and up to the present,—and simultaneously on both sides of the Atlantic, the pressures of social and economic forces on archaeology and its practitioners forced a political and, some argued, a moral dimension into archaeological thinking and behaviour as its 'resource base' was visibly and drastically eroded. As I write, archaeology is in a state of flux, conceptually, technically and organisationally, and it is too early to forecast what will emerge as 'main stream' over the next few years.[14]

The following subjective discussion of some approaches to archaeology, while very conscious of the historical development of the subject, must therefore reflect—and does

[11] S. Piggott, 'Archaeology and Prehistory', *Proc. Prehist. Soc.* 29 (1963), 2. The echoes of this paper throughout this book, noted now in this 'late insertion', were unconsciously created but doubtless accurately reflect a source in what was for me a seminal lecture. Professor Piggott's latest book, *Ruins in a Landscape* (1976), examines with learning and sympathy several of the aspects of men and their past touched on in this chapter.

[12] Sir Mortimer Wheeler, *Archaeology from the Earth* (1954); *Still Digging* (1955); *My Archaeological Mission to India and Pakistan* (1976).

[13] *Proc. Prehist. Soc.* 6 (1940), 30–111.

[14] Compare, for example, the first chapter of C. Renfrew, *Before Civilization* (1973); the last chapter of G.R. Willey and J.A. Sabloff, *A History of American Archaeology* (1974); P.A. Rahtz (ed.), *Rescue Archaeology* (1974) and the last chapter of G. Daniel, *op. cit.* note 9.

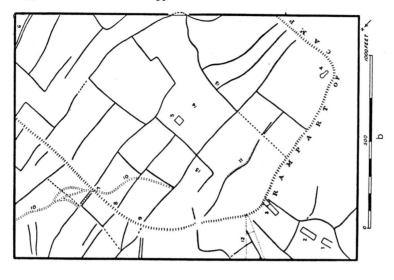

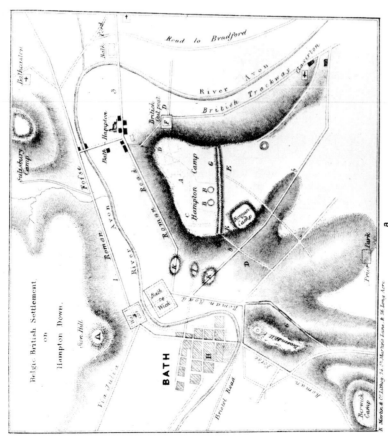

1.3 'The past is there and we want to find out about it': three illustrations of the same archaeological complex on Bathampton Down, Avon, published respectively in 1836, 1928 and 1967. Apart from demonstrating different styles of draughtsmanship which both represent changing attitudes to the past and affect appreciation of the evidence in what attempt to be objective statements of that evidence, the captions themselves are a commentary on the changing past: 'Belgic British Settlement', 'Bathampton Down' in a section on 'Ancient Fields', and 'Bathampton Camp' in a paper entitled 'The Excavation of an Iron Age Hillfort ...'. Significantly, the 1928 version is a diagram taken straight off a vertical air photograph demonstrating a relationship between fields and 'camp' which led directly to the excavation of the 1967 version.

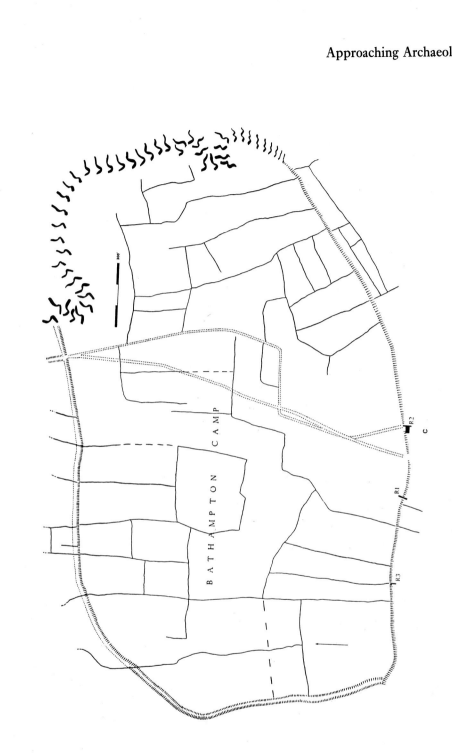

so consciously and willingly—the present state of uncertainty, of dynamism yet of potential fragmentation, in both archaeological studies and the archaeological community. Whatever happens, there can be no argument that the study of the past at the moment is an intellectually exciting field of human endeavour in which to be involved, whether as theorist or fieldworker, as amateur or professional, as teacher or taught.

Rationale of archaeology

'Human endeavour' may be too high-sounding a phrase to describe what many would regard—if they regard it at all,—as an irrelevant or at best incidental fringe activity on the skirts of 'real' life. There is of course no single, clear-cut reply to such a view but several suggestions can be advanced. The unexplained 'natural' curiosity of the human race, of societies, of individuals has already been mentioned and, though an unsatisfactory answer, it may be the basic one. Man is a curious animal, and much of what now differentiates him from the rest of the animal kingdom stems from this fact. In this context, his curiosity about his past is on a par with his curiosity about his own world and the worlds outside and beyond his own—the dimensions of time, space and spirit. In a sense then the answer to the question is that we cannot help it—we just want to try and find out. From this follows the element of challenge: the mountaineer answers 'Because it's there' and basically that is probably why Man has flown to the moon. We see the past as a challenge too: we know it is there, therefore we want to find out about it because it is there and we were (and still are) ignorant about it (fig. 1.3). Not only nature, but the human mind too, abhors a vacuum. And if the challenge is there, so too is the satisfaction of responding to it and beating it—in much of all this, archaeology is no different from many other fields of 'human endeavour', both physical and intellectual, and needs no more justification than they do—or needs just as much.

Equally unsatisfactory are those answers trying to explain the particular characteristics of archaeology which distinguish it from other activities. 'It's fun'—yes, so it should be, but so doubtless is kicking policemen yet personal entertainment cannot seriously be allowed as a prime justification for or objective of a destructive activity at the expense of the communal heritage. On the other hand, the disciplined execution and completion of an archaeological enquiry of whatever sort can, albeit incidentally, provide personal satisfaction, and undoubtedly many who now spend their spare time digging as volunteers on archaeological excavations do so because they enjoy it, particularly perhaps because of its physical demands in pursuit of a number of apparently readily identifiable and immediate goals, e.g. 'to uncover the building', 'to find out what is there', 'to recover what we can before it is destroyed anyway' (these examples are quoted without necessarily endorsing the validity of the reasons expressed). 'I just like the exercise after sitting at an office desk all week'; 'I enjoy the company'; 'I think it's marvellous to handle things that no-one's seen for 2000 years'; 'I hope to find something valuable'; 'I want to see my name on a museum label'; 'I'm

28

bored stiff with this site actually but if we don't do it who else will'—the pot-pourri of quotations culled from excavations over many years could be supplemented almost endlessly but this sample gives a range of motivations of people who are actually participating in that facet of archaeology which so many equate with archaeology itself. At the individual level archaeology, like other hobbies, can provide a form of social therapy appealing to the keep-fit enthusiast, the lonely, the extrovert, the greedy, the romantic (imaginative and amorous), a private wish for fame or immortality and to a sense of duty. In other words, it can offer a lot to individuals and they tend to find in it what they seek, but I do not think that this justifies, even if it partly and at a fairly low level explains, a particular form of archaeological activity (Pl. I.3). In any case, none of these approaches have much to do with the objectives of archaeology as an academic discipline. To say as much is neither to deprecate the one nor elevate the other: there is a genuine dichotomy and it is as well to recognise it though its sides are, fortunately for archaeology, not mutually exclusive.

Nevertheless, a social function must be taken seriously as part of the answer to the question of why we search for evidence of the past. We shall return to this point in Chapter 6 when we look at archaeology in operation in contemporary society but meanwhile a few more general and indeed theoretical aspects of its appeal can be aired.

I.3 'They tend to find in it what they seek . . .' Stonehenge as background for a family snapshot.

1.4 'It affords pleasure in countless ways . . .' Appreciation and enjoyment of the past is closely bound up with works of artistic and architectural merit, irrespective of their academic value as primary evidence about the past: the south-western doorway, Kilpeck Church, Herefordshire, September, 1975.

A lot of people find the past 'fascinating' and at this level probably the present popularity of archaeology is on a par with the vogue for the historical novel and indeed archaeological fiction (p. 188). To the serious archaeologist, 'fascinating' is among the less acceptable adjectives for his subject and he will feel almost a duty to speed the process of inevitable disillusionment of the person who thus describes it. On the other hand, many a person fascinated by the past, perhaps with romantic and mysterious longings, certainly with suspended or without any critical equipment to make a valid judgement, supports archaeology by subscribing to societies, attending lectures and visiting sites; and his lack of scholastic appreciation in no way invalidates the genuineness of his interest. Indeed, it is precisely the existence of an uncritical fascination with the past which can provide the background for the sudden revelation — the 'ah ha syndrome', —when a sight or site, a chance remark or a phrase in a lecture will trigger a movement of perspective as a result of which mental images fall into a different, more intelligible and more satisfactory pattern. This can of course operate against as well as towards a fuller understanding of the past and the proper study of it. Nevertheless, this wish to understand something about the past, particularly on the practical side—'So *that's* how they did it', —is a real force, a great aid in education and usually sincere. It may of course itself be motivated by other facets of our ambivalent attitude towards our past: I have had the impression from some questioners after public lectures, for example, that the real point of the question was to buttress a belief in the superiority of modern man over his predecessors—'They were only savages you know, my dear, not like us', —while, conversely, others seemed angled to seek reinforcement for perhaps hazily held ideas about the 'noble savage' and the inherent 'betterness' of times gone by. One can only add that those who look for achievement in the past on which to fasten their admiration seem, in the light of current archaeological research, to have picked the better bet.

Admiration for and fascination with the past, correct or otherwise, tend however to be a passive sentiment; more positive is a wish sometimes expressed to learn from the past. Certainly the past, including that derived from archaeological evidence, has often been searched for the 'lessons of history', perhaps at a straightforward cause and effect level and sometimes in more philosophical vein. The most serious attempts, like that of Toynbee,[15] have tried to establish a pattern, a series of cycles, in the past, based on the premise that if such can be recognised we can then perhaps locate our position in the cycle. The next step is not so much to learn from the past as to forecast the future. The method is very similar to that now employed to compile long-range weather forecasts; the principle is that history, or the weather, repeats itself. In the sense that archaeology provides many an undocumented example of the rise, maturity and fall of civilisations, there may seem to be a rational basis for such an approach, provided one does not worry too much about the time factor or the doctrine of Man's 'free will'. If people wish to find

[15] A. Toynbee, *A Study of History* (1934, 1939, 1954).

I.5 'Archaeology has an escapist value . . .', frequently given romantic expression in 'arty' shots of 'This is your heritage' type. View from the basement of the S.W. Tower up through the Great Hall towards the Solar, Goodrich Castle, Herefordshire, September, 1975.

a cyclical message of immutable processes in the affairs of human societies, archaeology selectively used can provide the evidence; archaeologists on the whole do not, however, consciously do so, even though nowadays their concerns are increasingly with the processes of cultural change through time. Whatever the merits of the case, undoubtedly a desire to learn from the past to avoid its mistakes and to try to read the future to mitigate the unease about the Great Unknown are factors in the study of the past, though perhaps not prime motivators of scholarship.

We have still not arrived at a clear-cut answer to the question of why study the past. Probably there is no one answer. People look to it out of curiosity at various levels, for comfort, for self-satisfaction, for profit; it affords pleasure in countless ways (Pl. I.4), its study is argued to be educative, and some pursue that study out of a genuine, disinterested wish to add to the sum of human knowledge. It can be used for political ends and it certainly has emotive overtones for those who seek them. Archaeology in particular has an escapist value offering the chance of academic retreat into the study of times and things past and of intellectual withdrawal similar to the absorbing unrealities of detective fiction and cross-word puzzles (Pl. I.5). But whatever reason the individual may give for an interest in the past, archaeology's main significance is in a communal context: the sites in the field, the material in museums, they provide the tangible evidence of a common identity, a society's history, and they both represent and foster a communal memory. In Britain this is unspoken except when pomp and circumstance require an overt appeal to the past, and it is assumed to be a 'good thing' unless financial expediency demands otherwise; in much of Africa and the United States at least some of the archaeological activity is motivated by a recognition of the role that archaeology can play in the development of social attitudes ranging from local pride to national consciousness.[16]

[16] *Cf.* the last chapter, respectively VII and VIII, of the 1939 and 1957 editions of G. Clark, *Archaeology and Society.*

Bibliography

Agric. Hist. Rev. 24, (1976), 49 (E. Kerridge review of *Studies of Field Systems in the British Isles* (1973))

Antiquity 50 (1976), 230–2

P. Ashbee, 'Field Archaeology: its Origins and development', *Archaeology and the Landscape* (1972); *The Bronze Age Round Barrow in Britain* (1960)

I. Berlin, *Vico and Herder: Two Studies in the History of Ideas* (1976)
D. Browne, *Principles and Practice in Modern Archaeology* (1975)
G. Clark, *Archaeology and Society* (1939, 1957)
B. W. Cunliffe, *The Past Tomorrow* (1970)
G. Daniel, *150 Years of Archaeology* (1975)
D. Dymond, *Archaeology and History: a plea for reconciliation* (1974)
P. J. Fowler (ed.), *Archaeology and the Landscape* (1972)
H. P. R. Finberg (ed.), *Approaches to History* (1962)
Guardian, The, 26 Feb. 1976 (Berlin *op. cit.*, reviewed by J. Rosselli)
R. Jessup, *Curiosities of British Archaeology* (1961)
W. D. Lipe and A. J. Lindsay, Jr. (eds.), *Proceedings of the 1974 Cultural Resource Management Conference, Federal Center, Denver, Colorado* (1974)
S. Piggott, 'Archaeology and Prehistory', *Proc. Prehist. Soc.* 29 (1963); *Ruins in a Landscape* (1976)
Proc. Prehist. Soc. 6 (1940), 30–111
P. A. Rahtz (ed.), *Rescue Archaeology* (1974)
C. Renfrew, *Before Civilization* (1973)
A. Toynbee, *A Study of History* (1934, 1939, 1954)
Sir Mortimer Wheeler, *Archaeology from the Earth* (1954); *Still Digging* (1955); *My Archaeological Mission to India and Pakistan* (1976)
G. R. Willey and J. A. Sabloff, *A History of American Archaeology* (1974)

2
TOPOGRAPHICAL
ARCHAEOLOGY

'. . . there is one document that no historian can neglect except at grave peril, and that is the face of the country' H. J. Randall, *History in the Open Air* (1934)

Archaeology is often regarded as synonymous with excavation and in practice, over much of the world, excavation *is* archaeology. One of the results of this is that much excavation is questionable—throwing 'pseudo-light . . . on non-problems' in Jim Dixon's epic phrase,[1] —and much archaeology is, in an intellectual sense anyway, bad archaeology (*see* Chapter 3). The reason for this is that there is another whole dimension of evidence bearing on man's history: the evidence that is *on* the ground as well as that buried in it. Of course, in practice it is difficult and probably ultimately indefensible to separate the two, although it has frequently been done to the detriment, indeed exclusion, of the above-ground evidence. Here, however, we shall concentrate on the earth's surface, the topography, as an approach to the past through visible but non-excavational evidence.

Archaeology in the field

In England, this approach is often called 'field archaeology' without further qualification, as epitomised in Crawford's book *Archaeology in the Field*; but unfortunately at least two other English books largely devoted to excavation are called *Field Archaeology*[2] so the phrase also has an inclusive sense embracing all that the archaeologist does out of doors, in the same way that 'field studies' or 'field geology' covers the whole range of out-door activities in other disciplines. 'Non-excavational

[1] K. Amis, *Lucky Jim* (1954) (Penguin, 1974, 14).
[2] O.G.S. Crawford, *Archaeology in the Field* (1953); R.J.C. Atkinson, *Field Archaeology* (1946, 1953); J. Coles, *Field Archaeology in Britain* (1972). *Cf.* E. Fowler (ed.), *Field Survey in British Archaeology* (1972), and Ordnance Survey, *Field Archaeology in Great Britain* (1973).

archaeology' is an unacceptable alternative, in principle because definition by a negative is an unhappy device, in practice because field survey should, and often does, both inform and lead to excavation. 'Field survey' is in fact a phrase often now used to cover much of what this chapter will discuss, but we are consciously reverting to the title at the head of the chapter because 'topography', particularly as practised in the seventeenth and eighteenth centuries, is fairly precisely our concern here: the description, representation and interpretation of both the natural and artificial elements in the landscape, and of the relationships between them. In a very real sense this is of course not a bad description of a combination of old-style 'physical' and 'human' geography and it comes very close to a definition of 'historical geography' if, as must certainly happen from the archaeologist's point of view, the phrase 'through time' is added to it at the end. Essentially, in recognising the landscape and the relationships through time expressed within it as central to its study, archaeology with whatever adjective placed before it—'topographical', 'landscape', 'total' and so on,—is sharing a common concern with many other disciplines. Ideally, each should inform the other and, nowadays, they frequently do so.

Many of the leading practitioners and scholars in the field of landscape management and landscape studies realise that, whatever their particular training, expertise or interest, academic or value judgements cannot authoritatively be made without knowledge and appreciation of conceptual and information inputs from a wide range of specialist studies. Archaeology here finds itself in distinguished and challenging company not always appreciative, however, of the distinctive contribution that archaeology in its topographical function can produce. Too often still, the archaeologist finds himself regarded only as a digger—'Still digging?'—a slightly-glorified technician scrabbling in the soil for finds, fame and fun, and it is not difficult to identify where the source of this misconception lies and is indeed perpetuated.

The landscape as artefact

Accepting for the moment that the 'world of archaeology'—what a deplorable phrase!—is not confined to digging, what else can it contribute to the real world of field studies? In general terms it can contribute signally to no less than the identification, record and, ultimately, understanding, of the artefactual component in the landscape, the man-made contribution to our present environment. Of course it is recognised that the geologist, the geomorphologist, the pedologist, the climatologist, the geographer, are all going to contribute to knowledge of the basic 'natural' framework with all its constraints on what Man would and would not do in any one area; but, welcoming that knowledge and the parameters it postulates, the archaeologist can make his distinctive contribution through study of the impact of Man on that area through time, in the first instance through the physically-existing artefactual evidence. That evidence will range from the single potsherd through archaeological sites in the conventional sense (which

II.2 'Areas of relict landscape . . .': fossilized ridge-and-furrow on Tyne Hill, Sibford Gower, west of Banbury, Oxon. 1975.

may or may not be excavated and in 999 cases out of a 1000 will not be) to areas of relict landscape like ancient field systems (Pl. II.1), on to 'old' elements in the present functioning landscape and on indeed into the future through the recognition now of potential archaeological resources amongst Man's recent and contemporary creations. Clearly this sort of approach involves recognition of a continuum both conceptually and practically, with the evidence, whatever its manifestation, existing in four dimensions i.e. vertically (above and below ground), horizontally in width and length, and through time. In this context, the prehistorian affecting superiority over the industrial archaeologist or the latter regarding his work as unconnected with other field archaeology is simply being myopic: period specialisation is conceptually the antithesis of topographical archaeology, although of course it may be necessary for practical reasons in any given instance. Equally, a narrow view of what is proper for archaeology to be doing would find the general argument here anathema, particularly when the argument is taken to its next step which is that this sort of archaeological approach fundamentally involves the use and understanding of a considerable range of, *sensu strictu*, non-archaeological evidence, notably from documents and the environmental sciences.

Of course, the archaeological record, strictly defined as a list and description of man-made landscape phenomena, can stand on its own, and serve a function—'Here be earthworks',—as a corpus of data in its own right; but the function in academic terms, let alone any other, remains very limited unless the record is transmuted, interpreted and synthesized in the light of other evidence. Often in practice this is simply not a problem because the researcher, having found his unexplained 'earthworks' (or whatever), will repair to the Record Office and Library in search of further enlightenment whether he thinks his archaeological evidence is prehistoric or later. This is the point of the topographical approach: whatever the estimated date and function of the physically-existing archaeological evidence, it has existed through time in a topographical or landscape context and, provided only that at some period the area was used by literate people, potentially the archaeological evidence can always have existed at some stage in a documentary context. In that sense, there is no such thing as 'text-free archaeology'. Of course, the concept of prehistory as the history of pre-literate peoples recovered by archaeological methods studying archaeological evidence is perfectly acceptable. The point here is that in many parts of the world that evidence will subsequently have existed during land-usage or perhaps merely visits by literate peoples whose contemporary documentary record may well illumine otherwise puzzling aspects of the much earlier archaeological evidence.

To take a simple example from southern England, understanding of settlement patterns in the last two millennia BC has been greatly enhanced in the last decade by study of the written and cartographic evidence bearing on medieval and later land-use history (fig. 2.1). Indeed, such evidence has not only helped us to understand some of the archaeological evidence in general and the history of some individual sites in particular, but it has also contributed to the recovery of previously unknown archaeological evidence both in the form of 'new' sites and, less tangibly, new relationships. Hence the recent invention of the phrase 'total archaeology' implying the use of all available evidence regardless of what form it takes, in order to study the interaction through time of Man and his environment in any given area. There is a very

2.1 A distribution map of various types of 'archaeological site' in central Dorset. In that the map represents information recently collected in a professional, comprehensive survey, the record is 'archaeologically complete'. Even if that were so—and new evidence is already to hand from the area—'obvious' deductions from the several distributions e.g. second millennium burials only occur on high ground; first millennium people only lived on the downs; there was a total change in settlement pattern at the end of the Roman period; medieval settlement was confined to riverside location, are simply not true. Such interpretation of even a full and accurate record as here ignores the limitations of archaeological field evidence—some settlements leave no superficial traces, the field evidence exists in a landscape with a constantly changing pattern of land-use e.g. medieval cultivation has affected the barrow distribution,—and the existence of documentary evidence.

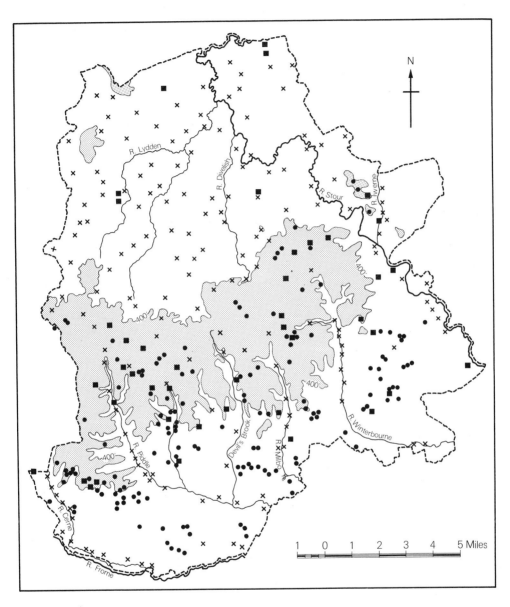

N

● barrows
■ Iron Age and Romano-British sites
✕ Medieval settlements

real point to this, granted the limitation of space—for practical reasons 'total archaeology' involves a topographical constraint: if the objective is to try and understand how an area has been used in the past, how indeed it has come by its present appearance, it really is conceptually irrelevant whether that evidence exists as a burial mound, a scatter of Roman pottery or an eighteenth century estate map. Of course different techniques and skills are required to elucidate the physically different types of evidence and because of this, group research (or only partial study) may be necessary; but the 'total archaeologist', individual or collective, should be taking the total evidential product of his area as the basis for his proper study. Whether he should be called, or should call himself, an archaeologist when he so does is a different matter.

Merits of field archaeology

Whatever the name of the person who carried it out, field archaeology in the restricted sense i.e. non-excavational, has considerable merits as an approach to the past. In the first place, its subject matter is all around most of us, varying only in range, variety and age. If we live in a 'modern' town or city we may lack locally the traditional subjects of field archaeological study—Indian mounds, prehistoric barrows and Roman forts, for example,—but the whole field of urban topography lies on our doorstep, a field which in Britain anyway has only recently come to be investigated seriously on any scale.[3] This point leads to the second great merit of field archaeology: not only can any one do it more or less anywhere, subject only to a few basic guidelines, but anyone becoming involved can be virtually guaranteed that they will make some 'discovery', not, may it be said, in the sensational, dramatic and treasure-finding sense so beloved of the media within their own concept of the 'world of archaeology' but quietly, seriously, in terms of making a contribution to knowledge e.g. about the evolution of a townscape, about the location of a Roman villa reported in the nineteenth century and since 'lost'. To quote such examples is in no way to limit or denigrate the significance of potential contributions from people whose time may be limited or whose initial motivation is no more than an untutored curiosity about their own house or village; they merely serve to indicate the minimal scope, emphasising how people can, and frequently do, first become involved in a small, finite piece of research and implying that many such pieces, if co-ordinated and directed, can build up into a considerable research project.

A third merit of field archaeology is that it is non-destructive. Unlike excavation, where the evidence is destroyed (and substituted by records—or not as the case may be, see Chapter 3) as the work progresses, fieldwork substitutes pencil marks for the original evidence but does not, or at least need not, affect that evidence at all. Theoretically, and again unlike excavation, fieldwork is repeatable and furthermore is

---

[3] I.e. from the archaeological point of view, *cf.* C. Heighway, *The Erosion of History: Archaeology and Planning in Towns* (1972); M.W. Barley (ed.), *The Plans and Topography of Medieval Towns in England and Wales* (1976); M. Aston and J. Bond, *The Landscape of Towns* (1976).

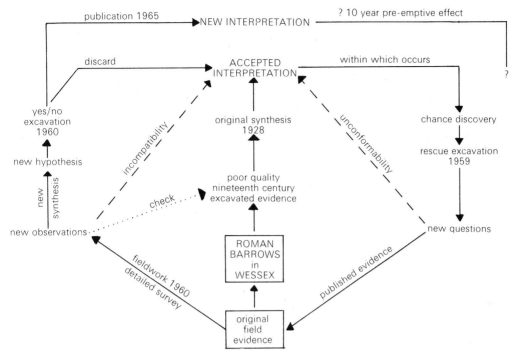

2.2 Diagram of the relationships between the stages in an archaeological enquiry.

repeatable by others at any time in the future; the fact that in practice this is not always the case owing to the land-use demands of contemporary society does not alter the principle. The author, for example, was able to check in the field in the 1960s a whole series of observations made by O. G. S. Crawford in the 1920s concerning the details of some burial mounds claimed to be of Roman date. The point was that new evidence, from a 'rescue' excavation as it happened (*see* Chapter 6), called Crawford's interpretation into question and it therefore became desirable to check not only his published material but also the field evidence that lay behind it. Despite some further damage to the sites in the intervening 40 years, enough remained in the field to confirm the basic correctness of his observations but to show that, in the one respect I was now looking for in the light of the new evidence, he had overlooked a critical detail. I was nevertheless able to go back to the original in exactly the same way as an historian, many historians, will consult the same document in the Public Records Office many times. It is a point which is emphasised by the fact that, in that same small piece of research, I was *not* able to go back to the original evidence in trying to re-assess the dubious and confused records of the few excavated barrows involved.[4]

4 'A Roman Barrow at Knob's Crook, Woodland, Dorset', *Antiq. J.* 45 (1965), 22–52.

The whole little episode, incidentally, illustrated quite neatly the interplay between fieldwork and excavation which often in fact takes place, despite the headings of Chapters 2 and 3, not least because it ended with a tiny excavation in a very specific spot to answer a very specific 'yes/no' question. The whole cycle, in this case in minuscule but illustrating one of a number of processes which can operate on a much larger scale, can be represented diagrammatically (fig. 2.2).

The main reason why the topographical approach to archaeology is absolutely vital is, however, because it alone gives that spatial dimension within which the past occurred and without which it is a meaningless, or at least a very limited, field of study. One has only to cope with some unlocated finds in a museum basement to realise this. Admittedly, in such a case, one can describe the material, probably say what it is and how it was made and even go into aesthetic rhapsodies if it includes items with some artistic quality; but unless its provenance is recorded, its potential value as evidence cannot be realised. Not that topographical archaeology is primarily concerned with 'finds' as such: its concern is with the landscape as evidence and with the archaeological elements in the landscape which contribute to our understanding of it now and of Man's relationship to it in the past. In trying to elucidate these themes, field archaeology accepts certain premises and follows certain principles. It assumes, for example, that all the evidence of Man's activity has not yet been found in the landscape, whether it is surveying an archaeologically virgin area in Africa or a much-investigated landscape such as we see in Denmark or England. It is a safe assumption, certainly for many decades to come, even for the well-trodden downlands of Wessex: new material comes to light every year, cumulatively making field archaeology's most important contribution to study of the past. This is the demonstration of the sheer density and variety of evidence on and in the ground in both town and country. This fact is so significant that it is worth examining its dimensions and implications, both for its own sake and for its relevance to other methods of archaeological research and to excavation in particular.

Maps and the cultural record

In many developed countries like Britain and Denmark a long tradition of recording the existence of archaeological sites has built up some form of national archive of information about their location, nature and date. Basically, this is the product of the initial data-gathering phase essential to the development of many academic disciplines. Some, but by no means all, of this information has been published on maps freely available and in common use. In Denmark, the maps of the Geodætisk Institut are gaily dotted with red and blue symbols showing the location and types of ancient and historic sites; in America, maps of the National Parks Service draw attention to archaeological sites that may be visited; while in Britain the Government through H.M.S.O., the Ordnance Survey and the Department of the Environment go to some pains to publish a variety of material, not least maps, showing the whereabouts of a plethora of archaeological sites or, as we still quaintly persist in calling them in officialese, 'ancient monuments'. Small wonder then that many people naturally think that all has been found, all that is known is shown on maps and indeed that the maps show the total distribution of archaeological sites. Field archaeology's greatest achievement, even if not yet everywhere realised, is to demonstrate the complete inadequacy, with very few exceptions, of all published maps in representing anything like the real distribution of archaeological evidence. The 'quantitative explosion of field data' is so great that it begs questions not only about distributions and former land-uses but also about some of the methods, premises and interpretations of archaeology itself.[5] And here we are thinking of conventional archaeological evidence alone, the sites of finds which constitute the traditional 'hardware' evidence of the archaeologist. How much more complex it all becomes when more general and less tangible landscape evidence is also considered (p. 49).

Topographical archaeology began with the obvious sites—the upstanding megalithic structures, the large mounds, the major 'camps', the Roman monuments and roads and it progressed, especially in England, to record and ponder upon the less obvious, the other hill-forts and smaller enclosures, the thousands of smaller mounds, the non-military settlements, field systems and ancient trackways. The approach, the range and the results, in all their limitations without a firm chronology, were impressively consummated in Allcroft's *Earthwork of England* (1908). Within that pre-war generation, the first British (1882) and American (1906) Antiquities legislation was passed, the first conscious and semi-political stirrings about the destruction and deliberate preservation of field monuments were witnessed and, in Britain, the first professional organisation specifically for state-financed archaeological field survey came into being in a typical cumbersome-sounding insular form—the Royal Commissions on Ancient and Historical Monuments (1908–10). Conceptually, it is interesting to note their brief to record those monuments 'illustrative of contemporary culture' up to 1714; for that phrase, shorn of pretensions to the grandiose, the aesthetic and the mysterious which had dogged so much of archaeological scholarship, opened the way eventually to an ever-increasing catholicity in what could and should be included in the magisterial pages of the Commissions' county surveys. The effect, acerbated by other reasons, has been a ponderous rate of ground-coverage, not least as the extension of the academic coverage has increased in range for standing buildings as much as it has for earthworks and sub-surface sites. The fact too that the Commissions always have paid great attention to buildings has had the effect, *inter alia*, of preserving the idea of the entity of the cultural record, creating the impression of long-term

---

[5] As is discussed or implied in, for example, M. B. Schiffer and J. H. House, *The Cache River Archaeological Project: an experiment in contract archaeology* (1975); P. J. Fowler (ed.), *Archaeology and the Landscape* (1972) and *Recent Work in Rural Archaeology* (1975).

institutional wisdom now that there are signs of a revival of popular and academic interest in buildings as evidence.[6] This is particularly so now that, in the context of 'total archaeology', standing structures are taking their rightful place and more archaeologists are accepting the view that there is no logical distinction to be made between evidence which, through the accident of time, is below, on or above the ground. This development alone is bringing about an enormous increase in the quantity of archaeological evidence and, further, makes the acquisition of yet more skills desirable in the tool-kit of the practising archaeologist. It is obviously silly, for example, to study only excavated evidence of medieval houses when many may still be standing round about the excavation (Pl. II.2).[7]

Aerial photography and its archaeological implications

The single most significant technical development in topographical archaeology occurred in the generation after the Commissions started work. This was the application of aerial photography to landscape study. Crawford must take full credit for this archaeologically speaking: his initial publications in the 1920s showed a remarkable grasp of the potential of the new tool technically and academically and his actual analyses of fossil landscapes in Wessex have not been surpassed in method or achievement (fig. 2.3, Pl. II.3).[8] He also showed, then and in his later writings, a growing awareness of the conceptual impact of air photography and regarded his own work in this field as one of his three main achievements.[9] It has, however, taken another generation of work and further advance in photographic techniques to bring that impact realistically to bear on archaeological thought.[10] The cumulative effect of 50 years of archaeological air photography (and it is still referred to as a new technique!) is to show in Britain at least a staggering wealth of artefactual evidence which was simply

[6] In addition to its normal publications on counties and cities—Dorset, Cambridgeshire, Yorkshire, Cambridge and York recently or currently,—the Royal Commission on Historical Monuments (England) has published E. Mercer, *English Vernacular Houses, A study of traditional farmhouses and cottages* (1975) almost simultaneously with the Welsh Commission's P. Smith, *Houses in the Welsh Countryside* (1975).
[7] The case is argued further in A. Rogers and T. Rowley (eds.), *Landscapes and Documents* (1974).
[8] O.G.S. Crawford, *Air Survey and Archaeology* (1924, 1925); (with A. Keiller) *Wessex from the Air* (1928).
[9] In a letter dated 16 Aug. 1955 to D.P. Dobson, now in the author's possession.
[10] D.R. Wilson (ed.), *Aerial Reconnaissance for Archaeology* (1975) now provides a modern and authoritative statement. *See also Rescue News* 10, 1975.

II.2 'There is no logical distinction . . . between evidence . . . below, on or above the ground'; and similar principles and methods can be followed and applied in the study of standing buildings in the vertical plane as in excavation and field survey. 'Stratification' exhibited in the multiphase facade of a building at Vezelay, Yonne, France, April, 1976.

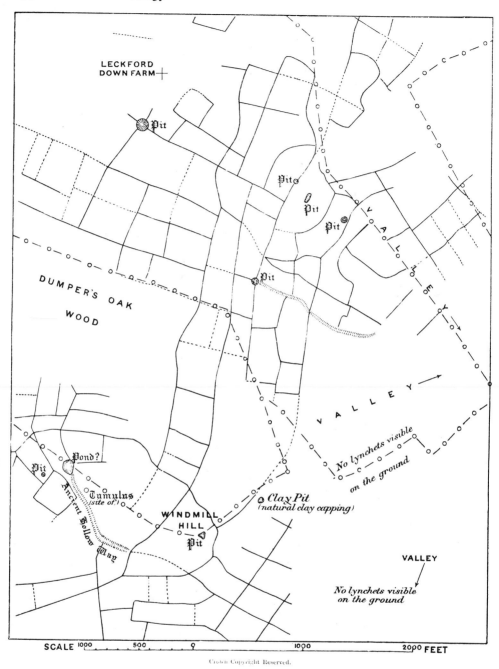

Crown Copyright Reserved.

2.3 Diagram of 'Celtic' fields, Windmill Hill, Hampshire, drawn from the air photograph illustrated in Pl. II.3.

II.3 'Celtic' fields on Windmill Hill, near Crawley, Hampshire, as recorded on a vertical air photograph by the School of Army Co-operation at Old Sarum at 4 p.m. on May 8th, 1922, from a height of 10,000 ft. The field system and other features are mainly showing up as soilmarks in arable. *Cf.* fig. 2.3.

not known previously to have existed. Over large tracts of countryside it is totally unrealistic to talk or think of a lesser or greater density of sites: if we must use somewhat archaic terms, the whole landscape is a single archaeological site.

No longer is it a question in many areas of photographing a known site here and there: the only adequate record is saturation coverage in colour and black and white, preferably by specific oblique views and by automatic, overlapping vertical cover, all repeated annually, seasonally and, ideally, weekly or daily. Some air photographers have been realising this as they have continually recorded new evidence on an annual basis in areas already well-covered. After 1975 and 1976, phenomenal years for air photographic results presumably because of two consecutive long, hot English summers punctuated by short, heavy rainstorms, it is quite clear from the way that evidence waxed and waned over very short periods of time that we are still a long way not only from understanding the differential factors affecting the archaeological phenomena but also from completing a full record of the phenomena themselves.

What exactly is this new wealth of evidence? The question is difficult to answer,

II.4 '. . . extensions into a sensitive floral medium'. Settlement features—multi-period enclosures, ditches, pits—showing as cropmarks in a field of cereal near Woodford, Northants. This is a typical example of the multitude of 'new' flattened archaeological complexes or buried landscapes recovered by recent aerial photography over much of lowland Britain now under arable and superficially without much in the way of 'archaeological sites'.

particularly as this is not the place to become too involved with technical discussion, but basically what the airborne camera is recording are fragments, sometimes extensive ones, from a palimpsest of landscapes preceding the existing one. They are 'new' old landscapes in the sense that they have already been flattened and smoothed over, in some cases a long time ago, and have not therefore been susceptible to identification by the superficial methods of traditional field archaeology. This has relied largely on the three-dimensional qualities of landscape evidence and specifically on the above-ground element in the vertical dimension. These flattened and buried landscapes also exist three dimensionally but their existence in the vertical plane is entirely below ground level i.e. there are with very few exceptions (*see* p. 53) no surface structural indications of their presence. Yet of course, since we are here mainly dealing with crop-marks, the phenomena do exist at and above ground level, albeit only seasonally or less, otherwise they could not be photographed on normal light-sensitive film. In the form in which they do become visible, the phenomena are not actually the artefactual features themselves but extensions of them into a sensitive floral medium (Pl. II.4).[11] Other methods now being developed e.g. infra-red photography recording other manifestations, do not affect the substance of the argument here.

Given the tool of air photography and an increase in the number of people using it, the other factor which has made it so revealing in the last two decades has been a large-scale turnover from pastoral to arable farming over much of England. Ironically, since some at least of the new arable has caused tremendous destruction of the traditional subject matter of field archaeology i.e. above-ground features, it is only the planting of cereals in particular on former pasture or marginal land which has revealed the buried landscapes previously masked by grass. Of course, air photography can produce, as Crawford soon showed, superb results from grassland (Pl. II.5) but it is then largely limited to the superficial, and though some complex sites in such circumstances can demonstrate succession, it is only when one can as it were peer through the topsoil by the agency of sensitive root systems of cereal crops in particular that we can appreciate the evidence in both its lateral and vertical dimensions and, by observing relationships, through time. The principle is exactly the same as for excavation evidence; it is merely that the techniques for acquiring the skills for interpreting the evidence differ.

Much of the new evidence now recorded from the English landscape has not yet been assimilated into archaeological thought. Indeed, in a very real sense it is not available to be assimilated and, by its nature, it will not be for some considerable time. We are thinking of tens, probably hundreds, of thousands of photographs, annually increased, most perhaps not yet critically examined and interpreted, the great majority unpublished in plate or map form, many not catalogued in a publicly available register

[11] Effectively demonstrated by R.C.H.M., *A Matter of Time* (1960), subsequently if belatedly followed by three air photographic surveys of the Thames Valley: D. Benson and D. Miles, *The Upper Thames Valley: an archaeological survey of river gravels* (1974); T. Gates, *The Middle Thames Valley . . .* (1975); and R. Leech, *The Upper Thames Valley in Gloucestershire and Wiltshire* (1977).

II.5 The Priddy Circles on Mendip, Somerset, a very difficult air-photographic subject because of their extent and low relief in scrub and grass, superbly caught in the right conditions of low, strong, oblique sunlight. 1973.

and some not even developed or printed. Impressions of the significance of this photographic evidence are therefore subjective, partial and empirical; but they are probably not entirely invalid, at least in general terms. In the first place and most significantly, aerial photography has in effect given a new dimension to the archaeological record and therefore to archaeology itself, certainly in Britain and apparently (though the author has no direct flying experience there) over large areas of France, Germany, and the Low Countries.[12] We really can no longer confine archaeological thinking by the so-limiting concept of the site (it is interesting that, starting from different premises, one aspect of the so-called 'new' archaeology argues to similar effect—*see* p. 145). Even the standard English types of site like the upstanding barrow or hill-fort do not exist as independent features on the ground: such exist in a temporal, physically-surviving landscape context which in many cases has now, at least in part, been recorded on film. So we can no longer think of sites as discrete cultural phenomena, existing as it were in isolation, as dots on an otherwise blank map: by and large, most of the sites mapped as earthworks and the like before say, 1950, are merely the tips of submerged landscapes which happen, through all sorts of local accidents, to have broken up through the ground's surface, rather like mountain peaks sticking through the upper surface of the continuous cloud cover so familiar to all fliers in Britain (Pl. II.6). Just as an earlier archaeology's predilection for studying the object had to be elevated to the concept of the associated group of material and then to the concept of the culture, so now it has to think its way out of a pre-occupation with the site to develop an appropriate intellectual framework not just for a site complex or a group of sites but for a whole series of cultural topographies interlocking in space and time. Within that concept, the previously known site—the upstanding barrow, the Roman villa—is seen in a new perspective which may require radical re-assessment of its significance, e.g. in its newly-appreciated context it may not be either the typical or unique phenomenon it was once thought to be or its significance may be completely altered by the new information that it is merely a small part of a complex series of landscape features. To put it crudely, the excavation of a particular site could subsequently be seen to have been misdirected or the preservation of an 'important' site might be seen to have been misplaced. This landscape dimension to field archaeology does in fact have considerable implications for both excavation and preservation policies (Chapters 3 and 6).

As has already been said, most of the evidence lying behind these generalisations is neither published nor readily accessible; even when and if it is, there is no substitute for seeing the evidence, three-dimensionally in colour, oneself. Words like 'exciting' and 'breath-taking' should not perhaps be part of the archaeologist's vocabulary but it is difficult to convey without using emotive language any impression of the visual impact the aerial view can occasionally provide for the informed observer. Some of the effects I

[12] See the papers by I. Scollar, R. Agache and C. Léva in D. R. Wilson (ed.), *op. cit.* note 10.

II.6 'The tips of submerged landscapes . . .' The outlines of a Romano-British settlement, its closes, trackways and fields, fortuitously preserved under grass on South Hill, Bleadon, Somerset. 1973.

have seen are truly staggering—though I find almost as staggering the fact that other people fly over the landscape daily and do not even notice what the landscape is displaying for them. For example, one particular flight over Cranborne Chase, Dorset, which I thought I knew intimately on the ground, caught the area just in those critical autumnal days when most of the fields had been ploughed but before they were harrowed. The effect was startling, partly because of the story it showed of wholesale destruction of not long previously preserved monuments but also because soil-marks representing earlier human activity in the area occurred in every field. Similarly, but in the different circumstances of the long, hot summer of 1975, one particular flight over southern Somerset was a revelation despite, or rather because, the Ilchester/Somerton area was already well-known as containing a marked density of Roman villas. From the air, however, on that particular evening, we saw extensive tracts of presumably Roman landscape, the context of the villas, laid out across the countryside as crop- and parch-marks in cereals and grass.

While experiences like these are personally significant, overall it is the cumulative effect of archaeological air photography which is so significant. It is quite clear that the extent, quantity, quality and range of archaeological evidence in the landscape is far greater than has hitherto been appreciated. One of the consequences is that we have to redefine our grammar of field archaeology, for the new evidence is producing types of sites morphologically outside the conventional range represented by the Ordnance Survey's authoritative *Field Archaeology*;[13] another is to increase the chances, on a numerical basis apart from any other, of existing and still-used features in the landscape being a perpetuation of a much older feature. A hedge along the side of a 'modern' field, for example, may be on the line of a buried prehistoric ditch, a piece of the living landscape fixed in space by a long-forgotten piece of a fossilised landscape. How many indeed of the elements in our present landscape perpetuate earlier land-arrangements?—of field patterns, boundary lines, country lanes and settlement location. In this context, aerial photography has another function: not only is it a means of discovering and recording 'ancient' and *buried* landscapes but it is also the most convenient way of looking at the *existing* landscape from the historic point of view. Here of course we are not looking for the conventional archaeological site but attempting to identify in the existing pattern of land-use those elements which, by originating in earlier times, both inform our understanding of the present landscape and, at the same time, provide direct contemporary evidence of earlier landscapes. In other words, the air photograph, particularly a series of vertical views, provides the basis for an analysis in historical topographical terms of the landscape as an artefact created through time. As such the object of study is somewhat more extensive and complex than the flint scraper or Roman villa, than the material which archaeology has conventionally studied; but the approach is essentially archaeological.

[13] Ordnance Survey, *Field Archaeology in Great Britain* (5th ed., 1973).

A third consequence of this approach in the light of the greatly extended scope and variety of germane evidence must surely affect archaeology itself, at least in respect of its dependence for new information (and for popular support) on excavation. The dichotomy is sharply put by bringing together two quotations from separate, recently published archaeological books: 'Excavation is the main source of new information to the archaeologist'; 'The wide extent of the remains precludes anything but a technical mite of the whole ever being excavated'.[14] Is in fact archaeology going to continue to be content, indeed ever be taken seriously, if the main source of its information is regarded as coming only from 'a technical mite of the whole'? The question becomes even more serious when it is appreciated that this 'technical mite' is selected for information-extraction with no known regard, at least in Britain, for standard sampling procedure (p. 125). The matter of excavation will be pursued in the next chapter and here we need only note that the first quotation reflects a proper traditional view of archaeology which can no longer be sustained. Excavation need no longer be the main source of information for the archaeologist and in parts of the world like the American south west and the Mississippi Basin, parts of Denmark, Sweden and France, and Britain for example, it has already been superseded.[15] The main source of information is in the landscape and is extractable by means other than excavation; the great bulk of it, over 99 per cent, will only ever be extracted by non-excavational means. In this context, air photography is not merely a technical aid in 'Finding an Archaeological Site',[16] the role to which it is frequently relegated in archaeological text-books on the usually unstated premise that excavation is the high spot of the archaeological process; air photography potentially is an approach to the past at least as valid in its own right as excavation, demonstrably in quantitative terms and convincingly in information-retrieval terms for some major categories of evidence.

'Air photography' is qualified by 'potentially' in that last sentence because not only are there many practical points to be overcome in the successful application of the technique but also because, like excavation, air photography is not a process for the revelation of self-evident truths. A set of skills, equivalent to those of the excavating archaeologist are necessary for the *interpretation* of air photographic images; and in any case, air photographic results, to be transmitted into accurate and usable data for cultural and landscape history, need to be used in conjunction with careful ground control. So the footslogging field archaeologist is not redundant: indeed his role is both

[14] D. Browne, *Principles and Practice in Modern Archaeology* (1975), 55; H. C. Bowen, 'Air Photography: some implications in the south of England', in E. Fowler (ed.), *op. cit.* note 2, 42.
[15] E.g. G. J. Gumerman, *The Distribution of Prehistoric Population Aggregates* (1971) and the Cache River Project, *op. cit.* note 5, illustrating methodology and interpretation without or with minimal excavation; T. Mathiassen, *Nordvestsjaellands Oldtidsbebyggelse* (1959); R. Agache, *Détection Aérienne de Vestiges Protohistoriques, Gallo-Romains et Médiévaux . . .* (1970); and the papers by J. Hampton (esp. fig. 2), D. Baker (figs. 1–3) and C.C. Taylor in D.R. Wilson (ed.), *op. cit.* note 10. *Cf.* also C.C. Taylor in P.J. Fowler, *op. cit.* note 5 (1975), 107–20.
[16] D. Brown, *op. cit.* note 14, 38.

necessary and more powerful as the significance of the airborne view becomes more apparent. That significance to a considerable degree depends on the *extent* of the view obtainable from on high and consequently of relationships which are simply not visible at ground level; but ground work is always vital for checking details (and often recovering new data at the same time) so archaeology should not delude itself with the fallacy that land-use changes in our present landscape do not matter very much archaeologically, provided we have a good set of air photographs covering the area. Few things are more frustrating than to find, when you have gone out to check an air photographic feature, that there is now a factory on the site or that a quarry has now taken its place. In these circumstances, and dealing with detail, an air photograph is second best to former reality. So there is only some, and that highly qualified, consolation in the fact that there are many thousands of archaeologically-uninterpreted air photographs of now altered or destroyed landscapes. Such evidence, in its degree of uncertainty and its uncheckability, is equivalent to a bad excavation report of a lost site.

The topographical art

While air photography has, therefore, now assumed a major role in topographical archaeology as a prime source of information, the topographical approach itself still relies heavily on the old virtue of 'seeing for yourself' (fig. 2.4). We are now better equipped to know what to look for, we have new questions and we have a deeper appreciation of landscape complexities; but the principles and practices of archaeology in the field remain largely unchanged, not least because the early English practitioners of the topographical art achieved, intuitively it seems, a remarkable correctness in both. They went, saw and recorded, and when they could not do that, they used first-hand accounts of 'correspondents', a tradition which has been continued almost to the present with the 'correspondents' of two of the British State agencies, the Inspectorate of Ancient Monuments and the Ordnance Survey. And the practice is reviving in a new form as archaeological societies, for example in Cornwall, appoint 'correspondents' in the various parts of their area of responsibility. The tradition is strong because, whatever the mode of transport, there is no substitute for the first-hand inspection in the field and, in many respects, better still if 'inspector' or 'correspondent' is a local person. A 'feel' for landscape, however unscientific that may sound in the 1970s, is essential; a sound knowledge of a locality, which by definition is almost bound to be empirical, can allow that 'feel' to be utilised effectively or, to put it minimally, should prevent the making of elementary mistakes in the intuitive appraisal of an area. It is, for example, all too easy to be misled by a simple-looking mound, recognising it because it has certain characteristics as a burial mound when in fact, as ten minutes in the local record office or in conversation with the proverbial oldest inhabitant (and most villages have several) would tell you, it was a windmill mound. Such a distinction might seem trivial but it is at the very core of field documentation of which the aim is, and can only

NAME and ADDRESS of OWNER/TENANT (if known)					PARISH		
AGE of HEDGE (if known)					GRID REF.		
TYPE	Dry stone	Stone and earth		Earth	Planted		
POSITION	Estate boundary	Roadside		Between cultivated fields	Between uncultivated fields Moor/Wood/Other		
ASPECT	North	South		East	West		
HEIGHT	0 - 1.5 m.	1.5 - 2.5 m.		2.5 m. & over	Mature trees		
WIDTH	0 - 1.5 m.	1.5 - 2.5 m.		2.5 m. & over	Recently repaired		
MANAGEMENT	Hand clipped	Layered		Mechanically cut	Unmanaged		
CONDITION	Bank sound	Bank disintegrating		Tipping	Litter		

In a 30 m. length

FAUNA	Ants	Bank vole	Birds' nests	Lizards	Rabbits	Rats	Snails
WOODY SPECIES	Ash	Beech	Birch	Blackthorn	Bramble	Broom	Cherry
	Elder	Elm	Gorse (Furze)	Hawthorn	Hazel	Holly	Hornbeam
	Oak	Poplar	Privet	Rose	Rowan	Sycamore	Willow
HERBACEOUS SPECIES (please list)							

DATE			

NAME of SURVEYOR _ _ _ _ _ _ _ _ _ _ _ _ _ _ _ _ _ _ _

ADDRESS _ _ _ _ _ _ _ _ _ _ _ _ _ _ _ _ _ _ _

_ _ _ _ _ _ _ _ _ _ _ _ _ _ _ _ _ _ _

INSTITUTE OF CORNISH STUDIES: BIOLOGICAL RECORDS CENTRE

HEDGEROW SURVEY

Hedges occupy a greater acreage than our National Nature Reserves, and support a large proportion of our lowland wildlife. The purpose of this survey is to define the distribution of the various hedgerow types, their management and their wildlife potential. The need for this study is urgent as the agricultural trend towards larger fields is causing a loss of hedgerows at a rate of approximately 5,000 miles a year.

HOW TO COMPLETE THE CARD

1. Put a diagonal line through each appropriate compartment to indicate that the feature is present. If unknown, please insert a query (?).
2. This is essentially a preliminary survey, and the animals and plants on the card are indicator species to help in assessing the character and value of the site. Further details or records, or a note that they are available, would be welcomed.
3. Please return the completed cards to: Biological Records Centre, Institute of Cornish Studies, Trevenson House, Pool, REDRUTH, Cornwall TR15 3RE

HEDGE TYPES: PLEASE MARK SKETCH THAT THE HEDGE MOST CLOSELY RESEMBLES.

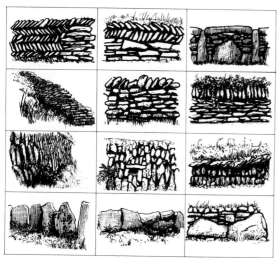

WALL INCLUSIONS	Trap holes	Bee bole	Deer leaps	Columbaria	Other
DITCH	Present		Absent		

2.4 'Seeing for yourself', to be most useful to others, needs to result in the *systematic* collection of information. As a result, various record cards have been devised to try and ensure that *comparable* information is collected from an area or about a particular type of site by different people at different times who, left to themselves, would work to different standards and by different criteria. This example, incidentally illustrating that archaeological data is no longer confined to conventional archaeological sites of the remote past, is that issued to its local, volunteer helpers by the county 'agent' of a national survey. Similar cards are available from the C.B.A. e.g. for the recording of industrial archaeological information, and from county archaeologists and some archaeological societies committed to field survey.

II.7 Training a group of adult students on a University Extra-Mural course in the techniques of instrumental field surveying as practised by R.C.H.M.; and, at the same time, producing an accurate plan of the deserted medieval settlement at Barbury Castle Farm on the Marlborough Downs, Wiltshire, as at March, 1976.

be, absolute accuracy (Pl. II.7); and academic considerations apart, the distinction could be vital if a practical decision had to be made whether to allow or oppose a proposed development, whether to excavate in advance or merely record during destruction (*see* p. 179). But the point here is that field observation can only be improved by using whatever other local sources of information exist. Since such sources are going to include documentary ones, once more our archaeological approach is on an interface with history; and in practice, the particular concerns of topographical archaeology make fruitless attempts to draw distinctions between archaeology and many aspects of local history. Any differences in approach are usually only ones of emphasis, in techniques, in objectives or in the personal background of the investigator. At this point on the spectrum of archaeological activity, the evidence used broadly overlaps with that of other landscape-rooted studies concerned with a locality. The only real argument is over who is the 'best' synthesiser of the various lines of investigation, and that can usually be settled on personal rather than abstract disciplinary grounds.

In fact it should be self evident that topographical studies must embrace documentary as well as artefactual evidence. What a superficial and indeed misleading picture can result if either or, worse, both are ignored is well-illustrated by the following quotations about the same village:

'THE LANDSCAPE

3.2.7. Until 1939 the landscape had probably changed little since the enclosures and was heavily hedged with a large number of characteristic hedgerow elms. Many of the gentler landforms would have been obscured by hedgerows but the ridge on which Leighton stands would have stood out then as now. The prominent position of many of the villages is characteristic of this landscape. They are mostly on high ground with the church tower or steeple rising above the villages trees . . .'[17]

'The area contains four specific types of site:

(a) *Ridge-and-furrow* Up until the early 1950s some 500 acres of well-preserved ridge-and-furrow remained in the parish. This has virtually all been destroyed, with the result that the pattern of medieval agriculture no longer exists . . .

(b) *Roman Road* The line of the Roman Road Godmanchester-Leicester (Margary 57a) marks the N boundary of the parish. Over most of its length it is followed by the modern road.

(c) *Site of Leighton Bromswold Hall* This lies immediately E of the village and is a Scheduled Ancient Monument. Minor damage has occurred . . . The remains have been misinterpreted and published as a 'castle'; in fact they represent abandoned gardens and the house, built in the early 17th century. Though the garden boundary bank and prospect mounds are obvious . . . the interior contains the very slight remains of the house foundations and garden layout. These are only a few centimetres in height and have not previously been recognized.

(d) *Shrunken Village Remains* These lie E and S of the garden . . . and have already been destroyed . . . when the scheduling of the garden remains took place the village earthworks were allowed to be ploughed . . . presumably because their significance was not understood . . .

 . . . The earthworks . . . not only represented a type of site rare in Huntingdonshire but also were important in explaining the whole development of the existing village. It is possible to see how the village grew up on top of a narrow E–W ridge, on either side of a track along the ridge. Subsequently the road pattern changed to a N–S one and part of the track and one third of the village was abandoned, presumably in late medieval times. The construction of the house and gardens in the 17th century was actually on the top of the deserted part of the village.'[18]

---

[17] Countryside Commission, *New Agricultural Landscapes* (1974), 16.
[18] Extract (by C.C. Taylor) from the submission (1975) by the C.B.A. to the Countryside Commission in response to the publication of *New Agricultural Landscapes*.

The second description incorporates not only greater technical skill in the analysis of the physical components of the landscape but also the all-important time, or historical, dimension. Furthermore its use of documentary evidence draws on maps, place-names and field-names as well as on the more conventional written sources; and doubtless, had it been appropriate, church dedication and local folklore on the one hand and, on the other, geological, pedological and other 'natural' environmental considerations could have been brought to bear too. The fact is that, in this topographical approach to the past, even if the starting point is archaeological the full assessment of its end-product demands consideration of a broad spectrum of source material by methods proper to their study and with an awareness of the nuances in the use of particular types of evidence in their own specialist fields of academic discipline. The ideal is of course difficult to attain and few individuals succeed by themselves. The definition of objectives in topographical studies is therefore important, primarily so that it can reach a state of 'completion' by its own terms of reference, partly to disarm unfair criticism. A typical local history, for example, may well demonstrate an unawareness of the archaeological dimension in the landscape with which it is concerned, but if its prime concern is with genealogy and the descent of the manor its limited scope may be deplored but not its failure to achieve what it never set out to do. Similarly, just as a great deal of descriptive and analytical work may usefully be devoted to a prehistoric settlement and its surrounding fields, so exactly the same archaeological approach can produce useful information about a deserted village and its fields or indeed an existing town and its context. A *full* study on either of these last two cases would obviously require a great deal of original documentary research just as a *complete* history would require a detailed and sympathetic treatment of the artefactual evidence; but just as a history of sorts can be written, *in vacuo* as it were, entirely from documentary sources, so can archaeology produce results of a sort, even for the medieval and later periods, without resort to documents. It is as valid to look at an existing village in Northamptonshire, for example, and describe its standing buildings, its street pattern, the earthworks of its former extent and its surrounding field pattern, to analyse these data and to make deductions from them as it is to follow the same procedure with an abandoned prehistoric settlement 'fossilized' on Dartmoor. An existing village is an artefact developed through time just like a prehistoric settlement and, as such, it can produce a body of information—its position, shape, size, methods of construction, stages of physical development and so on,—in an entirely text-free context. Its date, and the existence or otherwise of documents, are from this point of view irrelevant. Archaeologically, it must be insisted that this approach is valid or, by definition, there could be no knowledge, let alone understanding, of pre-literate societies and landscapes. There would be no point in even looking for, let alone studying, our fossilized Dartmoor settlement; ultimately, there would be no prehistoric Europe, no history of pre-European America and, ultimately, no knowledge of pre-literate Man.

While, however, the validity of the approach must be a basic premise (and it has after all validated itself by results), its *degree* of validity allows plenty of scope for debate. It may indeed provide, as many historians would argue, an inferior quality of evidence — but when, as in Neolithic Europe or in the later pre-European American South West, for example, topographical archaeology provides the *only* evidence of where people lived and of some of the things that they did, to what is the evidence inferior? It is either that or nothing. In the thirteenth and fourteenth centuries AD, England is in the full flood of medieval documentation but a great deal of the subject matter of topographical archaeology, e.g. the shape of settlements, the sorts of houses most people lived in, is still not covered by this additional source of evidence. On the other hand, of course, in that the documents tell us of named persons, provide dates and cover aspects of the human condition not detectable by archaeology, a fuller and richer understanding of English medieval life can be built up than American archaeologists can provide for the Hohokan or Sinagua Indians or English archaeologists can provide for life on prehistoric Dartmoor. But the approach from the landscape point of view remains valid, whatever the period and whatever other evidence is available; perhaps such validity is to be judged more in relation to the availability or not of that 'other evidence' than by reference to some abstract scale of values which sees history as 'better' than archaeology. In topographical studies the more, and more varied, the evidence the better, for each source can potentially complement the other. It is, however, quite unacceptable to regard an archaeological observation in the field as 'wrong' either because it is undocumented or because it is apparently contradicted by written evidence. Similarly, a documentary 'fact' is not wrong because there is no archaeological evidence to bear it out. The two approaches are each valid in their own right but they deal with evidence of different sorts and, by and large, produce results of different sorts. It is an assumption that the two approaches will coincide; it is presumptuous for one to denigrate the other when they do not. But lucky the locality when they do (fig. 2.5)!

Two case studies[19]

Two small examples from my own experience neatly illustrate these various points. Both concern the present parishes of Fyfield and West Overton in Wiltshire. The first time I went up on to Fyfield Down was in a purely field archaeological sense: it was to check on a site recorded on an air photograph by Dr. St. Joseph. The site was located and various observations made about it and its relationships to other features in the area e.g. it was later than the 'Celtic' fields here and contained a long rectangular structure. Subsequently the complex of earthworks and stones was surveyed in detail so that we had a 'cartographic' statement of the evidence supplementing the air photographic and

[19] Interim reports appeared in *Wilts. Archaeol. Mag.* throughout the 1960s, syntheses being in C. Thomas (ed.), *Rural Settlement in Roman Britain* (1966), 54–67; *Antiquity* 41 (1967), 289–301; *Current Archaeol.* 16 (1969), 124–9; and P.J. Fowler (ed.), *op. cit.* note 5 (1975), 121–36.

field notebook record. If work had stopped there, as it reasonably could, we would still have possessed a lot of new data, 'text-free' and valid in its own right, about a site and its context: the superficial evidence had been recorded accurately and thoroughly and from it certain deductions could be drawn. Soon afterwards, for various reasons, excavation began on part of the site, immediately showing it to be of twelfth/thirteenth century date and the 'long rectangular structure' to be a contemporary long-house. No wonder the site appeared to be later than 'Celtic' fields! Note though that the excavated evidence, in giving greater chronological precision to the relationship, in fact confirmed the correctness of the relationship produced by field observation. Nevertheless the research was entirely archaeological in motivation and method up to this stage, again one at which it could reasonably have stopped.

Unbeknown to me, however, a local historian had for long known of the existence of the site *as a series of documentary references* in the Winchester Custumal of St. Swithun's Priory. He did not, however, know where the site was, nor did his source material tell him much about the site as such even though full of detail about the name of the man who lived there, his stock, and his duties to the lord of the manor for being allowed to farm up on the Down. Fortunately, the publicity attendant on the excavation brought us together, providing me with a chronological and tenurial framework within which to continue the excavation and the local historian with a three-dimensional context within which to re-examine his source material. Of course, both sorts of evidence, archaeological and documentary, not only could stand but in this case had stood as perfectly valid but separate bodies of information; but both were constrained for interpretative purposes by the inherent limits of each type of evidence. Put together, each illumined the other, even though there was only partial concordance between the types of evidence. The documents did not say what sort of house or other buildings existed at the farm; archaeology provided that evidence very clearly but could not produce the name of the man who lived in it or indeed the name of the farm. Put together, we can state that a man called Richard lived at a farm called Raddun in the second half of the thirteenth century in a long-house 58 ft. by 14 ft. with two entrances in the east wall, one in the northern half (blocked) and one in the southern half for animals. We can add that, archaeologically but not documentarily, the southern half of the building drained into a sump and that the northern half contained a hearth against the west wall; but we could not have excavated the information that Richard was privileged to grind his own grain because of the distance of Raddun from the manorial mill (though we might have deduced that had we found the mill-stones). Chronologically, the interplay of sources is illustrated by the earliest reference in 1248, a century or so later than the start of the farm on archaeological grounds; and the archaeological end of the site in the early fourteenth century generally with the precision of 1316 as the date of the last 'Raddun' entry in the Custumal (which does not, however, state that Raddun was abandoned then: to think so is to interpret and, in that sense, the documentary evidence is no more precise than the archaeological). Since I have mentioned earlier other sources of

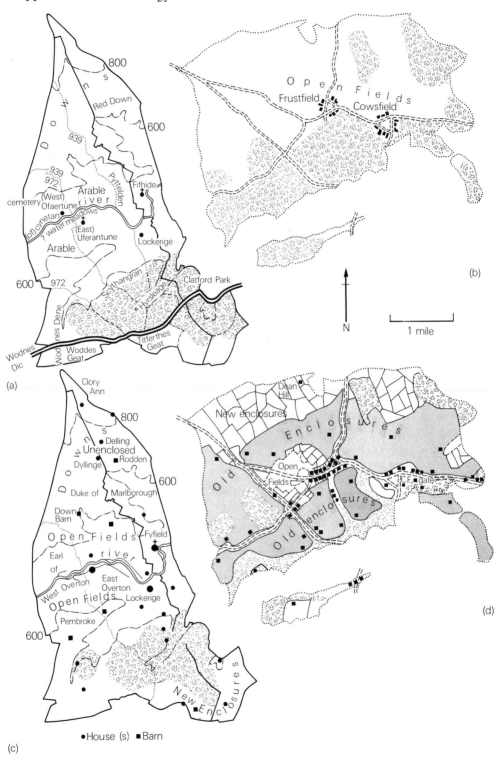

(a)

(b)

(c)

(d)

• House (s)   ■ Barn

N

1 mile

evidence, perhaps I could add that we were told locally that the wood adjacent to the farm was called Wroughton Copse after a certain Colonel who was alleged to have shot there in the 1920s whereas in fact the name can be traced back, through for example Rodden in 1562, to the thirteenth century Raddun. That name itself is independently attested as having nothing to do with the late version of the Copse name by the field in which the site exists being called Rowden Mead on a map of 1773.

For my second illustration, we turn from a single site to an area of landscape that is now largely embraced in the Fyfield Down Nature Reserve which includes, nevertheless, much of Overton Down. For a long time well-known through Major Allen's famous air photograph, the Downs in fact contain much more evidence of fields, settlements and related features than had been appreciated. A detailed archaeological field survey recorded most (it is hoped) of this evidence which now exists on paper as a statement of what is there on the ground. Inevitably the question 'What does it mean?' arose during and after its collection. At first glance, the mass of data seemed to confirm the thesis of prehistoric and Romano-British preference for settlement on the high downland and various attempts were made cartographically to refine and express this preference by plotting the distribution of settlements in particular against heights above Ordnance Datum, slope, soil type, water sources and all the other conceptual residue of geographical determinism (happy days!).

The correct explanation of the apparent density of surviving evidence on these Downs came, however, from a completely different source: an attempt to reconstruct from documentary and field evidence the arrangement of the medieval field system in the two parishes (or, more correctly, four tithings). Here, this could be done relatively easily and with some degree of certainty, and it was then apparent that the controlling factor in the distribution of the visible prehistoric and Roman period field evidence was the extent of the medieval field system i.e. what was outside the permanent arable survived, what was inside had long since been flattened. In other words, the concentration on the Downs of the upstanding archaeological evidence was an accidental by-product of medieval farming practice. Here indeed is a case of 'pure field archaeology', 'text-free archaeological evidence' capable of being correctly interpreted only in terms of later agrarian practice and later still documentary evidence. The 'proof'

2.5 West Overton/Fyfield parishes and Whiteparish, Wiltshire: two examples, slightly differently expressed, of landscape analysis. a and b show the reconstructed landscape in the early Saxon period, c and d in the post-medieval period. Each map is merely one of a series attempting to show the evolution of these particular local landscapes from prehistoric times to the present; and, conversely, to demonstrate the extent to which historical constraints are a factor in present appearances and indeed in existing land-use and settlement pattern. a/c is a typical (?) long, thin, cross-valley chalk downland parish, just touching the edge of Savernake Forest; b/d is a forest edge parish on chalk, sand and clay in the Hampshire Basin. Both reconstructions depend heavily on detailed field study and documentary evidence.

of the thesis is the subsequent recovery by air photography of archaeological sites and features as crop- and soil-marks from *within* the areas of the former 'North Fields' of the different field systems stretching across the valley floor inside their long, narrow tithings (fig. 2.5, a and c).

Distribution maps

As is clear from these examples, maps are an essential tool for presenting and indeed interpreting the data from field archaeology; implicit in a lot of them is the concept of settlement pattern. Again it was Crawford, with his contemporary Cyril Fox, who almost literally put British archaeology on the map in landscape terms. Previously, archaeological maps of any sort were rare although, as we have noted (p. 42), the inclusion of archaeological sites on 'public' maps already had a long pedigree. But conceptually there is a big difference between showing antiquities on ordinary maps and using a map as a tool from which to make cultural deductions in a topographical context. The first maps show where sites are and probably what sorts of site they are: it fixes them in space. From this, the next step is the distribution map for which a group of material—sites or finds—is abstracted from the rest and plotted on the same map. Similarly, several groups of different dates can be plotted on the same map to demonstrate that they do or do not have relationships in space and time (fig. 2.6). This is one of the critical differences in map-making: primarily to show location or, by selecting intentionally, to show relationships as well. Either way, the presumption is that the symbols on the map 'mean' something in terms of human activity and that this 'meaning' is something different from our knowledge derived from single sites and indeed the sum of our knowledge as added together from single sites. In other words, the distribution of data in space is itself meaningful, can tell us something in addition to what we can learn from the known existence of a burial mound or the discovery of a coin hoard at a Roman villa. Conceptually, a distribution map is a model (p. 147) to test the hypothesis that the distribution of data in space forms a pattern which, being an artefact, is capable of examination and allows the making of deductions in terms of human activity. When such archaeological data is additionally plotted against topographical data (and not just shown in space on an otherwise blank map), we are refining the tool in an attempt to make it provide greater understanding, more meaningful patterns; but at the same time, by emphasising one additional set of data, we are also narrowing the interpretative options and may indeed be foreclosing on a non-critical factor in the known distribution pattern. In a minor way, the Fyfield Down example discussed above (p. 63) illustrates the point. We can now recognise therefore a critical distinction between, on the one hand, a distribution map seeking to demonstrate by an assumption of spatial pattern a cultural relationship between data or between one set of data and another; and, on the other, the use of the map as a tool to test and demonstrate settlement patterns.

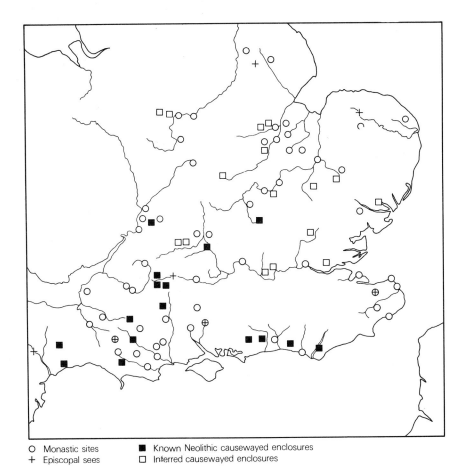

O Monastic sites   ■ Known Neolithic causewayed enclosures
+ Episcopal sees   □ Inferred causewayed enclosures

2.6 How not to make a distribution map: this shows two discrete but similar distributions of respectively Neolithic causewayed enclosures (fourth millennium bc) and English monasteries in the ninth–eleventh centuries A D. Each distribution *separately* represents a statement of fact i.e. the incidence in space of a particular cultural phenomenon as known at present. There is no implication that either distribution is finite (in fact the circles and crosses are knowingly incomplete, sites to north and west being omitted to make the map more 'convincing'; the squares will certainly be added to by new discoveries); but of course the criteria behind the identifications are completely different (documentary evidence for the circles and crosses, morphological similarities in earthwork or air photographic evidence for the squares). Apart from the cartographic quibbles that the symbols would be more appropriate if transferred and are too big anyway in relation to the map scale (not given; the size of the symbols makes nearly all the sites appear to be on riverbanks, which is not so, and the rivers shown are themselves carefully selected), there is no rational justification for bringing two such disparate distributions together and certainly not with an interpretative goal in mind e.g. to 'demonstrate' a connection between ritual/religious sites separated in time by four millennia. Though distribution maps are 'objective' statements which can reveal significant spatial relationships, their use is a matter of judgement and is therefore subjective. This is a major problem for 'scientific' archaeology: academically, this map is a nonsense in terms of cultural history yet it is a gift for anyone wanting to 'prove' continuity from Neolithic ritual to early Christianity. Perhaps it will grace the pages of a book cultivating the 'mysterious past' approach for it exactly demonstrates the method of non-sequential juxtaposition so often used (*below* p. 188).

In practice the distinction may be slight and indeed the same data may be used for the different purposes. For example, the round burial mounds of Wessex in the second millennium BC have been exhaustively recorded and collated in recent decades by the unremitting endeavours of one man, Leslie Grinsell, who has been able to produce comprehensive maps showing where the barrows are.[20] In addition he has also shown that overall they have a non-random distribution, within which morphologically distinct types have discrete distributions e.g. one version of the disc-barrow only occurs in Dorset. Subsequently, others who have not visited every barrow on the ground have been able to use this data and replot it using different criteria and different techniques to support a thesis of a particular economy and land-use practices in Wessex contemporary with the round barrow-building activity. And indeed, adding other data to that of the round barrows, a thesis concerning how contemporary society developed in organisational terms has been further adduced. So here we can see a process of interpretation, of 'model building', going through four distinct stages, all of them depending on maps and ultimately on the field record. Grinsell produced plans of single barrows, maps of barrow groups, and location maps, and then the distribution maps though with little interpretation; Fleming produced settlement pattern maps as an interpretation of that data in landscape-economic terms; and Renfrew, bringing in other data and stretching the time-scale, used maps showing presumed relationships apparently observable in the field data to generate a socio–economic explanation of that data and indeed designed to be of wide applicability in later British prehistory.[21]

Such use of maps ultimately goes back to the field record which comprises not only that which exists now but also that which no longer exists, visibly anyway, but has been recorded as existing in the past. This applies particularly to barrows in England where the topographical literature of past destruction is voluminous. Since so much depends on the accuracy of this record, since it can be used to carry such a weighty superstructure of interpretation, we should perhaps look at the factors affecting its nature. In the first place, an archaeological landscape feature be it barrow, bank or ditch owes its existence to human activity in the past at the place where it now exists. In that sense, the main factor in the field record is what Man has done in causing the feature to be created and, further in that sense, the field record can represent such creativity because of other, subsequent factors which affect the product of that creativity. If a community built entirely of wood, for example, only in unusual circumstances will their products be detectable by the field archaeologist without resource to excavation for the simple reason that, by and large, wood rots and does not leave much above-ground evidence of its former existence. Products of more durable material can also

[20] To the bibliography of Grinsell's publications in P.J. Fowler's (ed.), *op. cit.* note 5 (1972), 250–6, should now be added 'Disc-Barrows' in *Proc. Prehist. Soc.* 40 (1974), 79–112.
[21] A. Fleming, 'Territorial Patterns in Bronze Age Wessex', *Proc. Prehist. Soc.* 37 (1971), 138–66; and Fleming's chapter, together with one by the editor, in C. Renfrew (ed.), *The Explanation of Culture Change: Models in Prehistory* (1973). *See also* Renfrew's *Before Civilization* (1973), ch. 11.

disappear, their stones for example perhaps removed for other purposes like road-making. Evidence can become deeply buried or washed away by 'natural' erosion, and of course all sorts of later land use like ploughing or gravel extraction are constantly eroding the evidence. So the field record, even if intensively compiled, contains only that which is recordable and that, by definition, is only a variable proportion in any area of that which once existed. Furthermore, the pattern of land-use at the time or times of field survey is a crucial factor, and so too is the pattern of archaeological activity. The somewhat sick in-joke that distribution maps merely reflect where archaeologists have worked still contains a substantial element of truth. Another critical factor is the quality of the field archaeologist himself and of the recording system in any given area. A museum or journal, for example, which encourages the receipt of information will quickly build up a reasonable bank of information which can be made available to others and assimilated into the archaeological thinking about the area involved; but an equal amount of field activity in a neighbouring area can be to little avail if there is no such facility.

An archaeological distribution map is then compound of and constrained by a whole range of factors, some of which have nothing to do with the original distribution of whatever it is that is being mapped. As such it must be used with caution, not least as it is all too easy to jump to 'obvious' conclusions staring out of the completed map e.g. earthworks of prehistoric settlements occur on the Wessex Downs and not in the valleys; therefore prehistoric people lived on the downs (which is correct) and not in the valleys (which is false). Other examples are: hill-forts in Wessex with two or more ramparts occur mainly west of the Salisbury Avon (correct) and, since multivallation is a late development (correct at time of writing but actually false), were so fortified against the Belgae (false); pit alignments occur only in eastern England (correct at time of writing but actually incorrect) and can therefore best be explained in an Anglo-Saxon context (false because of new discoveries further west and excavated dating evidence). Perhaps the most striking example of all from Britain is the way in which the deduction from the negligible field record that little if any prehistoric settlement of the Midlands occurred has been reversed by photographic results in recent years.[22] The 'obvious' overall deduction is that any distribution map is no more than an interim cartographic statement which could be not just amplified but actually changed completely by further work. The field record may be ultimately finite, and that finiteness is certainly already sufficiently reduced by destruction to affect its value as an interpretative base in the topographical archaeology of certain areas; but meanwhile so much of it still remains a potential rather than an actual record that, for many parts of the world, the main archaeological task for the rest of this century is quite clear.

[22] Beginning with G. Webster and B. Hobley, 'Aerial reconnaissance of the Warwickshire Avon', *Archaeol. J.* 121 (1965), 1–22. The bibliographies attached to the several papers in D. R. Wilson (ed.), *op. cit.* note 10, give good coverage up to 1974.

Bibliography

R. Agache, *Détection Aérienne de Vestiges Protohistoriques, Gallo-Romains et Médievaux* . . . (1970)

K. Amis, *Lucky Jim* (1954)

Antiq. J. 45 (1965), 22–52 ('A Roman Barrow at Knob's Crook, Dorset')

Antiquity 41 (1967), 289–301

M. Aston and J. Bond, *The Landscape of Towns* (1976)

R. J. C. Atkinson, *Field Archaeology* (1946, 1953)

M. W. Barley (ed.), *The Plans and Topography of Medieval Towns in England and Wales* (1976)

D. Benson and D. Miles, *The Upper Thames Valley: an archaeological survey of river gravels* (1974)

H. C. Bowen, 'Air Photography: some implications in the south of England', *Field Survey in British Archaeology* (1972)

D. Browne, *Principles and Practice in Modern Archaeology* (1975)

J. Coles, *Field Archaeology in Britain* (1972)

Countryside Commission, *New Agricultural Landscapes* (1974)

O. G. S. Crawford, *Air Survey and Archaeology* (1924, 1925); *Archaeology in the Field* (1953)

O. G. S. Crawford and A. Keiller, *Wessex from the Air* (1928)

Current Archaeol. 16 (1969), 124–9

A. Fleming, 'Territorial patterns in Bronze Age Wessex', *Proc. Prehist. Soc.* 37 (1971)

E. Fowler (ed.), *Field Survey in British Archaeology* (1972)

P. J. Fowler (ed.), *Archaeology and the Landscape* (1972); *Recent Work in Rural Archaeology* (1975)

T. Gates, *The Middle Thames Valley* . . . (1975)

L. V. Grinsell, 'Disc-Barrows', *Proc. Prehist. Soc.* 40 (1974), 79–112.

G. J. Gumerman, *The Distribution of Prehistoric Population Aggregates* (1971)

C. Heighway, *The Erosion of History: Archaeology and Planning in Towns* (1972)

R. Leech, *The Upper Thames Valley in Gloucestershire and Wiltshire* (1977)

T. Mathiassen, *Nordvestsjaellands Oldtidsbebyggelse* (1959)

Ordnance Survey, *Field Archaeology in Great Britain* (1973)

R.C.H.M., *A Matter of Time* (1960); E. Mercer, *English Vernacular Houses, A study of traditional farmhouses and cottages* (1975); P. Smith, *Houses in the Welsh Countryside* (1975)

C. Renfrew, *Before Civilization* (1973); (ed.), *The Explanation of Culture Change: Models in Prehistory* (1973)

Rescue News 10 (1975)

A. Rogers and T. Rowley (eds.), *Landscapes and Documents* (1974)

M. B. Schiffer and J. H. House, *The Cache River Archaeological Project: an experiment in contract archaeology* (1975)

C. Thomas (ed.), *Rural Settlement in Roman Britain* (1966)

G. Webster and B. Hobley 'Aerial reconnaissance of the Warwickshire Avon', *Archaeol. J.* (1965), 1–22

D.R. Wilson (ed.), *Aerial Reconnaissance for Archaeology* (1975)

3
BURIED ARCHAEOLOGY

'. . . the light of simple veritie,
Buried in ruines, . . .'
   Edmund Spenser, *Complaints: The Ruines of Time* (1591)

We have already noted that a distinction between above and below-ground evidence is untenable (p. 35) and this chapter, in being physically separate from the last, is therefore merely an organisational device. We have also already discussed one of the larger components of 'buried archaeology', that is the mass of evidence recorded from the air as crop-marks which, by definition, relate to buried features (p. 49). Indeed, the existence of the air photographs poses in an acute, practical form the basic, philosophic question which has to be answered anyway: 'Why excavate?' If the air photographs are so good, why does the archaeologist want to dig up (and spoil) the features they reveal? If the air photographic results really are so overwhelming, what is the point of excavating?

These are not merely idle questions since the approach to the past through digging in an ever more systematic way is not only the *raison d'etre* of archaeology in many people's minds but it is also *the* activity which differentiates archaeology from the other field sciences. Without excavation, archaeology could probably be subsumed into one or more of them, or possibly even into history, as its academic disciplinary base. Traditionally, and perhaps conceptually too, excavation is therefore at the core of archaeology and central to the work of archaeologists. Even the great non-excavating line of British field archaeologists in recent times—Crawford, Grinsell, Bowen—has had to concern itself with the *results* of much excavation while having the sense not to become involved in the personal direction of the *act* of excavation. Tradition and conceptual necessity hardly explain and certainly do not justify the act of excavation, however, even though they may suggest the existence of long-term and basic reasons for

III.1 'Excavation, even from its earliest days, . . . has been effective in finding material things . . . durable building materials'. Two published, early twentieth century excavation photographs: (a) 'remains of Buildings, C. Block XIV. Pillar and south-west corner of building' at Newstead, Melrose, Scotland; (b) 'Western side of Room T', Hal-Tarxien, Malta.

what is, particularly in its modern form, a very curious, complex and expensive type of activity.[1]

Until recently, one of archaeology's greatest assets was a belief that it dealt primarily with the surviving material from the past—the tangible things, the solid structures, the demonstrable evidence. Its role was to uncover, to reveal, to discover forgotten civilizations, lost worlds, mysterious ruins and fine art. Though such a circumscribed approach to the subject and its objectives is no longer adequate, nevertheless archaeology retains a big advantage over straight history, for example, in that it can literally deliver the goods and appeal directly to a public audience. Whether in so doing it also produces good, i.e. academic, archaeology is a different matter, and risks are of course attendant, as in all public relations exercises, in playing to the audience. Recent episodes in Britain, for example the excavations at Silbury Hill, South Cadbury Castle, *Vindolanda* and Bayard's Castle in London, illustrate some of the facets of the complex relationship between what the public expects (or is led to expect) and what archaeology actually produces in terms of visual discoveries and instant results.

The nature of excavated evidence

By and large, the mythical 'man in the street', equating excavation with archaeology, still expects archaeology to produce, and indeed to be aimed at producing, two things: treasure and skeletons. Stone buildings come third. Drama, excitement and visual impact apart, archaeological evidence of course includes such material, particularly skeletons and stone buildings though 'treasure' very seldom indeed. (Nearly all of the treasure from British soil has been found by accident, e.g. in ploughing or, particularly in recent years, by self-styled treasure-hunters deliberately attempting to exploit part of the national heritage, *see* p. 186.) Archaeological excavation, even from its earliest days, always has been effective in finding material things—pottery above all but also coins, brooches, stone and metal tools and other objects, durable building materials, glass, in fact anything which survives when buried (Pl. III.1). In particular circumstances, as in the damp of Danish bogs, the ice of Siberia or Arizonan desert aridity, it has recovered organic materials like wood, textiles, basketwork and even corpses, much of them before the development of modern excavation and conservation techniques. The contents of museums in both the Old World and the New attest only too well to the success of archaeological excavation as an instrument of discovery and recovery. All of this material forms the bulk of archaeological evidence as found and now stored, as a

[1] At the moment there is no authoritative textbook on the conduct of modern excavation to the best current standards though it can be anticipated that P. A. Barker, *Techniques of Archaeological Excavation* (1977) will meet the need. The basic available publications are Sir Mortimer Wheeler, *Archaeology from the Earth* (1954); J. Alexander, *The Directing of Archaeological Excavations* (1970) and G. Webster, *Practical Archaeology* (2nd ed. 1974). Personally, I would still recommend R. J. C. Atkinson, *Field Archaeology* (1953) for its clarity and S. J. de Laet, *Archaeology and its Problems* (1957) for its sensitivity.

III.2 'Lack of dramatic interest . . . on the frontiers of knowledge'. Drs. J. G. Evans and S. Limbrey taking soil samples during the sixteenth year section through the Overton Down experimental earthwork, Wiltshire, July, 1976.

physically existing corpus of finds on which our edifice (or is it facade?) of archaeological knowledge has been constructed.

Excavated evidence now includes not only the post-holes of timber buildings but also much more fugitive traces of structures, perhaps established over a whole sequence of excavation and never visible at any one time as a complete entity, either to the archaeologist or to the day-visitor. The latter is naturally disappointed, probably puzzled and possibly cynical if he comes and sees nothing when he has read in the local press about the discovery of large timber halls or rows of wooden buildings (fig. 3.1). The ultimate in excavation so far is not to find anything at all in the conventional sense but to demonstrate a series of relationships, e.g. between the ephemera of fugitive timber structures and genuinely blank areas in a settlement in the horizontal plain, or between a vegetational sequence and a series of C14 dates in the vertical plane. In the last example, the main 'finds' could well be nothing more at face value than a dozen soil-filled polythene bags. Their lack of dramatic interest for the public, expecting to find

73

the archaeologist on the frontiers of knowledge, hardly needs emphasising (Pl. III.2).

There is then, this other type of evidence which is now more or less a standard product of excavation. It does not consist of finds of the sort the archaeologist can display on site or in a museum. It consists of samples like those we have just used in our example, samples of soil and other deposits in the ground, collected partly to examine the soil itself and also to extract from it the wealth of environmental evidence, fossil creatures and floral fragments in particular, it could well contain. It is often now literally true that the excavator does not know what he has found until months, even years, after his work on site has finished; for he may well need an enormous amount of laboratory analysis, probably carried out by others, before he has the information on which to start making an assessment of his excavation. Even when he has the data its 'meaning' may not be clear, and further analysis, with or without a computer, may well suggest patterns not previously perceived. Any such patterns are themselves just as much evidence as the pottery and stone walls 'revealed' on the site. The macro-visibility of evidence is really irrelevant to its validity as evidence. We can see then, even at this preliminary stage, that the range of evidence produced by the search for the past is enormous, even within the confines of archaeological research. It certainly extends well beyond the 'treasure and skeletons' image with which archaeology is still lumbered by its paymasters and customers.

Why excavate?

Rather than look first for answers to the question 'Why excavate?' in the history of archaeology, let us take some recent reasons given to explain why a particular excavation was carried out. They come from a 'grab sample' of reports picked off my book-shelves, almost but not quite at random since I am confining myself to modern examples and deliberately chose from a range of *published* excavation reports (thereby excluding a very large number of excavations). Perhaps the most revealing fact is that

3.1 General plan showing all the features recorded in the horizontal dimension during three small-scale excavations outside the present standing east end of St. Mary's Church, Deerhurst, Glos. The fragment of the polygonal apse is also still standing; and the semicircular apse, uncovered in an earlier excavation, was visible before 1971. Its interior had been almost completely cleared out but none of the features shown here, or those outside, had previously been noted. Though expressed here in a two-dimensional drawing, they belong to a long sequence of activity, of at least seven detectable structural phases, spanning the five or six centuries between Roman Britain and Norman England. Though apparently 'meaningless' in plan, and actually meaningless without the stratigraphical/time dimension, detail of this sort, patiently built up over weeks of painstaking work, is now observed and recorded as the norm on modern excavation and there seems no academic point in excavating unless this standard is accepted and achievable. *Cf.* fig. 3.2.

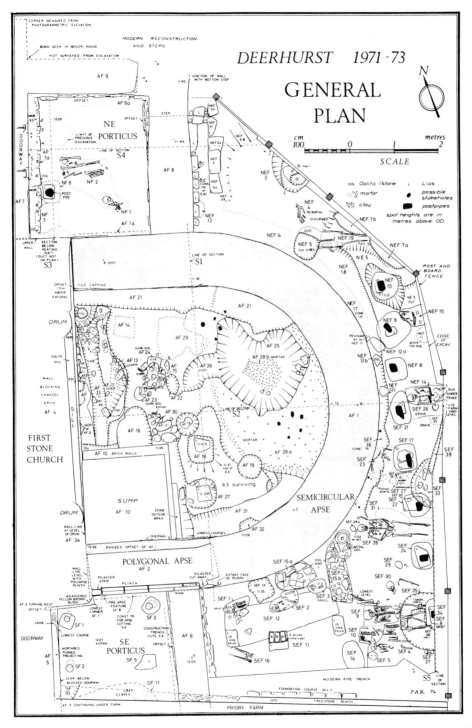

DEERHURST 1971-73

GENERAL PLAN

nearly half of the reports gave no reason at all for the excavation, rather confirming a suspicion that, in archaeologists' minds anyway, excavation is self-justificatory. One dip into a pre-1940 journal was enough to produce as a starting point a statement representative of old-style excavation objectives:

> 'The purpose of the excavation . . . was to expose the ring wall . . . and to trace out . . . the plan of the interior buildings, as a prelude to a systematic exploration of the site . . .'[2]

Another traditional reason for an excavation, the wishes and/or interest of a landowner, also immediately appeared in my sample:

> '. . . the new owner . . . approached the County Museum expressing his interest in the villa and the possibility of future excavations . . . the curator then asked the (Society) if they (*sic*) would be interested in the site, and negotiations were opened . . . the writer was invited to direct the excavations . . .'[3]

Basically the same reason can also be expressed by an individual through an institution:

> '. . . the . . . Trust, at the instigation of the late Wellesley Tudor Pole, initiated a programme of archaeological excavation in the hope that it would clarify the early Christian legends . . . further work . . . has been suspended indefinitely because of the death of Major Tudor Pole . . .'[4]

The same reason too continues in modern institutional form:

> '. . . the entire fort and a large part of the surrounding area . . . was opened to the public as an amenity area. At the request and under the sponsorship of the County Council, excavation began . . .'[5]

Institutions have a big advantage in being able to pursue long-term objectives, in another case adding the element of preservation i.e. on-site consolidation for public display:

> 'The excavation . . . was undertaken . . . in pursuance of the Ministry's policy to elucidate and preserve the monuments of national importance under its care.'[6]

The public interest in excavation, and archaeology's need for trained diggers, has

[2] *Proc. Soc. Antiq. Scot.* 70 (1936), 175.
[3] K. Branigan, *Latimer* (1971), 8.
[4] P. Rahtz and S. Hirst, *Beckery Chapel, Glastonbury 1967–8* (1974), 7.
[5] *Antiq. J.* 51 (1971), 240.
[6] R. J. C. Hamilton, *Excavations at Clickhimin, Shetland* (1968), xv.

resulted in Britain especially but also in America in a curiously introspective type of excavation, the publicly-available training excavation:

> '. . . the author supervised a trial excavation . . . as part of a training course in the techniques of archaeological investigation . . . the primary object was to recover the plan of the fort and its defences, and ascertain when the site was in use . . . it was also considered desirable that at least a little should be learned about its internal layout.'[7]

We see there but first mention of detailed objectives, the plan of the site, its date and its internal arrangement, giving in that case an academic justification to a training exercise. The former comes first in a similar statement:

> 'My attention was drawn to the site . . . when I was looking for a villa on which to plan a long-term research project which could also be used for training purposes.'[8]

In other words, the excavator is trying to marry two different and perhaps incompatible reasons for carrying out an excavation, using educational means towards a research objective. At its grandest, research excavation can sound very grand indeed and need have no regard for such conceptual hair-splitting or practical ambiguity:

> 'The excavations were conceived and initiated . . . on behalf of the Department . . . as part of its efforts to investigate various aspects of the physical and cultural evolution of Man.'[9]

Research excavation can also be designed to meet a very practical academic need, in this next case the context of a large and archaeologically important nineteenth century collection of objects in a national museum. It is interesting to note how that reason is further justified by the research potential of a 'unique' site:

> 'A native hill-fort thus occupied by an established Roman garrison is a unique site, and it was clear that its excavation should produce invaluable information on the character and effects of the Roman conquest in Wessex . . . The need for establishing an historical context for this (Durden) collection, and of relating the types of object represented . . . to the different structures on the site, provided another weighty reason for excavation. In consideration of the British Museum's special concern, excavation was undertaken . . .'[10]

---

[7] *Proc. Soc. Antiq. Scot.* 104 (1971–2), 147.
[8] *Trans. Bristol Gloucestershire Archaeol. Soc.* 86 (1967), 74.
[9] *Proc. Prehist. Soc.* 39 (1975), 9.
[10] J.W. Brailsford, *Hod Hill I* (1962), vii.

The Hod Hill excavation was initiated very much as an *ad hoc* and finite piece of research. A research excavation can begin with a very specific, problem-oriented objective yet avowedly have wider objectives, not least in fitting into a long-term research design:

> 'The . . . excavation . . . sought to answer specific questions, primarily about the context of the post-Roman sherds in order to establish whether their (previous and unstratified) discovery was evidence of a genuine re-occupation. This renewed interest in the site was to a large extent stimulated by excavations at South Cadbury and Glastonbury Tor . . . which had highlighted the whole question of 'Dark Age' settlement types . . . and the distribution and significance of imported Mediterranean pottery in particular. In a more local context, the excavation fitted . . . into a detailed study of the land-use history of the Vale . . .'[11]

In addition to research, excavation can also be viewed as but a stage in a larger project involving the community in its archaeology and designed to result quite specifically in a publicly available product:

> 'The excavation was designed to form the local part of a programme leading directly through to a book incorporating all that is known of Manchester's archaeological past.'[12]

That Manchester programme arose out of the archaeological opportunity provided by urban redevelopment. It was originally an emergency or rescue excavation, carried out then and there for that reason. Such destruction or threat of destruction is probably now the most frequent reason for excavation and is commonly regarded as reason in itself:

> '. . . the Society was informed that part of a tesselated pavement had been ploughed up . . . (in a field) known to contain a Romano-British building . . . an emergency excavation was considered necessary.'[13]
>
> 'In view of this accelerated rate of destruction, and in the knowledge that it would continue, a decision was taken to excavate the site immediately.'[14]
>
> 'The standard parochial histories . . . generally agreed that the site must have been of importance . . . excavation of this site was arranged . . . at the time of the clearing and afforestation of the valley. (It) continued . . . to reveal the complete area of occupation and to examine the defences.'[15]

---

[11] P.J. Fowler *et al.*, *Cadbury Congresbury, Somerset 1968* (1970), 10.
[12] G.D.B. Jones, *Roman Manchester* (1974), 31.
[13] *Proc. Devon Archaeol. Soc.* 32 (1974), 61.
[14] *Trans. Bristol Gloucestershire Archaeol. Soc.* 88 (1969), 38.
[15] *Medieval Archaeol.* 18 (1974), 94.

Those three quotations relate to known sites. Air photographs may have made known previously unrecorded sites, the 'newness' of which can of itself be regarded as justification for excavation:

'The sites . . . were first discovered from the air . . . and until their excavation . . . air photographs constituted the only evidence for their nature and position . . . a new gravel pit was started in (their) immediate vicinity . . . As the rapid destruction of the sites appeared inevitable, permission for their excavation was obtained . . .'[16]

The fact that a site was completely unknown has itself been advanced as a reason for a salvage excavation, despite the fact that thousands of known sites are simultaneously being destroyed:

'. . . burnt material and scraps of bronze were being found in a trench cut into a small, previously unrecorded mound . . . The site was visited and, since a small pit was visible in section, and the finds were apparently from it, further investigation was planned.'[17]

Ideally perhaps, conscious academic objectives can be sought in the rescue situation, replacing the hit-and-miss, instinctive and probably emotive reaction to the destruction of sites with a problem-oriented research design:

'The influence which the Little Woodbury excavations and their interpretations have had on Iron Age studies in Britain is all-pervading, and yet the evidence was obtained from a partial excavation . . . For many years it had been apparent that the total excavation of a Little Woodbury-type enclosure was a prime necessity for the advancement of socio-economic theory in Iron Age studies . . . the author reviewed the known enclosures in Wessex . . . with a view to excavating one such site totally . . . Eventually the enclosure at Gussage All Saints was selected and totally excavated . . .'[18]

Overall perhaps it is not too unfair to say that British archaeologists are not apparently very good at explaining, at rationalising, why they are doing particular excavations. As the above quotations illustrate, and others would substantiate, there is some confusion about the objectives of an excavation and the reasons for doing it. Strategies and tactics are mixed up even if they consciously exist; and we have not yet touched on a range of other reasons, sub-academic or sub-professional, for some excavations being carried out. Though they do not primarily concern us, since our

[16] R.J.C. Atkinson *et al.*, *Excavations at Dorchester, Oxon.* (1951), vii.
[17] *Antiq. J.* 45 (1965), 22.
[18] *Antiquity* 47 (1973), 110–11.

subject is archaeology, it nevertheless has to be recognised that a lot of digging on archaeological sites, sometimes in the name of archaeology, is executed primarily though perhaps unconsciously for reasons other than academic research: to cock a snook at the professionals and academics; for self-aggrandizement, physical relaxation, excitement, masochism; out of local pride, curiosity, innocent enthusiasm, selfishness, greed; as social therapy or vandalism—all these and many other reasons come to mind. Scratch anyone thus digging and his reason will probably be found amongst these, often in combination, often muddled, and often not really thought out coherently. Amongst 'volunteers' on a large excavation in Britain anyway, the need to earn money and to meet academic course requirements may well be the immediate reason for a person being on that excavation, whatever the motives of the institution or director in mounting it.

Academically, there is really no doubt that the main reason for excavating is to acquire new information and thereby new understanding of the past. The older idea that the main reason was to acquire new objects, preferably display-worthy, persists, however, and still remains a principal reason for collectors and museums supporting excavations financially. There need be no conflict here, but conceptually and sometimes in practice there is. If the excavation's aim is truly to acquire new information, then it really is irrelevant from the purely academic point of view in what form that information is recovered (fig. 3.2). Normally, it will come as visible structural remains and tangible artefacts of baked clay, glass, metal and other durable material but it could come as well, and perhaps exclusively, in the form of drawn plans of transient soil differences and of soil samples. Indeed, excavations producing just such results are commonly carried out by geologists and palaeo-botanists, for example, though their diggings have none of the complexity or sophistication of archaeological excavation. Ideally of course the palaeo-scientist should be on the archaeological site obtaining his samples from cultural contexts observed and recorded with normal archaeological precision; but even to say that probably assumes an initiating and dominant role for the archaeologist. He could well be hired in fact to provide the technical expertise in digging on an excavation primarily being conducted for environmental research. Either way, 'finds' in the conventional, museum sense need not be the object of the excavation, though unusual would be the excavation in southern England if there were none. Even if there are, however, the spatial relationships between 'finds', horizontally as well as

3.2 A reconstruction in plan of the eight main structural phases through which the 'lost' church of St. Pancras, Winchester, passed during its thousand or so year history, as witnessed by evidence obtained from archaeological excavation. None of the church survived above ground and the results of its excavation, as expressed here, are derived as much from the evidence of 'transient soil differences' as of masonry remains. A similarly expressed sequence was possible from the Deerhurst excavation, fig. 3.1.

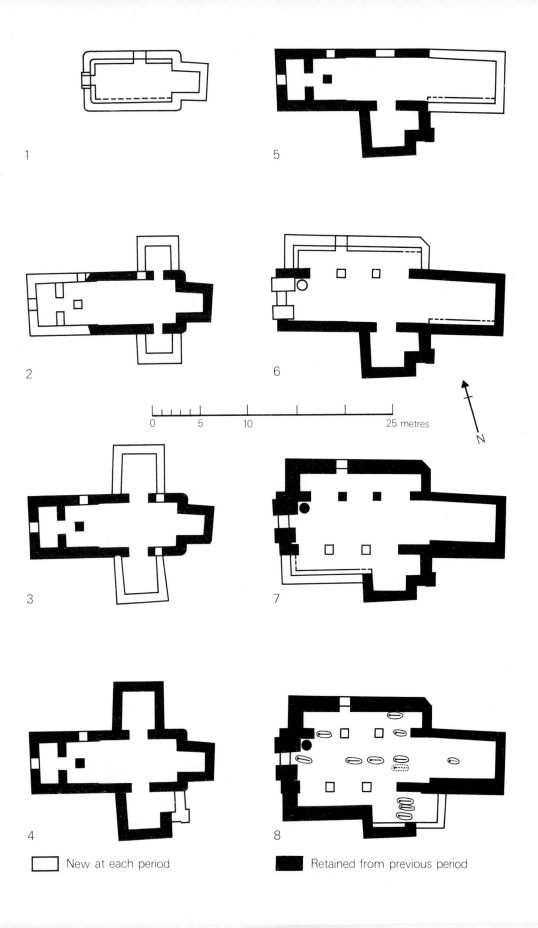

1

5

2

6

0   5   10   25 metres

N

3

7

4

8

☐ New at each period   ■ Retained from previous period

vertically, represent 'new information' as much as the objects themselves, and they have to be recovered with appropriate recovery techniques just as the 'finds' themselves have to be recorded.

Once this is accepted, then clearly an excavation can very quickly become a technically complicated process of 'finding' many thousands of new pieces of information of which the significance will almost certainly not be apparent until long after the publicly-viewable part of the exercise is over. It is in this context that the difficulty, even reluctance, of the excavating archaeologist in answering the commonest question he is asked has to be seen. 'What have you found?' or more usually 'Have you found anything interesting?' is understandably not satisfied with 'I don't know' or 'I hope so', though such answers may well be the literal truth. Despite this, it must be said that there are probably more excavations now than ever before conducted with an eye to the public interest in the activity of excavating *per se* and making some provision for meeting and indeed encouraging that interest. Particularly where that interest is based on a local patriotism, informing it could well be high on the list of reasons for the excavation in the first place. In contrast, however, there are many excavations in remote places all over the world without a thought for public interest at the time, conducted purely for scientific, research reasons. Basically excavation remains a disciplined exercise in curiosity: whether the exercise is acceptable archaeologically depends to a large extent on the intellectual and technical level at which the curiosity is expressed and satisfied.

The burial of cultural evidence

Rationalising apart, however, the main reason why we excavate to infuse our knowledge of the past with new information and, hopefully, new understanding is quite simply because things tend to become buried through time. If this did not happen, excavation would be unnecessary. Its *raison d'être*, and therefore that of archaeology as a field science or merely a field technique, is as simple as that. Because evidence of the past becomes buried, the purpose of excavation is in a simplistic but real sense to uncover that which has become hidden by being buried. In that sense, therefore, the functions of excavation are very similar to those of air photography (p. 44) and various sub-terrestial and sub-aqua surveying techniques (p. 124) in that they seek to reveal what has become buried and is consequently hidden. Why we, human beings, should want to see what is buried and to seek to know not only how it became buried but also what it 'means' is difficult to explain rationally and is not satisfactorily answered by reverting to the word 'curiosity'. Nevertheless, whatever the reason for and motivation of 'curiosity', its power is strong and even recognised by non-psychological interests such as urban developers as they provide public platforms for the curious to watch their big mechanical excavations dug for construction purposes.

The chance of a 'discovery' being made is one of the attractions of such works—

attractions for the public, that is, since developers and archaeologists fear precisely that happening (p. 182). Nevertheless, deep holes in towns provide a useful starting point briefly to consider why and how things — old buildings, ancient pottery and so on — do in fact become buried. It is a common belief that very old remains are buried very deeply and indeed that the older something is the deeper it will be (*cf.* p. 87); and it is indeed confusing that a Neolithic site of *c*. 4000 bc like Windmill Hill, near Avebury, or indeed Avebury itself of *c*. 2500 bc, should be visible on the present ground surface while medieval Oxford is some 4 m. deep below Carfax. Even more perplexing in a way is finding on the surface of a ploughed field Mesolithic flints, Roman building debris and modern tea-pot and willow-pattern pottery, or looking at a museum case and seeing that Palaeolithic flints of *c*. 10,000 BC have been variously found on the present ground surface, 5 m. deep outside a cave and 10 m. deep in a gravel terrace. In most such cases, what is determining the depth is not time but the situation of the original site and the uses to which it has subsequently been put by Man, Nature or both.

Before considering how natural processes bury a site, let us first look at Man's activities. These alone would in many cases make excavation necessary, granted a 'need' to find out the history of a site from unwritten sources. We can distinguish four stages in the history of a site which lead to its being now in the state where it is deemed worthy of excavation. The first stage is 'natural': the development of the site to the state it is in when Man first affects it; second is the period, brief or long, during which Man uses it; and the third and fourth phases are again 'natural', assuming for present purposes that the site is eventually abandoned. The third stage is that of collapse, in which the man-made features disintegrate, and the fourth is as the natural processes take over completely, reducing the site to its present state (Pl. III.3). This model is, of course, grossly simplified, but it serves to illustrate why and how sites are buried — or not, as the case may be.

Once stage 2 has started, excavation is almost certainly going to be the only way in which evidence can be acquired about the site in stage 1, for Man's use of the site or area will affect both its 'natural' state and the evidence for that state. The building of structures and the digging of pits will disturb or bury it, the laying of floors will cover it. In stage 2, if use of the site is of any duration and particularly if the use is for habitation, that use will, in creating its own archaeology, tend to bury or otherwise obscure features. Early arrangements of buildings will be altered, structural features will be modified, parts will fall out of use and new parts will be added, soil will be moved around and rubbish will be deposited. So that, even before stage 3 started, excavation could usefully be employed to find out about the history of the site from the evidence which is already buried below ground or obscured in standing structures. In addition to evidence deliberately buried, like rubbish in pits or burials in graves, earlier occupation levels could be sealed beneath later floors, early foundation trenches could be covered by later walls, timber structures might have been replaced by stone ones. So a site such as an existing farm or village has really acquired its excavation potential during its

III.3 'The natural processes take over . . .' Kilpeck Castle, Herefordshire, in September, 1975, looking up the slope towards its overgrown ditch, rampart and high surviving wall (on top of which two figures are standing). This is a typical case of how even substantial remains deteriorate and barely rank as visible history in popular or educative terms without careful, and expensive, maintenance.

man-made life, before it subsequently collapses and is handed over to Nature for stages 3 and 4. These stages usually make the elucidation of the evidence more difficult. Except for proving evidence of the post-occupation history of the site, which can of course have an interest in its own right, theoretically those stages are not basic as such to the function of an archaeological excavation if it is defined as one primarily concerned with artefactual evidence and cultural history. In practice, however, there are so many exceptions to such a theoretical position that the generalisation can best be disregarded. It is only by studying the changes in the site in stages 3 and 4 that an appreciation becomes possible of why the site is in its present state and of how the evidence of stage 2 comes to be in its observable state as recovered by excavation.

In stage 3, for example, even though the site may already have been abandoned, it is vital to establish how the 'collapse phase' occurred: was the site left in pristine condition, was it demolished, was it left to rot and decay? Apart from contributing to its cultural history, such considerations bear on how the site came to be buried: demolition of a site, for example a Roman fort, will create a different burial pattern from that of a medieval stone castle merely left to the elements, and both will be different from a wooden building burnt to the ground. Whatever the immediate cause of stage 3, the effect will be to cover up stage 2 as building materials of all sorts collapse and

84

disintegrate. In stage 4, by and large this process will continue depending on where the site is and on a complex of climatic and land-use factors. In a valley or on a flood plain, it could become deeply buried by alluvium, gravel or erosion products off the hill-sides. If somewhere not subject to such factors, its own collapse could create a vegetation which gradually buries it in humus, perhaps to survive as grass-covered earthworks if the area is not subsequently ploughed. The thousands of examples of deserted and shrunken medieval settlements in England illustrate this. Alternatively, a dry site, through a change in climate or in local drainage patterns, might become waterlogged, stopping the decay of its organic components but creating new conditions in which it becomes buried by the growth of peat. In sharp contrast, sites can become completely desiccated, perhaps through climatic change, and be buried and largely preserved by sand, either in desert conditions as in Egypt and Arizona or during dune-formations along coastlands. Cases of this last occur, for example, around St. Ives Bay, Cornwall, and in the Orkneys and Shetlands.

The commonest reason for the deep burial of archaeological deposits, however, is the continued use of the site: hence the tells of the Near East and the several metres of material above the Roman levels in cities like London, Lincoln and Gloucester. The levels are buried by the rubble and rubbish produced by people living for centuries on the same site and gradually rising on their debris. The area around the cathedral in Dublin or behind the quays at Bergen, Norway, are splendid examples of this, all the more so because the damp conditions have preserved all the organic materials, especially wood, making up the archaeological layers on which the present streets and pavements lie. But most historic town sites are the same: Jerusalem and Jericho sit on their own rubbish of millennia, and so do Cologne, York and Colchester. The slight rise up to Carfax along the four roads leading to it through Oxford is caused by the accretion of rubbish on the gravel terrace some 4 m. below the present tarmac, an accretion of barely 1200 years. There is really no problem of why sites are buried: in a way the marvel is that so many are either not really buried or lie immediately below the present surface.

The point needs stressing since people seem to expect excavations and archaeologists to go down a long way, perhaps on the unstated assumption that deeper is better, older and richer. Until the advent of systematic air photography, however, most known archaeological sites in Britain were known precisely because not only were they not buried deeply but because they actually stuck up above the general level of the surrounding ground. Here one is thinking not merely of the many ruins of medieval sites marked by upstanding masonry but of the much larger number of earlier sites — Roman and prehistoric — which survived until recently in Lowland England as earthworks and still do survive extensively in the north and west of Britain and in Ireland. Such sites have not been buried in any real sense, and now they are merely covered by grass on a thin layer of humus or, in the west and north, by heather or nothing at all. In such cases, climatic and other factors have prevented burial of sites, as the many examples of hut circles, stone ramparts and burial mounds attest, for example, on Dartmoor and in Gwynedd. Such factors may even have had the opposite effect by exposing features through the processes of erosion and soil leeching. This is why so many of the visible 'ancient monuments' in Britain are in the west and north and why air photography has been so successful in recording many of the surviving, surface sites in England. In excavation terms, such sites lack stage 4, and their investigation can begin almost with a study of stage 3, their collapse. This really applies to sites of all post-glacial periods in Britain: in such circumstances, especially of denudation and erosion, depth has no relation to age; the palaeolith can be just as near the surface as the teapot sherd, and hence the field above (p. 83) with material from a wide time-range all on the surface. From the excavator's point of view, such areas and sites are of course attractive in the sense that a prehistoric layer 5 cms. rather than 5 m. deep is much more accessible; but, on the other hand, such sites will lack long, clear-cut vertical sequences and, in all probability if severely denuded, artefacts other than those of stone.

The evidence of sequence and artefacts is among the most important products of excavation, despite what has been said above (p. 74), simply because change (or lack of it) is archaeologically one of the most interesting facets of cultural behaviour to study. Furthermore, archaeology prides itself on being good at studying (or at least at detecting) cultural change. Certainly we could excavate a single period site (though even that must basically have a before, during and after) and find nothing in the way of normal archaeological material, yet still be able to say a number of worthwhile things about it. On the other hand, unless we can place that site in absolute time or in a relative time sequence, and unless we can relate its inhabitants to other people and to a life-style, our interpretative ambitions must be strictly circumscribed. An excavation would by no means necessarily be a failure if it did not discover 'finds' of pottery, stone or metal for, as we have seen, it might produce crucial environmental evidence instead (p. 74); in Britain anyway, it would actually be of considerable interest if it *was* only of a single-phase since virtually all sites appear to be multi-phase (so much so that a report of a single phase site would probably be suspect as being that of a poorly conducted excavation!). Nevertheless, to be able to place a site with all its phases in a sequence is a basic objective of the archaeological approach (p. 109), and it can only be realised if the principle of stratification and the technique and art of stratigraphy are followed.

Stratification and stratigraphy

Both, like so much else in archaeology, were adapted from the natural sciences, in this case from geology in the mid-nineteenth century. Stratification is the process whereby the rocks of the earth's surface are laid down naturally in a sequence with the earliest at the bottom and the latest at the top. In practice, of course, there are exceptions due to faulting, upthrusts, inversions and other natural phenomena; and stratigraphy, the process of recording and interpreting the observed strata, is further complicated by features such as discontinuous layers and indeed the absence of layers from sequences in which stratigraphically they should occur. But the principle remains correct and, granted that there are similar but much smaller-scale complications in an archaeological context, it can be applied as the guide-line in establishing an archaeological sequence. The lowest layers, features and 'finds' recorded in an excavation should be the earliest and are certainly earlier than similar evidence originating higher up the strata or 'layer-cake' constituting an archaeological site. The man-made stratification, perhaps interleaved with natural layers formed, for example, by a flood, consists then of deposits created in a sequence through time, with the newest or youngest at the top and the oldest at the bottom. One of the aims of excavation must be to expose and record this sequence, whether the technique employed is a deep, straight-sided trench with the layers exposed to view or a more sophisticated three-dimensional area record with no standing sections. The principle is the same, and has been the basis of good excavation, though not always followed, since technically mastered by General Pitt-Rivers in the 1880s (fig. 3.3).

Granted that the main objective of excavation is to recover information rather than objects *per se*, the necessity for stratigraphy is obvious. We need to know not only what has been found but also where it came from in relation to other objects and to the features constituting the site (for present purposes a layer is a feature). Furthermore, we need to know not only the absolute and relative context of objects but also the relative position of all the features so that all the constituents of the site —pots and all the other objects, structures, layers, the variety of environmental evidence, —are related not only to a context but also to each other; and the key to those relationships is stratigraphy. The relationships can of course be expressed in absolute terms —a is 1·25m. below b, c is 2·7 m. west of d —but, since cultural stratification possesses all the complexities of geological stratification, such measures express nothing more than a spatial relationship in one dimension. In cultural and sequential terms such absolute expressions are meaningless unless they are simultaneously related to the real sequential development of the site in which it would be surprising if there were not the archaeological equivalents of fault-lines, upthrust and inversions (fig. 3.3).

During the use of a site, layers are disturbed by Man's activities. He digs parts of layers away and redeposits the material elsewhere. He digs trenches, graves, pits and post-holes. He excavates ditches and builds banks with the spoil, he alters the bank's construction, he replaces wooden structures with stone; he alters the shape, size and function of buildings, he lays floors on top of existing ones, he digs cellars with floors well-below his contemporary ground surface by cutting down into earlier levels and redistributing their materials in later contexts. All the time he is fighting a battle with the rising tide of his rubbish: he buries it, he heaps it up, he spreads it around, he dumps it elsewhere. And in more recent times, he is forever digging trenches in which to put pipes, wires and drains, while his modern ability and apparent need to dig bigger and deeper holes can cause more confusion to the existing stratification in a day than

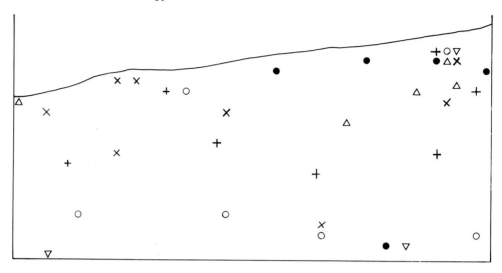

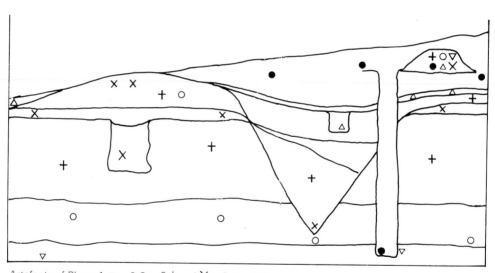

Artefacts of Phase 1 ▽   2 ○   3 +   4 ✕   5 △   6 ●

3.3 A simple illustration of why finding 'things', even if their positions are noted, is not a very informative exercise unless the stratification is noted too. Diagram (a) shows a section on which the positions of numerous objects of six different dates are accurately located. Diagram (b) is the same but with the stratification now added, showing layers, pits, a ditch, a bank and a well, together providing a context for the artefacts, a relative chronology and potentially an absolute timescale too if the artefacts are independently datable. It must be stressed that this is a *simple* diagram: real stratification is often much more complex with thousands of 'things', hundreds of features and dozens of phases *cf.* fig. 3.4.

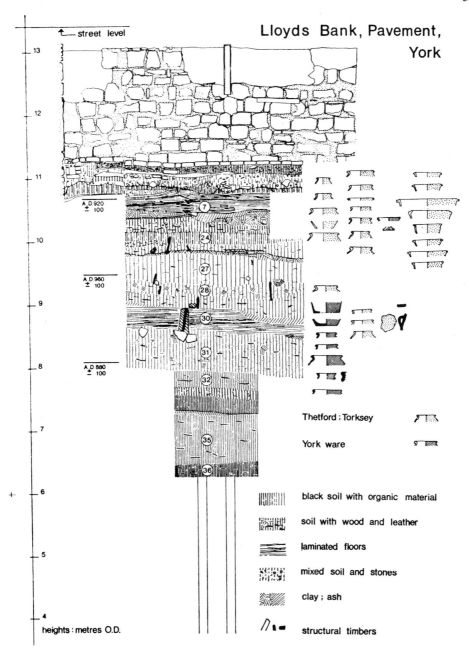

Lloyds Bank, Pavement, York

street level

heights : metres O.D.

A.D 920 ± 100

A.D 960 ± 100

A.D 880 ± 100

Thetford ; Torksey

York ware

black soil with organic material

soil with wood and leather

laminated floors

mixed soil and stones

clay ; ash

structural timbers

3.4 A real archaeological section as published, from Lloyds Bank, Pavement, York, showing some 40 layers of Anglian and Anglo-Danish deposits. The absolute chronology is indicated in this case additionally by C14 dates, although there appears to be a contradiction between the upper two (but *see* p. 113).

89

that produced in two millennia. No wonder then that stratigraphy on site is usually much more complex than the theoretical model of stratification; but nevertheless the principle holds good, and archaeological stratigraphy involves the exercise of a very demanding skill in recording and interpreting the observed stratification in the light of that principle. Only in such a way is it possible to begin to give the site, the excavation, a significance in terms of human activity through time, to be able to say rather more, on the basis of demonstrable evidence, than that which sadly applies to so many excavations i.e. 'Here was an archaeological site (settlement, building, cemetery, defence work etc.), now denuded by me of some/much of its cultural and environmental content in the name of excavation which produced 759 potsherds, 316 flints and a bronze brooch, probably Roman but since lost'. Such results and their equivalents hardly further the sum of human knowledge, or indeed the cause of archaeology.

Excavation and 'revelation'

Excavation is not then a finite and objective exercise. It is a process involving many choices before, during and after its execution, and it is therefore, however high the level of technical expertise brought to the task, a qualitative and subjective exercise. One wonders indeed if two archaeologists would produce the same results if both were able to excavate the same site; but the query is of course uncheckable since the excavation of the one would render such an experiment unrepeatable by another. This aspect of excavation is worth emphasising because, despite the remark above that in a sense one of the functions of excavation was to 'uncover' buried evidence, it would be quite wrong to imagine that hidden beneath the ground is a self-evident, well-defined quantity of evidence which the correct application of certain techniques will reveal in a way which will 'mean' something fairly obvious. What is 'revealed' is conditioned in the first place by the type of site chosen for investigation and by the history of that site during its use and subsequently. It is also conditioned by the circumstances of the excavation, including the skills and experience of the excavator, the objectives of the excavation, the strategy and tactics of the exercise in the field, and the resources available to the field team before, during and after the excavation itself. There are so many variables here that it is not really surprising to find excavation 'results' of very uneven quality. And this unevenness is not merely a function of time, though on the whole standards of excavation have improved over the last century; but in practice today, excavations are being conducted at widely different levels of competence and the results from many of them, for example on similar types of site or on different types of site from the same period, are not usefully comparable in any strictly scientific sense of enquiry or synthesis. A usually unstated but nevertheless real wish to ignore, to write off, the great bulk of excavated 'evidence' and to start again from first principles with fresh evidence is often to the fore in archaeologists' private thoughts. This general lack of quality, of reliability, indeed of relevance, in the available excavated data can be seen as one of the (unconscious?) motivations behind the fashionable trend towards the 'theoretical' archaeology promoted in the last decade. The attractiveness of flight to the purity of an intellectual un-world untrammelled by the dimly-lit reality in a museum basement of thousands of unwashed potsherds from an unpublished and unlocatable nineteenth century excavation can easily be appreciated (Chapter 5).

Excavation does not, then, reveal a self-evident truth, even when it visibly and tangibly uncovers something obvious like a Roman villa or a medieval stone castle. The meaning or significance of what it reveals is directly related to the questions asked of the site; they will in their turn affect the way in which the site is excavated. There is no standard, fool-proof method of excavation, though all excavations should attain certain minimum standards. There are, however, basic categories of excavation which should be specified, not so much for their technical differences but because their differences radically affect the nature, type and quality of evidence excavated; and such differences in the evidence produced in their turn affect not only interpretation of the site but also what can and cannot be done with that site and its evidence in cultural and comparative syntheses, i.e. in trying to convert archaeological data into prehistory or history.

Excavation as a sample

One of the basic choices facing the excavator is to decide on the nature of his sampling strategy i.e. how he is going to reveal the evidence. If the choice is made for him by circumstances, for example in a salvage situation, he should at least be aware of the extent to which his sampling options have already been foreclosed. This use of the word 'sampling' may be puzzling, but it is used here deliberately in recognition of the fact that, however an excavation is carried out, it essentially represents the exercise of a number of choices, of picking and choosing which parts of the site to excavate and by what means for how long. Even if a site is totally excavated, as is possible with a relatively small and finite structure such as a burial mound or a Roman villa, the total excavation is nevertheless but a sample of a larger whole since no site existed in isolation: it was part of a landscape, its people were involved in external social and economic structures, and the whole complex of human and environmental relationships existed within an ecosystem (p. 144). So even before excavation starts, basic decisions affecting the sampling strategy have already been taken once one site rather than any other has been chosen as the target. Hence the logical trend today to think in terms of projects or programmes involving a series of excavations (and related activities) over a period of years rather than the one-off 'discovery' or 'salvage'-type excavation (fig. 3.5).

Given that a site has been chosen for whatever reason, further choices then have to be made about how it is to be excavated. All sorts of factors affect such decisions, not the least of which is the time available; and however logical such decisions may be in the light of information available before excavation begins, they must always be capable of equally logical modification in the light of new information which becomes available

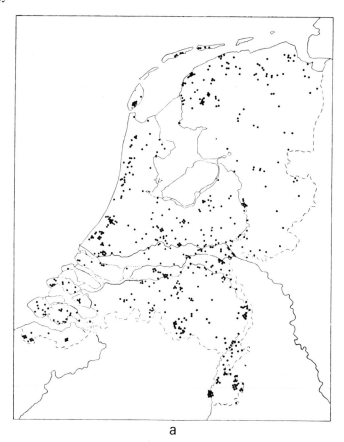

a

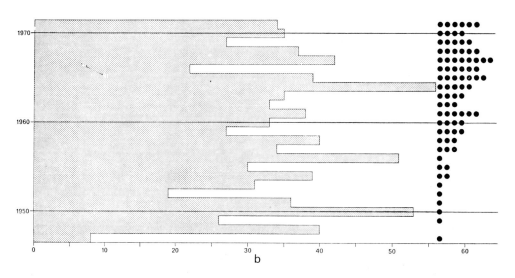

b

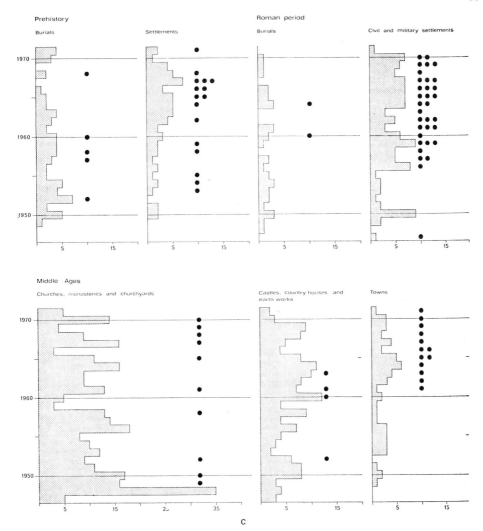

3.5 An analysis of the R.O.B. (State archaeological) excavation programme in Holland, 1947–71: (a) spatially; (b) temporally; (c) by period and type of site. Most parts of Holland have received some attention though (a) indicates a slight favouring quantitatively of the southern part of the country and the coastal belt. The significant factor in (b) is not so much the wildly fluctuating histogram of the crude total of excavations per year as the increase in the number of dots to the right. They represent excavations which lasted more than three months i.e. there was a big increase in the excavation input in the 1960s. (c) is rather like reading a pollen diagram (fig. 4.3) e.g. as the excavation of prehistoric burials declined so that of settlement increased, representing a general shift in the focus of European prehistoric research in the 1960s. In contrast, the input to the Roman period remains generally of a level while for the medieval period an overall decline in the excavation of religious sites presumably represents a general switch of resources to urban archaeology and a miscellany of other medieval sites. Interestingly, all the histograms except, ironically, that for prehistoric burials, show fewer excavations taking place in 1971 than in the late 1960s. Overall, the falling off in effort the further back in time we go is a marked and constant characteristic i.e. medieval studies have claimed more resources than Roman, Roman more than prehistoric.

daily during the excavation. The distinction to draw here is between the strategy and the tactics of conducting an excavation. The strategy may be merely to 'test' the site: does it exist? Is it medieval or prehistoric, a settlement or religious site, of timber or stone, with or without organic remains, well-stratified or disturbed?—and so on. No one method of test excavation would answer all these questions, but a strategic decision to mount a sampling excavation specifically to test some of the points would be a viable way of proceeding and would largely dictate the method of excavation. Similarly the methods, the tactics, would be different if the strategy was to excavate a large part of the site completely, perhaps with the aim of obtaining a 'typical' sample of the industrial quarter of a town through time; or if it was to elucidate the defences and gateways of a fortification, to establish the evolution of house-types in a settlement, or to investigate questions of population and pathology in a cemetery. Techniques, tactics, flow from such excavation strategies, though the point must not be taken to imply that evidence unrelated to the prime objectives is not examined or indeed not looked for. All, in an excavation, is grist to the interpretative mill—the excavator cannot pick and choose what he notes once the excavation has started,—and indeed it is not unknown for an excavation planned for one reason to be completed for another (p. 61 gives a simple example). In practice, however well designed, the actuality of excavation tends to be repetitively unpredictable, almost always in detail and sometimes on the grand scale. Yet, overall, one of the main reasons for continuing to excavate is the hope of establishing patterns of human behaviour as expressed through cultural material distributed in space and through time.

We can see, for example, from many excavations of defences of Roman towns in Britain, a pattern of activity represented by the insertion of stone walls into the front of existing fortifications, even though the evidence allowing this generalisation comes from excavations carried out at different times for many different reasons and even though controversy persists as to why this mural activity was general.[19] Similarly, the observation of a pattern of repeating and sometimes associated features and artefacts in burials beneath the round barrows of central southern England led to the hypothesis of a 'Wessex Culture' there in the mid-second millennium BC. The hypothesis is now challenged but the observation of the pattern existing from many, mostly poor-quality, excavations holds good.[20]

Results and techniques

Most of those barrow excavations were designed to find things, the burials and their

---

[19] *See now* J. Wacher, *The Towns of Roman Britain* (1974).

[20] Initially S. Piggott, 'The early Bronze Age in Wessex', *Proc. Prehist. Soc.* 4 (1938), 52–106, with subsequent discussion reviewed and referenced most conveniently in C. Renfrew, *Before Civilization* (1973), chap. 11, and by C. Burgess in C. Renfrew (ed.), *British Prehistory: a new outline* (1974), 165–232, exhaustively referenced pp. 292–329.

accompanying grave goods. From observation and instinct, the best chance of finding such was in or beneath the centre of the mound so, the 'strategy' being what it was, a hole dug down from the top of the mound was the favourite technique employed; and as many museums, particularly in Wessex and Yorkshire, demonstrate, it was an effective method of achieving the required objective. Various practical difficulties led to the use of an alternative method which was to dig a trench through to the centre of the mound from one side, sometimes continuing it right across on a diameter particularly when the practice showed that burials also existed in the mound off-centre. It was in the course of such work that the first archaeological sections came to be observed and indeed recorded—a significant breakthrough because it immediately showed that excavation could ask and answer questions other than the prime one of 'What is buried here?' For example, 'How was this mound built?' 'Was it built all at once or in several stages?' Once this conceptual jump was made, though it required a man of genius, Pitt-Rivers, and several generations of archaeological trial and error to exploit it, the way was open for the strategies of excavation to change and be reflected in the techniques used on site. The nineteenth century trench through the centre of the barrow became the section cut through a hill-fort's defences, a technique still of great use provided it is used to answer the appropriate questions and provided interpretation of its results is suitably qualified. If the archaeologist wants to know the sequence of construction in a bank and ditch around a hill-fort, a Roman fort, a castle or a town, then basically a trench through the feature should provide some relevant evidence, at least minimally in the vertical plane of the section or side of the trench. The crucial word, however, is 'minimally', as we shall discuss below (p. 97); the point to stress here is that such a technique is inappropriate if the evidence being sought is meant to throw light on, say, how and where the hill-fort builders lived or grew their crops. Conversely, it is silly to criticise such excavations—hole in the mound or trench through the rampart,—for not answering such questions when they were not designed to do so. There is, to repeat, no objective truth buried in the ground waiting to be revealed by the archaeologist: he and his results are creatures of himself, his times and his techniques (fig. 3.6). And the best of modern practice will be out-dated more quickly than the holes of the barrow-diggers.

'The best of modern practice' can still of course include the trench through or across some feature if that is the most appropriate way of answering the questions asked. It may, for example, be desirable to know the shape of a filled-in ditch, the structure of a road, or the structural relationship between a ditch and road crossing each other, and for all such simple, specific questions, the section across the feature should provide some evidence and, with luck, a definite answer—*but for the point in question alone.* A single cut cannot be used as the basis for a valid generalisation. The evidence from such a trench is specific to its position alone and, if the trench is narrow i.e. 2 m. wide or less, could well be positively misleading. In excavating hill-fort defences, for example, a favourite subject of the long, narrow trench type of excavation, it is clear now, even if the questions asked are still the simple ones about structure, sequence and date, that

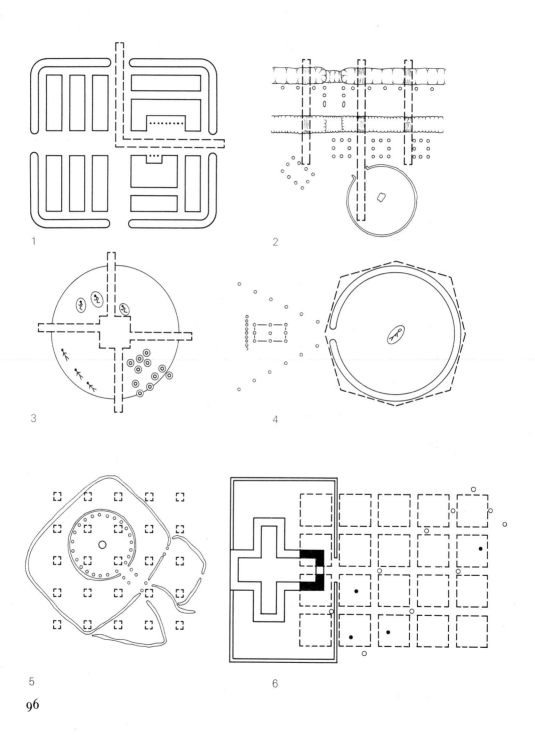

1

2

3

4

5

6

either many 5 m. + wide trenches or at least two 30 m. + wide trenches are required to establish the validity of the basic data, to demonstrate the constants and to isolate the oddities. So it is not just a question of a single narrow cutting perhaps missing an important piece of evidence but that structurally, statistically and almost certainly culturally, a single trench is totally inadequate as an acceptable sample, even within its own frame of reference. Certainly in practice, and theory apart, different sections across the same feature tend to produce different data, in detail at least, and make one very wary of placing much reliance at all on the single section. Yet interpretation of many sites is based on precisely that.

The principle lying behind the trench type excavation was and is that of stratigraphy (p. 86); the assumption, usually unstated, is that not only will the sections along the trench sides reveal the stratification but also that the stratification will be representative, typical or, in unquantified terms, a 'fair sample' of the site. In order to overcome one of the obvious limitations of the method i.e. that it only gave a view of the stratification in one plane, the vertical, and in one direction, along the sides of the trench, the grid method of excavation was developed. Essentially this brought control to the excavation of areas and allowed a three dimensional view of the stratification: every 'box' in the grid contained four sections in two pairs at right angles to each other, and the line of each section could be continued in both directions into neighbouring boxes while the sections themselves continued to exist physically as the excavation developed downwards and horizontally. The quadrant method of excavating circular

———— areas excavated

———— buried features NOT found by excavation

○ ○ ○ ○ (nos 2, 4, 5, 6) postholes

⚲ ⚲ ◎ ◎ (nos 3, 4) respectively inhumation and cremation burials

▥ • (no 6) excavated wall and postholes

3.6 Diagrams to illustrate in plan the limitations of different methods of excavation. To make the point visually, all six examples are exaggerations but all are theoretically possible and all, to a greater or lesser extent, are based on (private thoughts about) excavations seen by the author:

1 Method: trial trenching at right angles; possible interpretation: there is no Roman fort.

2 Trenching in a parallel; excavation showed a single phase, stone-faced rampart, a berm and a ditch but there was no evidence of an entrance or internal structures.

3 Offset radii plus clearance of central area of a presumed burial mound; this is not a burial mound.

4 Total excavation of a mound and surrounding ditch; this is a simple, isolated mound covering a single, central inhumation and surrounded by a circular ditch broken by a causeway on the west.

5 Trial excavation on a grid basis; despite the scatter of occupation material, no structural evidence of a settlement existed.

6 'Total' excavation on a box-grid basis: the main discovery was the eastern half of an isolated stone-based, probably square, building, east of which were only four unrelated post-holes.

features such as barrows was a similar development. Both methods were based on the correct premise that stratigraphy was the key to understanding a site but assumed that, in order to meet that need, it was necessary to keep the section permanently standing as a record of the stratigraphy until the very end of the excavation. One of the major technical advances of recent years has been to develop excavation and recording procedures entirely meeting the needs of the stratigraphical principle, while giving much greater flexibility to respond during excavation to the archaeological needs of the site rather than the clerical needs of the archaeologist. As a result, 'open plan' excavation is now widely followed, at least in north western Europe, and while it may not look so obviously controlled as the neat-edged symmetry of the box-type excavation, it does in fact require a very high degree of managerial control and professional skill (fig. 3.7; Pl. III.4).

This, however, is not the place for further discussion of the technical aspects of excavation since our concern is with the 'why' and not the 'how' and, in relation to excavation method, its bearing on the nature and quality of the information retrieved. And it must be said that even with the relative sophistication of modern techniques in the field, excavation remains a clumsy, increasingly slow and progressively expensive way of approaching the past. Even though in some respects its development now seems to be creating more problems than it is solving, unfortunately there is no alternative to excavation as a means of approaching much of that past. Complementary approaches, but not so far alternatives, have been developed across a wide range of the sciences, adding not merely to the technical battery which can now be brought to bear on the past but bringing a new dimension to its study and, potentially, to our understanding of it.

Bibliography

J. Alexander, *The Directing of Archaeological Excavations* (1970)
Antiq. J. 45 (1965), 22; 51 (1971), 240

3.7 (a) Plan of area excavation at Elsloo, Holland, showing part of a Neolithic settlement characterised by long, rectangular, timber-framed buildings and irregular hollows (stippled). *Cf.* the hit-and-miss methods of excavation in fig. 3.6. Despite the lack of deep vertical stratification on this site, by careful observation of the intersections and overlappings of the ground plans of the 33 buildings present, the excavator was able to divide the settlement into two main phases, each with subdivisions (a, b, c, d), i.e. there were probably less than 10, and perhaps as few as 3 or 4, buildings standing at any one time so the settlement was not as densely occupied in this area as the overall plan might initially suggest. This classic example of 'horizontal stratigraphy' illustrates how a completely wrong interpretation could be placed on the evidence as 'revealed' without close attention to detailed observation of that evidence.

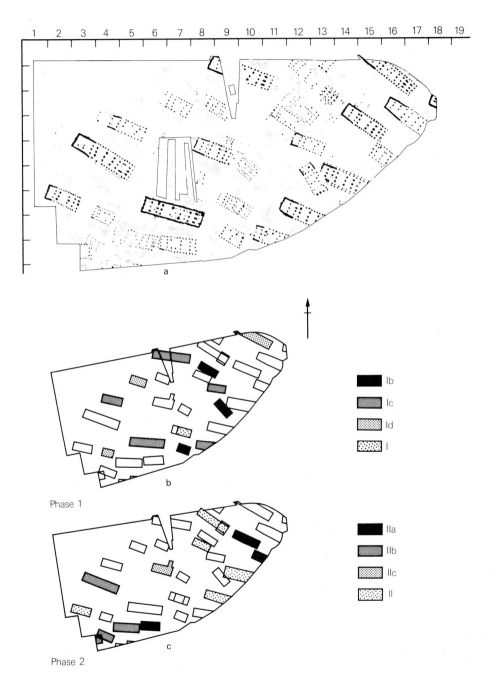

Phase 1

Phase 2

Ib
Ic
Id
I

IIa
IIb
IIc
II

III.4 'Open plan' excavation (requires) a very high degree of managerial control and professional skill'. A general view of only part of the 1976 excavation inside Winklebury hill-fort, near Basingstoke, Hampshire, carried out in advance of further housing development. The total plan of occupation features, circular and rectangular buildings, ditches, pits and post-holes, is revealed simultaneously after mechanical removal of the topsoil, enabling each to be examined in detail in at least a known horizontal context.

Antiquity 47 (1973), 110–1

R. J. C. Atkinson *et al.*, *Excavation at Dorchester, Oxon. 1951*); *Field Archaeology* (1953)

P. A. Barker, *Techniques of Archaeological Excavation* (1977)

J. W. Brailsford, *Hod Hill I* (1962)

K. Branigan, *Latimer* (1971)

S. J. de Laet, *Archaeology and its Problems* (1957)

P. J. Fowler *et al.*, *Cadbury Congresbury, Somerset 1968* (1970)

R. J. C. Hamilton, *Excavations at Clickhimin, Shetland* (1968)

G. D. B. Jones, *Roman Manchester* (1974)

Medieval Archaeol. 18 (1974), 94

S. Piggott, 'The Early Bronze Age in Wessex', *Proc. Prehist. Soc.* 4 (1938)

Proc. Devon Archaeol. Soc. 32 (1974), 61

Proc. Prehist. Soc. 39 (1973), 9

Proc. Soc. Antiq. Scot. 70 (1936), 175; 104 (1971–2), 147

P. Rahtz and S. Hirst, *Beckery Chapel, Glastonbury 1967–8* (1974)

C. Renfrew, *Before Civilization* (1973); (ed.), *British Prehistory: a new outline* (1974)

Trans. Bristol Gloucestershire Archaeol. Soc. 86 (1967), 74; 88 (1969), 38

J. Wacher, *The Towns of Roman Britain* (1974)

G. Webster, *Practical Archaeology* (1974)

Sir Mortimer Wheeler, *Archaeology from the Earth* (1954)

4
SCIENTIFIC
ARCHAEOLOGY

'historic data, empty of all ghosts'
  Bernard Bergonzi, *The Times Literary Supplement* (6 August 1954)

The chapter title is ambiguous since, in a sense, all study of the past by archaeological means is or ought to be scientific. Equally, however, a great deal of archaeology has been carried out without any awareness of scientific thought, method or technique; and of course, if history is the yardstick of archaeology, then by definition, some would argue, archaeology is not science. 'Archaeology, art or science?' is, however, a pointless argument because the fact is that the study of the past, particularly through traditional archaeological methods and material, has been and is greatly influenced by principles and techniques developed in unambiguous fields of scientific endeavour such as geology, as we have seen, and more recently, palaeobotany, nuclear physics and electronics.[1] In this chapter, however, I am not concerned only with the impact of scientific developments on approaches to the past (and I am not concerned at all with how the various techniques are applied) but with the general influence of scientific, as opposed to humanistic, modes of thought on archaeology.

Science in the history of archaeology

In the sense that in Europe it developed largely from the traditions of Classical and historical scholarship emerging from the increased intellectual and national consciousness of the Renaissance and its aftermath, archaeology enjoyed a distinctly non-scientific background; yet much of the earlier field work (p. 24), basing its

---

[1] The compendium edited by D. Brothwell and E. Higgs, *Science in Archaeology* (rev. ed. 1969) covers many aspects of the field and is well-referenced. Subsequently the *Journal of Archaeological Science* (1974–) and a series entitled *Studies in Archaeological Science* (Seminar, subsequently Academic, Press, 1972–) have expanded the available coverage and begun to produce much more detail.

progress on discovery, observation and careful record, was truly scientific in spirit and in no way distinct in method or results from comparable experimental work in, for example, the natural and chemical sciences in the sixteenth and seventeenth centuries. But two of the main temptations seemingly inherent in the nature of archaeological material—the quest for treasure and the abuse of evidence to support theories on the 'lunatic fringe' of scholarship,—strongly influenced the development of the subject thereafter and certainly threatened, as is the case again today (p. 188), its claim to scientific status. It required the achievements of nineteenth century scholars like Worsaae, Evans and Pitt-Rivers,[2] achievements based on and influenced by thorough-going scientific principles and methods, to place the study of the past through material culture on a disciplined foundation of observation, classification and logical deduction. In this respect, archaeology came to possess a scientific basis for a tradition of research which, although largely expressed in artefact studies over the last century or so, helped create the situation today in which both scientific principles and methods borrowed from the sciences are consciously an integral part of the archaeological approach to the past.

Since archaeology is largely taught as an Arts subject in British universities, however, and since the books by which it is known are characteristically to be found in libraries alongside History and in bookshops rubbing shoulders with Folklore, Witchcraft and the Occult (and occasionally the History of Art if not, ultimate degradation, Hobbies including Cookery, Judo and Soft-Toy Making)—in view of this popular definition of archaeology's place in the order of things, two other points are worth mentioning. First, the present increasing practical co-operation and conceptual integration of archaeology with the sciences is, in a sense, but a reversion in modern terms to a view of scientific research and discovery common in the decades after *c*. 1860. For many educated people, conceptually there was no division between archaeology and other intellectual strivings on the frontiers of knowledge. This mental framework is very clearly expressed, for example, in many of the Presidential addresses to the relatively new county archaeological societies of the 1870s and 1880s: one man, not necessarily an original scholar himself, would stand up and deliver a world-wide survey of developments across what we would now regard as a tremendous range of subjects spanning the Earth and Natural Sciences, Chemistry, Physics, Astronomy and Prehistoric and Classical Archaeology. This was the time of the scientific polymath, exemplified by great men like Darwin and Pitt-Rivers, before the age of the specialist. My point is that speakers and listeners unconsciously assumed that it was meet, right and proper for the well-informed person to have such a range of interest: the division of that interest into subjects and specialisms represents an intellectual fragmentation accentuated in the twentieth century not least as a product of mass higher education.

---

[2] The place of such men in the development of archaeology is still best examined in G. Daniel, *150 Years of Archaeology* (1975), with reference to other 'archaeographies'.

Approaches to Archaeology

The titles of those county societies bracketing Archaeology and Natural History meant precisely what they said; they were indicating a range of scientific interest over what we would probably now call Man and Environment, with the little word 'and' linking two branches of research into one natural conceptual whole. It was only later that that word tended, as it still does today, to carry the meaning 'or'; it is only with the growth of a new 'conservation' awareness in the last decade that the significance of its real meaning has come to be appreciated again.

Archaeology and anthropology

My second point on the historical background to archaeology's relationship with science is that the Classical/Historical roots of European archaeology are not a unifying characteristic of the discipline. In America particularly, archaeology if it exists at all as a distinct discipline is very much an offspring of anthropology, the scientific nature of which can hardly be questioned even if it is classified as a social science. While Classical archaeology has flourished in and from its transatlantic base by and large in harmony with European scholarship in the same restricted field, the archaeological discovery of the Americas themselves has proceeded from quite separate, anthropological bases, physically in museums, Federal institutions and university departments of anthropology, conceptually in the writings of Lewis Morgan and Franz Boas.[3] Of course, point was given to the anthropological emphasis and allied ethnological and ethnographical studies by the existence of an indigenous population. The 'Indians' were denoted as 'primitive' by the explorers and settlers of the 'advanced' white civilization from the Old World and were therefore conceptually impossible to connect with the archaeological field evidence of pre-European 'lost civilizations'. Even now, it is interesting to note the, perhaps unconscious, inclusion of archaeology within anthropology as suggested by this sentence in a recent book about American archaeology: 'From the very beginning, American archaeology was in close alliance with *the rest of* anthropology' (this author's italics).[4] This comes from a book which, despite its dedication to a scholar 'to whom archaeology has always been anthropology', nevertheless quotes as 'depressing' the statement that 'Archaeology . . . is doomed always to be the lesser part of anthropology'.[5]

The contrast between archaeo-scientific developments in Old and New Worlds is, however, neatly and concisely expressed:[4] 'The obvious importance of a related archaeological-ethnological attack upon the problems of the American Indian and his origins was an upshot of Thomas' mound survey and the demonstration that the earthworks had, indeed, been constructed by the forebears of the Indian. The physical anthropological study of skeletal material from the mounds was also found to be

[3] L. Morgan, *Ancient Society* (1877); F. Boaz, *Race, Language and Culture* (1940).
[4] G.R. Willey and J.A. Sabloff, *A History of American Archaeology* (1974), 86.
[5] *Op. cit.* note 4, 131.

relevant to the solution of such problems, and this third major branch of anthropology [the other two apparently being ethnology and archaeology—PJF] was brought into the American alliance. All this stands in notable contrast to the situation in the Old World where the three disciplines tended to develop separately. Many of the differences [between European and American archaeology] can be traced to this time [1880–1900] and to this turn of events in the Americas.

American archaeology has, undoubtedly, benefited greatly from this association with the house of anthropology yet, [in the earlier twentieth century] archaeology enjoyed little esteem and soon became the intellectual 'poor boy' in the field of anthropology.' Yet, in the decades mentioned, British archaeology had the option of at least physical anthropology open to it through, once again, the scientifically *avant-garde* work in this field by Pitt-Rivers, a percipient cultural anthropologist himself before hereditary fortune turned him into a Dorset landlord and an archaeological genius. It is interesting to remark too that a fellow county archaeologist, Charles Warne, began his *Ancient Dorset* (1872) with 'An Introduction to the Primeval Ethnology of Dorset', listed on the Contents page as '. . . Primeval Archaeology . . .' The distinction between the scientific bases of Old and New World Archaeology, subsequently fossilised by two generations of virtual non-contact, need not have happened, and British Archaeology's status as the 'poor boy' in the field of history and Classical studies need not have persisted for so long either.

The identification of cultural material

The scholar, when presented with an original document or a Classical text, may well be tempted to try and answer the obvious question first—'What does it mean?'. In fact, his first question should be 'What is it?' i.e. is it genuine? In this respect, there seems little difference between the student looking at archaeological or written evidence on the one hand and at scientific evidence on the other. We have to know what we are dealing with as a pre-requisite. 'What?' is one of the basic questions to be asked of archaeological evidence in constructing knowledge about the past. It is a question archaeology is quite good at answering—'What is it? It is a coin'—at the level of straightforward identification of common artefacts. It is obviously a little difficult, though not impossible (*see* p. 122), to proceed to further understanding unless one knows what it is that has been found. Of course, even some excavated objects cannot be identified or may be identified wrongly but on the whole archaeology proceeds without too much difficulty on this score.

Problems begin to arise when evidence has to be considered in space—'Where was it found?' The answer to this question is fundamental from the strictly archaeological point of view, though museum and art historical interests, concentrating on the object *per se,* do not rate it so highly. Unless the archaeologist, however, knows for certain where the material comes from in the horizontal plane—from this country or that country down to from this side or that side of that stone?,—and in the vertical plane— was it above or below that stone?,—unless he knows the physical context of the material, he is severely handicapped in using it. Indeed he is reduced, like the museum curator and art historian, to considering it merely as an artefact with a relatively low information potential rather than as a cultural expression in particular circumstances of time and place which were *observed and recorded* at the time and place of discovery. Of course, much can be done with circumstantial information and through erudition to make up for the lack of basic evidence about context which affects so much of archaeology's material available for study; but this must not obscure the ideal, and in practice the actuality of the best-organised fieldwork and excavation programmes, that every piece of evidence, artefactual or otherwise, should be recovered in a three dimensional context. Then the question where? can be answered fully and unequivocally, and the next question, when?, can be tackled on a firm basis of recorded observation.

The measurement of past time

The now common-or-garden concept in archaeology of cultural change occurring through time in essence also goes back to the mid-nineteenth century, in this case to Darwin's *Origin of the Species* (1859). Just as the species of the plant and animal world have evolved (to the point of extinction in many cases) so, in archaeological terms, do human societies, their technologies, economies and cultures, also evolve. Evolution is essentially a concept of change through time and not, as many tend to assume, necessarily a change for the better or the more complex. The evolutionary concept, linked to that of stratigraphy and applied, with increasing technical competence in the recovery of data, to the surviving and recoverable evidence from the past, essentially form the theoretical and working platform for the practice of archaeology as a viable intellectual discipline. Without those two concepts, both be it noted related to time, and an appropriate field technology to meet their data-demands, we would still be mentally threshing around with Stukeley amongst his Druids in the mid-eighteenth century or, a century later, with William Henry Harris, one of the earlier misguided American Presidents, looking for the 'lost race' of the mysterious Moundbuilders. The concept of the passage of time and the concept of change occurring as that time passes, plus an ability to detect both—these are of the essence of archaeology; and the first two come from field sciences, specifically two with which archaeology has always maintained links, and links which are now maturing into significant co-operative partnerships. What a contrast such scientific co-operation makes, basing itself on controlled, patient and verifiable field experiment, with the speculative maunderings of those Atlantis-seekers, ley-liners, druid-dramatists, treasure-hunters and similar intellectual fossils left floundering in the timeless, unstratified past of a century and more ago (p. 188).

Time is of the essence; and the measurement of time has been given considerable scientific priority in recent research. It is in the measurement of time past that some of the most fruitful co-operation in scientific archaeology has been achieved in recent decades. At least a dozen different non-archaeological techniques of dating are now in use and others are at the experimental stage. Clearly we cannot discuss them all, and in any case my concern is much more with their influence upon the archaeological study of the past than with the principles and methods of the scientific techniques themselves. Before attempting to assess their impact, individually or collectively, we must clearly establish why dating is important and how it is achieved in archaeological terms alone. Unless we sketch this outline, it could be difficult to appreciate why so much scientific expertise and research money all over the world has been devoted to the elucidation, particularly over the last twenty years, of this one particular question: how old is it?

It is in fact a basic question, because unless we know where we are in time it is extremely difficult to proceed with archaeology's function of observing and explaining the nature and processes of change as time passes. So we must have a date, which is another way of saying we must know how old it is but with a critical difference; for there are two sorts of date, and one of them can tell us where we are in time without telling us how old 'it' is. A date is normally taken to mean a point fixed in time and expressed in terms of a commonly-used time-notation system or calendar. Thus we can talk of AD 1066 and we can immediately place that date not only in terms of how old it is in relation to the present day but also in a time sequence related to years before and after that date. Within our own terms of reference, it 'means' something: the Norman invasion of England was 890 years ago i.e. 890 years before 1976, and 1121 years after Caesar's invasion of 55 BC (for present purposes, the minor adjustments in the Christian calendar over the last two millennia are ignored). We know, however, that these dates mean nothing to large numbers of our fellow human beings today because they are using different calendars i.e. time-notation systems with different starting dates, though most are based, like ours, on units of time defined by the passage of the earth around the sun (solar years; cf the similar concept based on different criteria expressing distance as well as time-values of a completely different order contained in the phrase 'light years'). Similarly, we know that different peoples in the past have also followed calendars both different from each other's and from our own; but by and large we are able to reconstruct the bases of such measurements of time, in for example the Egyptian Middle Kingdom and Imperial Rome. We can thus not only understand their own expressions of date but also, by correlation of calendars where they overlap in time or by extrapolation of ours backwards to create an overlap BC, we can convert such alien expressions into terms of our own calendar. Thus year 7 of Sesostris III (Egyptian Middle Kingdom) can be expressed as 1872 BC and the ninth year of the tribunician power of Tiberius Claudius Caesar Augustus as AD 49. We know where we are in time because the cultures concerned were numerate *and* literate, because enough evidence has survived and been recovered for us to break the various codes used, and because all were using *absolute* dates. AD 1066 is an absolute date and so is 55 BC: but there are no such absolute dates earlier than 55 BC in British history and of course for the Americas the equivalent date is AD 1493 or later.

It is the peculiar fate of archaeology, and specifically prehistoric archaeology if the lack of documentary evidence is taken as *the* criterion of prehistory, to be faced with the awkward fact that, until relatively recently, most of the world has not provided itself with written dates for its history; and archaeology's chief challenge over the last century has been in many ways not just to provide dates but to produce a temporal framework within which human life on earth can reasonably be accommodated and realistically expressed. In this it has, by and large, succeeded in world terms, though a myriad of micro-chronological problems remain at continental, regional and local level. Fundamental to this success in the early stages was archaeology's recognition in its own terms of a type of date other than the absolute one. This was, and is, the *relative* date, and recognition of its value takes us back to stratification, sequence and scientific cross-fertilisation. We can now examine the main considerations which will probably be in an archaeologist's mind as he arrives at his albeit cautious and qualified reply to one of the most frequent questions he is asked—'How old is it?'

The questioner must in fact be fair: very little archaeological evidence actually has a date on it and equally there is no magic formula the archaeologist can apply universally to produce an answer. He is likely to be forced back to the balancing of probabilities again. Even when he is fortunate enough to have evidence like coins or inscriptions with dates actually written on them, his answer may be infuriatingly qualified, and with good reason. What are we asking to be dated when we ask 'What date is it?'—the date at which a coin was made, the period when it was in use, when it was lost or the feature in which it was actually found? To pursue this simple coin example, it would cause no archaeological surprise in London, for instance, for a Roman coin to have been minted in the second century, to have continued in use into the third century, to have been kept as a souvenir in the fourth, to have been lost in the fifth and to be found in a medieval rubbish pit in 1975. What indeed are we dating even though we can say that the coin itself is 1750 years old precisely? i.e. that 1750 calendar years have passed since it was minted (assuming it was not made from an old mould and that it is not a forgery). If it is not always easy to arrive at an answer when dealing with material firmly inscribed with a date (or with an inscription which gives sufficiently precise information from which a date can be adduced), what hope then for the other 99% of archaeological evidence?

Relative chronology

Archaeological dating depends on three different ways of ordering archaeological evidence: by sequence, by association and by typology. All three methods can produce relative dates; none of themselves can produce absolute dates. A relative date is nothing more than being able to say that something is earlier or later than something else e.g.

railways are earlier than motorways. We are simply expressing a temporal relationship. We are saying nothing about how much earlier, or how long either lasted, how either was made or why the change occurred; but we could demonstrate the truth of the generalisation, and prove it to be true in many specific instances, by pointing to cases where motorways cross over or under railways or actually cut through disused railway embankments, all in a way indicating beyond reasonable doubt that railways existed before motorways were built. Stukeley made closely comparable observations in 1720 when noting correctly that what he took to be a Roman road, Ackling Dyke, cut part of a disc barrow on Oakley Down, Dorset. He concluded that the barrows were earlier than the Roman road, though he had no means of knowing how much earlier.[6]

This exemplifies the sort of phenomenon the archaeologist is faced with in the field. Looking at a stretch of countryside, he can note that a modern road (a) cuts a disused railway embankment (b) which itself overlies ridge-and-furrow (c) carefully respecting a mound (d). It requires no great intellectual effort to deduce that (a) is later than (b) is later than (c) is later than or contemporary with (d). We then have a relative chronology. We begin to convert this into an absolute chronology when we find out from documentary evidence that the road was built in 1959 and the railway in 1847; both (c) and (d) are therefore earlier than the mid-nineteenth century. Further research might then produce evidence that a castle existed here in the mid-twelfth century and we might have reason for arguing that our mound (d) was that castle. Chronologically, we could then say that the ridge-and-furrow (c) was no earlier than c. 1150 and no later than c. 1850.

The principle observed in that example derives from geological observation of the strata (p. 86). Exactly this principle applies in deriving a relative date from an excavation. Fig. 4.1, Site 1, shows in simplified form how, by correctly observing the superimposition of layers, we can say not merely that k is earlier than a but can rank all the components of the layers in a relative chronology:

> abcd are broadly contemporary, d begins earlier than a
> e–k are all broadly contemporary but earlier than a–d
> g begins earlier than ef
> hjk begin earlier than ef contemporaneously with g

The stratification therefore can be seen as expressing a period of time, we know not when or how long, during which certain cultural characteristics, individually and collectively, change (a–t could be anything from palaces to pin-heads, from settlement form to economy— anything which could be a cultural trait).

The principle is then extended spatially or horizontally to other sites where similar independent sequence can be observed (l–o are all earlier than e–k at Site 2 and p–t are earlier than l–o on Site 3). The more such sequences are observed, the more the relative

[6] *Iter Curiosum* (1776), *Iter VII* (quoted in R. Jessup, *Curiosities of British Archaeology* (1961), 40).

SITE 1	SITE 2	SITE 3	SITE 4	
a b c				
b c d				H1
e f	e f			
e f g	e f g			
g h j k	g h j k		i k	H2
	l m n	l m		
	m n o	m n o		H3
		p q		
		p q r		
		r s t		

4.1 Diagram to illustrate the principles of relative dating and association (pp. 108–11).

chronology can be refined and the more secure it becomes if the character-ordering is confirmed. Furthermore by noting correlations between one site and another, or between Sites 1 and 2, and 2 and 3, the sequence in an area can be lengthened: whereas with Site 1 alone we had five layers, by linking the three sites we now have ten layers with twenty features distributed in a sequence through them. This data begins to become predictive and self-checking e.g. if we find pqr we should not only not expect to find ghj or k but should check our observations if we did. And we can begin to be confident when finding pqr that we are dealing with a period of time earlier than that represented by a–o. Laborious though this sounds, and is, this is exactly the way in which the prehistoric chronologies of Europe, the Americas and, now, Africa have been built up; and even with the scientifically obtained dates we shall shortly discuss, a relative chronology is essential to exploit fully 'absolute' dates.

The little model in fig. 4.1 has also introduced the idea of association which can also be used for dating purposes. Another site may produce two unstratified, stray finds, ik. By reference to our relative chronology and to the *association* of groups of characteristics in the sequence, we can fit these new finds both into our floating time-scale and into a cultural context. We have noted elsewhere that k occurs with g and h and j so we would expect further work at Site 4 to produce g, h and/or j, and possibly e and f characteristics too since g is associated with them too; but we would not expect it to produce a–d or l–t from the same layer, and indeed only to produce either one group or the other unless it was, by comparison with Sites 1–3, an exceptionally long-lived site. We have noted that in our regional sequence there are breaks in the cultural succession at H1–3, not only in sequences spanning those breaks but in the ways individual sequences tend to stop at these horizons e.g. Site 2 stops at H1 and Site 1 begins at H2. Though the sequence at Site 3 spans H3 no cultural components below H3 appear above it and none of p–t appear on Site 2 which begins at H3. All this is idealizing, of course, but hopefully the principles are clear. They are in fact very simple as 'rules of the game', which makes it all the easier to condemn as non-archaeologists those who do not observe them, whatever they call themselves.

Absolute dating

Somehow we now have to introduce at least a minimal element of absolute time into our relative chronology. In practice, the odds are that somewhere either amongst our horizons or layers, which might run to hundreds in fact, or amongst our cultural traits, which might amount to tens of thousands, there will be something which quite independently of our regional sequence carries some absolute chronological connotation. A direct import from a literate culture is perhaps the most useful. Say, for example, that one of those stray finds, i, was a piece of Samian pottery. By following the process already outlined we could then cautiously insert a date of, say, AD 100 just above H2. Indeed, assuming the sherd itself was of a well-dated type in its place of origin, and was in an undisturbed context, and bearing in mind what has already been said about the grouping of the traits, we could, at least as a working hypothesis, propose that H2 had a *terminus ante quem* i.e. a date before which it was formed, of *c.*AD 100 and, furthermore, that h and j were also to be dated to the early second century AD with g continuing somewhat later. The details do not matter here: the point is that we now have one reasonably firm fixed point, as it happens near the middle of our sequence, around which our sequence can contract or expand in time as more evidence accumulates. Indeed, as happened in the real life episode lying behind this fictional illustration,[7] there would now be a good case for mounting a research excavation programme to test the hypothesis and in particular to try and find more Samian pottery in stratified sequences. The previous work in establishing the relative chronology should have provided firm leads as to the most likely contexts for it to occur. Such excavation might or might not support the hypothesis but at least there is now an absolute chronological base from which to work. Chronological horizons provided by

[7] Sir Mortimer Wheeler, *Still Digging* (1935), chap. 11.

dated exotic material intruding into local sequences, comparable to the Samian pottery in India are, for example, 'Egyptian' faience beads (fourteenth century BC) in southern Britain, North African pottery (sixth century AD) in western Britain, Arabian material in East Africa (ninth century AD), fifteenth-seventeenth century European material in America and West Africa, and eighteenth century Oriental material in the American South West.

Other archaeological methods of dating are really variations on these two principles of sequence and association, plus contact in some way at some time with an independently dated source to give an element of absolute chronology. Even that really only applies over the last 5000 years so is irrelevant for the many more earlier millennia of human history. We must, however, specifically mention typology, although it too is essential sequential and evolutionary in principle. The concept is of linear change through time in artefactual material such as tools, building types, and decorative and art objects. Indeed, the method is very similar to that of the art historian dividing the works of his artist into early, middle and late phases. So too the development of flint hand-axes, bronze axe-heads, sickles, houses, fields, indeed almost anything man-made, can be arranged in a typological sequence showing progressive evolution or devolution of its design as affected, individually or in combination, by function, materials and fashion. The changing external appearance of the motor car over the last 80 years provides a vivid illustration of an evolutionary typological sequence. While the method is primarily one for purposes of cultural study, it clearly carries chronological implications of the same order as our 'vertical' stratified sequence; for if the typology is arranged along its line of evolution or devolution correctly, then clearly the further along the line an artefact is the later it should be in relation to the early types. It provides a relative chronology and one too that can, with fortune, have a fixed date inserted into its sequence, most likely by one of the types being associated somewhere with something else which can be independently dated.

This relatively long excursion on archaeological dating is necessary for two main reasons. Chronology, rather than dates, is of fundamental importance to the study of the past, and the quest for dates has occupied a high proportion of serious archaeological effort and much more speculative time-wasting. Without a temporal framework, not only can archaeology not proceed to its higher tasks but it lays its evidence open to the timeless speculations of the spurious, the romantic and pseudo-scholarship. Secondly, despite all the effort, archaeology from its own resources had not been very successful in expressing its results in anything like a sufficiently precise or accurate absolute chronology, either for its own research purposes or for purposes of communicating its results to others, professional and lay alike. The realistic pathos of that situation is succinctly captured in a book composed during precisely those years, 1950–1955, when the stage was being prepared for a more or less completely new play: 'Let us admit it: archaeology is in fact a science in its infancy . . . it has not yet reached a stage, except in some very rare cases, in which absolute dates can be given to prehistoric cultures. For the most part, archaeologists have to be content with relative chronology; in other words archaeology can determine the relative sequence of the different civilizations which have left their mark in the soil of one country and work out the chronological affinities between these cultures and those encountered in neighbouring lands.

Relative chronology such as this is clearly begging the question, and absolute dating remains our constant goal'.[8] The accomplishment of major steps towards that goal in the two decades since 1955 have with little doubt been among the two or three most signal recent developments for archaeology.

Carbon 14 chronology

Radio-carbon dating has so far had the most impact on archaeology, on the thinking about archaeology and on the thinking of archaeologists about the 'meaning' of their studies. The nuclear physics and statistics on which the method is based are adequately described elsewhere and need only concern us in as far as they affect the validity of the 'dates' for archaeological purposes.[9] It must be stressed, however, that radio-carbon dating is but one of a whole battery of scientific techniques now in use for, or experimenting with, the provision of dates from archaeological or culturally associated material. The last two decades have seen a veritable explosion of chronological methodology, not supplanting but certainly complementing all the 'old' methods discussed above. An important feature of these new methods is that they depend on natural phenomena, the properties of the physical and chemical world, and not upon the somewhat cumbersome practice of stratigraphy, sequence, association, cross-dating, typology and so on. To be of use archaeologically, however, the independent dates from these new scientific techniques have to be from materials and samples safely recorded from known contexts in the field. Indeed, one of the first implications of the new scientific archaeology has been a requirement for even greater practical stringency in the observation of relationships and the collection of samples. There is little point in being provided with the age of a piece of wood when the context of the wood is unknown or uncertain.

The new types of date have already been referred to as 'independent'. By this is meant that the date given to them by whatever scientific means is not in itself in any way derived from any of the archaeological methods we have been discussing. The scientific estimate by the radio-carbon method of the age of a piece of wood found in an Egyptian pyramid, for example, is arrived at by virtue of the properties of that piece of

[8] S. J. de Laet, *Archaeology and its Problems* (1957), 58–9.
[9] For C14 and dating generally, *see* J.W. Michels, *Dating Methods in Archaeology* (1973) and M.S. Tite, *Methods of Physical Examination in Archaeology* (1973). C. Renfrew, *Before Civilization* (1973) explains the method briefly and with clarity in an Appendix (pp. 255–68); at the time of writing, the 'last words' are in *Antiquity* 49 (1975), 252–72, and 50 (1976), 61–3, and in T. Watkins (ed.), *Radiocarbon: Calibration and Prehistory* (1975).

wood without regard to its archaeological context in that pyramid. Its radio-carbon 'date' owes nothing to its context; yet of course it is precisely that context which alone can give the 'date' a cultural significance. Indeed, the estimation of radio-carbon dates for material from already dated contexts, such as Egyptian pyramids, has been in part responsible for showing that the radio-carbon dates were not firm, absolute dates, as some at first believed and many had hoped, but were consistently too young in relation to calendar years as expressed by our system of time notation. Characteristically, for example, radio-carbon dates of material from Egyptian tombs were about 2000–2100 BC when the known dates of the tombs were c. 2400–2500 BC (known, that is, from internal documentary evidence like the regnal lists and inscriptions in the tombs giving dates in Egyptian terms which could be converted into our calendrical terms). Recently, since the realisation that a 'radio-carbon year' does not express the same length of time as a solar year, a great deal of research has gone into producing data which will enable radio-carbon dates to be converted into true calendrical dates: the latest available 'curve' is shown in fig. 4.2. From this, it can be seen that from the third millennium BC backwards in time there is a variable but increasingly large discrepancy between a radio-carbon date and an absolute date. Since there has been uncertainty in recent years about the scale of this discrepancy, and further changes in the correlations can be anticipated, the practice has developed of expressing uncalibrated radio-carbon dates in years bc and only using BC for absolute dates i.e. when the date is derived from impeccable, literate sources, is a calibrated or corrected radio-carbon date, or is

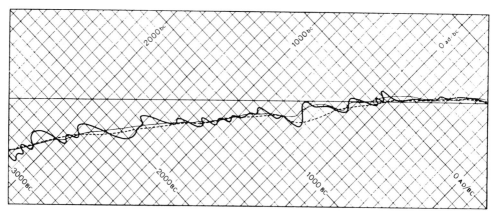

4.2 Three calibration curves (1970, 1973, 1975, respectively the bold line, the dashed line and the thin line) correlating radio-carbon 'dates' bc with an absolute time-scale BC derived from dendrochronology, the 'tree-ring dating' method here applied to the American bristlecone pine. Though the general agreement between the three curves and therefore their generally similar relationship to 'real' time in calendar years is impressive, problems arise at particular points in time bc e.g. to put it crudely, a C14 date of 500 bc could be c. 530 BC, 600 BC, 650 BC, 780 BC or 790 BC, and 2400 bc could be 2990 BC, 3050 BC, c. 3100 BC, c. 3180 BC or 3350 BC (and cf. p. 115 for other caveats).

otherwise expressing what the writer believes to be 'real' time in terms of solar years and the Christian calendar. In other words, to put it crudely the main agent of the scientific revolution in chronology has not yet attained that goal of absolute dating to which de Laet referred (p. 112).

There is another respect in which the 'dates' are imperfect. We have already referred to them as estimates and that is what they are in statistical terms. The 'date' provided by a laboratory will be expressed like this:

1	2	3	4	5	6	7
HARWELL REF.	SENDERS REF.	TYPE	DELCI3 (%/10)	AGE bp (YRS)	bp-1950	COMMENT REF.
HAR-1213	744090	Wood	−26·0	1600·±90·	ad 350·	

The date bp means 'before the present' and for these purposes the present is AD 1950. Thus 1600 bp is ad 350. Another convention is that the accepted 'half-life' of radio-carbon—the time taken for half the radio-carbon component of an object to decay since its death—is still assumed to be 5568 ± 30 years in all published dates, even though it is now generally agreed that 5730 ± 30 years is a more accurate estimate. So there is a second calculation to be made with the 'raw' laboratory date in edging it nearer to an absolute date. Then thirdly there is the calibration with the latest-available or 'best' curve, plotting radiocarbon years against calendar years as mentioned above. Even with that it is possible to be faced with more than one date BC as alternative calibrations of a date bc cf. around 2000 bc on fig. 4.2 where the wobbles in the curve are sharp and frequent.

After all that there is no finality, no absolute certainty, nor would there be were the curve perfected; for the 'date' we have been progressively modifying is but an estimate, not a firm date like AD 1815, and as can be seen above is expressed by the laboratory as 1600 ± 90 bp. This is a form of statistical expression meaning that the laboratory considers there is a 66% probability that the age of the sample lies between 1510 and 1690 bp. And any one year between those brackets is as likely to be the correct age as any other year, so the central date, the one specified, has no greater validity than any other within those 180 years. Yet the temptation is very strong to use AD 350 as a date in the same sense as AD 1815 is the date of the Battle of Waterloo; and even if the temptation is resisted, the danger remains for the data is there to be used and it is unrealistic to expect the user to make all the necessary cautionary qualifications every time he quotes a radio-carbon date. To expect that would be like expecting the E.T.A. of every airline flight to be qualified over the P.A. system with all the technical data qualifying the estimate. In view of the variable correlation between such E.T.As. and the actual times of flight arrivals, the analogy is perhaps more apt than we know.

The point should be clear that a single radio-carbon 'date' must be used with caution in archaeological interpretation. Yet the impact of such dates has been profound. Here it is their cumulative effect which is important because, despite all the variables and potential errors, they demonstrate an overall and internal consistency as applied across the world and particularly in their application to Old and New World prehistory. In other words, even if the absolute values of individual dates are suspect, their relative values are extremely useful in confirming archaeological hypotheses of sequence, in showing up previously unnoted breaks in sequences and in questioning temporal links suggested on the basis of cultural similarities. The value of radio-carbon dates from a sequence, on a single site as at Sitagroi, northern Greece, from a number of comparable sites like the southern British henge monuments, or over an area like the Somerset Levels, is enormous since they can not only support physically observed successions and link into a regional stratigraphy features not physically associated, but of course they also give a relative temporal dimension to the sequences.[10]

Other dating techniques

Radio-carbon dating depends on the properties of organic material—wood, charcoal, bone, anything that has 'lived' or been part of a living organism and has therefore absorbed C_{14} and C_{12} from the earth's atmosphere. Other dating techniques depend on quite different properties, including those of inorganic materials. Archaeologically, this is most helpful since checks can be run on different materials from the same contexts and materials not associated with organic samples can be 'dated' independently. Although radio-carbon dating has been most widely applied and has made the most influential impact on archaeological studies as a whole, in many specific instances other methods are more appropriate. Again the question is all-important: is a relative or absolute date required as the answer? Are we dealing with material thought to be of post-glacial times or much earlier? What is the nature of the material, the circumstances of its deposition and the conditions of its survival?—all such questions affect not merely the method used but the value in cultural terms of the 'date' obtained. So whatever the marvel and sophistication of the technique applied in archaeology's interest, there is no comparison between obtaining a 'scientific' archaeological date and the local historian asking 'When were the tithes in my parish redeemed?', going to his Record Office, getting out the Tithe Map and related documents, and coming up with the answer '1839'. That date, a fact, is of a completely different order from the 'age-estimate' obtained for, say, a tooth submitted to the fluorine test to answer the

[10] Sitagroi: *Antiquity* 45 (1971), 275–82; henges: *Proc. Prehist. Soc.* 38 (1972), 389–407; Somerset Levels: *Somerset Levels Papers* 1 (1975), 54–5.

question 'Is it or is it not old?'; or from the results of 'dating' a piece of pottery by its thermoluminescent properties, a hearth by the characteristics of its thermo-remanent magnetism or an obsidian blade by measurement of its surface hydration layer.

The problems which arise when attempts are made to interpret such 'dates' for cultural purposes are currently and very appositely illustrated by the latest phase of one of the longest-running bores of the archaeological fringe, 'l'Affaire Glozel'.[11] It is amazing that such a disreputable and prolonged incident of fraudulence and incompetence, irrelevant to the cultural history of mankind, should absorb so much academic effort and continue to arouse so much interest. With all the battery of scientific sophistication newly applied, the issue remains a psychological rather than an archaeological one, though ten days' untrammelled application by a professional English excavator on the site could settle the matter of date and authenticity once and for all. Doubtless, however, that would spoil the fun: the 'conundrum syndrome' dies hard in non-scientific archaeology and in this case, applied science, perhaps characteristically in some ways, is feeding it rather than breaking it down with the cold light of undisputed data. Incidentally, the episode beautifully underlines the essential place of context in scientific dating (p. 106): without it, 'dates' *in vacuo*, as from Glozel, tend to be contentious or, at best, ambiguous. 'Although we believe these conclusions to be soundly based it will be up to each archaeologist to make his own assessment of the evidence'.[12] In other words, scientific dating brings new data, opens up indeed new perspectives in world prehistory, but it also enlarges the field of uncertainty for the archaeologist, for whom the rules of the game remain the same with or without scientifically-obtained dates i.e. the judicious balancing of all available evidence in the interests of cultural history.

Environmental archaeology

That remains basically true if we look briefly at other fields where initially purely archaeological and purely scientific interests overlap. In one such they have indeed coalesced into what we may call 'environmental archaeology'. In material terms, we are here thinking of evidence not popularly thought of as being a major product of excavation (except for human bones). The range includes what, by definition almost, are usually the bulkiest materials removed by excavation—soil, stones and animal bones,—down to the micro-finds of floral and faunal evidence—pollen grains, snail shells and insect skeletons. Not that environmental archaeology can be confined to the study of excavated evidence: its full dimensions only become apparent when related to the mature approach of field archaeology discussed in Chapter 2 and raised again in

[11] Both wittily and ponderously discussed in *Antiquity* 48 (1974), 261-4, 265-72; 49, (1975), 219-26, 267-72.
[12] *Antiquity* 49 (1975), 268.

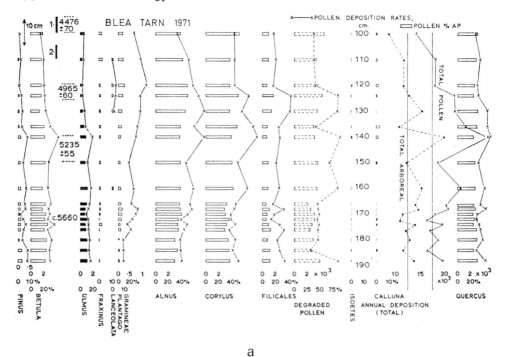

a

4.3 (a) An example of a pollen diagram (from part of a core taken from Blea Tarn, Langdale, Cumbria). Pollen values are given as percentages of total arboreal pollen (histogram blocks) and as annual pollen deposition rates (line graphs). 1 and 2 (top left) are C14 dated charcoal samples with three further C14 dates below. To read the information expressed in this very precise but superficially complex form requires practice but essentially the sort of feature to look for is how changes in the proportion of one or more species are echoed in the proportions of others e.g. the grasses peak as the elm declines c. 5660 bc. The diagram expresses *vegetational* changes however; interpreting it botanically is difficult enough and to do so in cultural terms adds another dimension.

Chapter 5. Nevertheless, it is in particular the laboratory-based, microscopic study of environmental evidence, especially from known cultural contexts, that has exercised such an influence on thinking about the past. Since major research is often thought of as involving large numbers of people, perhaps it is worth stressing that the number of palaeo-minded, archaeologically-aware scientists who have yielded that evidence is very small—a dozen or two in Britain recently, with the number increasing a little now as the academic impact gradually comes to be converted into teaching and research posts.[13]

It was Crawford and Fox in Britain from the 1920s onwards who first made a specific environmental interest a respectable part of archaeology, not only by placing Man in his

---

[13] Two were advertised on the same day (*The Guardian*, 14 Oct. 1976) some months after this was written.

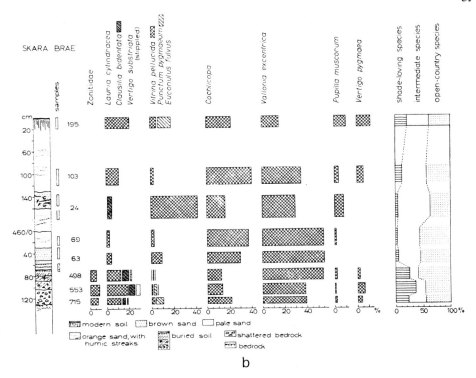

(b) An example of a molluscan histogram (from Skara Brae) showing the absolute number and relative proportions of different snails in the various layers of the section on the left. The column on the right could suggest a phase of land clearance, as the percentage of the total snail population at the buried soil level declines sharply.

geographical setting but by trying to reconstruct the flesh of that physical skeleton. Subsequently, from the 1930s onwards, it was the enormous developments, technically and conceptually, of palynology, associated in particular with Godwin and his Cambridge 'school', which gave an ascertainable verity at least to the floral clothing of that skeleton. Though the study of vegetational change through time is a study in its own right, and is carried out as such, archaeology was able to contribute by supplying material—soil containing pollen grain,—from 'dated' cultural contexts and of course from stratified sequences. Broad vegetational assemblages identified from fossil pollen carried chronological implications for the archaeologist since the botanists themselves could order such assemblages through time e.g. a floral spectrum in N.W. Europe of mixed oak forest was likely to be earlier than one of beech and herbs; but, relatively quickly in fact, the co-operation has moved well-beyond the post-excavation 'Will you look at my samples?' stage to integrated research exploring not just ancient flora and fauna but ecological systems of which Man is but one part. One reason why this has happened is that it soon became apparent upon detailed examination of pollen spectra that some changes in Nature could not satisfactorily be explained by natural causes; hence phrases such as 'the anthropogenic factor in vegetational change' and, more crudely, 'Man's impact on the environment'.[14]

Just as recently we have learnt to appreciate some of the effects we are having on our environment, so simultaneously and not entirely unrelated we have been learning to appreciate not merely the fact but also the significance of what earlier men were doing to theirs. They were not merely felling trees, domesticating animals and cropping fields but were integrally involving themselves directly and indirectly in a vast range of dynamic bio-cultural relationships. Man's activities affected not merely the size of the forest but also its nature; by cropping weeds, he developed cereals; his herding of cattle affected not only them individually and as a species but, over any one area, it affected too the plant cover and therefore the populations of light-sensitive snails, spiders, beetles and bacteria in the soil, and consequently the soil itself. Man himself would be affected by such changes, even to the extent of being forced to leave a previously habitable niche by ecological forces of which he may well have been an instigator. We can therefore think in terms of the 'natural' factor in cultural change, or perhaps more properly of Man as an active participant in an ecosystem, rather than merely of Man the logical and dominant mammal calmly surveying a static landscape and rationally choosing to settle and farm one area rather than another (fig. 4.3).

The impact of the Natural Sciences on the archaeological approach has been forcibly stated in this context by Dimbleby: '. . . I have long thought that the archaeologist should be aware of the potential scientific value of ancient sites. Indeed, I see no reason why archaeology should have exclusive claims on sites occupied by ancient man; they are equally important for botanists, pedologists and zoologists . . . the archaeologist is not justified in liquidating a site without reference to other possible interests . . . sites are valuable not only for the history of man, but for the history of his environment, with which he is inextricably bound up'.[15] It is significant that since those words were written a Journal of Archaeological Science, with Professor Dimbleby as co-editor, has been founded and is publishing papers of archaeo-scientific content in their own right rather than their content being relegated to an undigested appendix at the back of archaeological excavation reports.

We have briefly discussed pollen analysis because it is the environmental technique which has probably had most impact on archaeology so far, both directly in terms of results and generally in approaching the past. As with dating, however, the range of environmental evidence and appropriate techniques is now considerable, and all its components serve to emphasise that the study of the conventional elements of archaeological hardware purely in artefactual terms is an inadequate response,

[14] Cf. J.G. Evans et al. (eds.), The Effect of Man on the Landscape: the Highland Zone (1975). The C.B.A. should be publishing an equivalent volume for the Lowland Zone in 1977.
[15] G. Dimbleby, Plants and Archaeology (1967), 13.

120

Conventional ¹⁴c dates years BP	North Sea sea-level (to O.D.)	pollen zones	Great Britain	Netherlands	Northern Germany	Denmark	archaeological periods	
5.000	− 5 m	Sub-boreal		TRB	TRB	TRB		5.000
			Windmill Hill	Swifterbant	Ellerbek	Ertebølle	Neolithic	
6.000	− 7	Atlantic						6.000
				Bandceramic Late Mes. surv.	'Oldesloe'	Vedbaek		
7.000	− 10		Lower Halstow	De Lijen-Wartena complex / Late Mesol		Bloksbjerg		7.000
8.000	− 20		Skipsea Broxbourne	Boreal Mesol.		Kongemose	Mesolithic	8.000
		Boreal				Holmegaard Svaerdborg		
			Leman and Ower	Early Mesol. Bank	Hohen Viecheln	Mullerup Øgaarde I		
9.000	− 40		— Brown { Star Carr	Basal Mesol.		Klosterlund		9.000
	− 50	Pre-boreal			Pinnberg			
10.000								10.000
		Younger Dryas		Ahrensburg	Ahrensburg	Lyngby	Palaeolithic	
11.000		Alleröd	Creswell Cheddar	Tjonger	Federmesser	Bromme		11.000

4.4 A chart correlating and synthesising a vast amount of environmental, cultural and chronological evidence from the areas around the North Sea from c. 9000–3000 bc.

archaeologically or any other way, to the past. In a general but very real sense, archaeology is both part of and contributor of evidence to environmental research world-wide, for the present environment cannot be understood without an understanding of its development over the last millennia and not just over the last century. Climate and weather, for example, are crucial factors, and so too is soil, and the evidence for their changes as well as the effect of those changes on Man comes in part from archaeological investigation (fig. 4.4).[16] The study of crops through time,

[16] J. G. Evans, *op. cit.* note 14, gives many references, supplemented in J. G. Evans, *The Environment of Early Man in the British Isles* (1975), S. Limbrey, *Soil Science and Archaeology* (1975) and W. Pennington, *The History of British Vegetation* (2nd ed. 1974).

palaeoethnobotany, as distinct from the 'natural' vegetation (if there is any!), depends very much for its source material such as grains and grain impressions being found in archaeological contexts: the lack of progress in this field until recently bears the generalisation out because it was due to excavators' inability, mentally and physically, to find the data.[17] Though dendrochronology can proceed, using medieval timbers in England and desiccated timber in Arizona for example, without reference to excavated material, gaps in its sequences can be filled by fresh buried wood from archaeological contexts and, in its turn, it can feed back chronological and climatic information to illumine the cultural record. That record itself becomes more comprehensible as knowledge of human and animal pathology, diet, blood grouping and even genetic structure grows, with the raw material often coming from archaeological excavation and certainly the more valuable when it does so.

Analytic techniques

To balance this major research exploitation of what, in old-style terms, is conventionally non-archaeological material, we can look at the traditional materials of the archaeologist, the conventional 'finds' of his excavations and the museum display. These too are the subject of scientific archaeology, the history of co-operation here being somewhat longer. Naturally, since pottery, stone and metal objects were the province of the archaeologist, the application of scientific techniques to archaeology developed in this field relatively early—the hang-up has been in other areas on which archaeology bears, though it did not realise it, and perhaps did not want to know very much. Basically, however, there now exists another range of applied scientific techniques directed towards answering one of archaeology's oldest questions 'What?' and specifically 'What is it made of?' rather than 'What is it?' (p. 105). As a result, a question which archaeology thought it was quite good at answering is proving to be complex in detailed resolution and of considerable implication in and well beyond the field of technological enquiry. The constituents of the commonest artefacts, pottery, stone, bronze and iron, are coming to be identified with considerable precision through techniques such as analysis with the petrological microscope, optical emission spectroscopy and x-ray fluorescent spectrometry. On the better excavations metal artefacts are x-rayed as a matter of course since an x-ray photograph is a fuller record than a drawing of the object. This sort of approach to the artefactual data is now continuously supplementing (and sometimes correcting) the archaeologist's macro-assessment of objects. We are learning of the chemical and mineral components of our 'bronze' dagger and 'native' pottery, and of their trace elements too; and in addition to learning what they are made of in scientific terms, the various analytical techniques often tell how they were made

---

[17] J. Renfrew, *Palaeoethnobotany* (1973).

and, by revealing usage-patterns on or in objects like hammer-stones and sickles, what they were used for and indeed how they were used. So scientific analyses of archaeological material now provide a hugely increased, much more precise and quantified body of data than was previously available. Perhaps in this context it is fair to say that archaeology has become more obviously scientific than in other respects because here we are dealing with the raw material of conventional archaeology itself.

Much of this new information also has economic implications. Indeed it is deliberately sought for its economic uses as much as for its technological interest. By identifying the type of rock used to make a stone axehead, for example, it is possible, in some cases with precision, to say where the rock (though not necessarily the axe) came from; similarly, the mineral constituents of pottery can be traced to source or at least identified as local or non-local to the place where the pottery was found. Repeat the identification many times, and the result should be patterns of movement. In the Near East, for example, obsidian, a mineral with localised sources, can be seen to have 'moved' over a wide area in the early stages of agricultural development; in Wessex, as another example, many of the stone axeheads are of rocks which only occur naturally, as far as geological fieldwork shows at the moment, in West Cornwall, North Wales and the Lake District.[18] These are the observable scientific phenomena; their interpretation in cultural terms is a different matter to which we turn shortly in Chapter 5. Using different techniques but to similar ends, it is possible to analyse other materials like metals, glass and slags to try to identify the sources of their constituents too, again with a view to reconstructing any patterns of economic activity which may once have existed. So here again the application of scientific techniques to archaeology has had a profound effect on the study of the past as well as on our understanding of that past itself. Archaeologically we are not, for example, quite so glib now in our assumptions about trade and its sociological implications, about the housewife making her time-honoured pots outside the hut door or indeed about the cultural validity of pottery in general. In this respect, scientific data has shown a little cultural knowledge to be a dangerous thing indeed.

Laboratory conservation

One of the other scientific developments which is having an increasing effect on archaeological thought and practice is in the field of conservation, that is in the laboratory conservation of archaeological material. This is already established professionally as a field of such expertise that the poor archaeologist is exhorted more or less to do nothing with his finds without proper professional advice. I exaggerate, of course, but not much, and undoubtedly there is a strong case for leaving conservation not only to the trained expert but to the conservator with proper equipment and

[18] *Proc. Prehist. Soc.*, 30 (1964), 111–33; 38 (1972), 235–75.

facilities. Indeed, just as the botanist has argued that sites are too important to be left to the archaeologist (p. 120), so the conservator also wants to break the same monopolistic tradition of the archaeological excavator: 'finds' are also too important to be left to his ignorant ministrations. Again, there is much truth in this, in the sense that full, scientifically-based conservation now is technically sophisticated, time-consuming and expensive. Provided material can be recovered and brought to a laboratory, much that was previously 'not worth keeping' can be conserved, stabilised and retained for posterity. Enormous strides have been made, for example, in the treatment of organic materials—wood, parchments, cloths,—and the cleaning and stabilisation of metals now offers a future to objects whose lifespan was previously limited from the moment they were exposed to the air and lifted from the stable environmental context in which, by definition, they had survived. Among the problems here, however, are those of cost and expertise: in practice, the potential of conservation is but a pipe-dream for many excavators, at least in Britain, and strict application of the principle that no excavation should start without first securing an adequate short- and long-term conservation facility would put a stop to most current work. Perhaps that would be no bad thing; and it must be recognised that there is a certain strength in the argument that to dig up material without taking steps to conserve it is somewhat silly and at worst academic vandalism. On the other hand, there is a certain irony in the situation that archaeologists are being forcibly enjoined to take their 'finds' more seriously at a time when, for some anyway, 'finds' are the least of the problems thrown up by excavation and in many respects far from the most important part of an excavation's product. Nevertheless, it is important for the archaeological continuum that material which would previously have been lost can now, potentially if not always actually, be preserved to inform future studies.[19]

Field survey and sampling

Finally, in this selection of aspects of scientific development which have affected archaeology, I want to return to the field to mention three more, surveying, sampling and experimenting. As discussed above (p. 82), in a sense excavation is a last resort in default of any other way of seeing what is buried in the ground i.e. if soil was translucent, excavation would be unnecessary. The argument cannot be sustained, but nevertheless a range of equipment has been developed which in effect tries to 'see' through the overburden. Initially, these devices were thought of as an aid to excavation; like air photography, they were thought of primarily as devices helping to identify 'good places to dig' i.e. where something would be found, an approach involving, as we have

[19] H.J. Plenderleith, *The Conservation of Antiquities and Works of Art* (1956); G. Thompson (ed.), *Recent Advances in Conservation* (1963); U.N.E.S.C.O., *The Conservation of Cultural Property* (1968); E.A. Dowman, *Conservation in Field Archaeology* (1970); D. Leigh (ed.), *First Aid for Finds* (1972).

seen, a misconception about the nature of excavation (p. 80). Now, however, data from surveys carried out by magnetometers, gradiometers and soil conductivity meters in particular have established a validity in their own right. While an excavation might be guided or even wholly planned on the basis of such a survey carried out in advance, granted that the whole site could not be excavated and in the light of correlations between surveyed and excavated data, the survey results from the unexcavated part of the site can be used both as scientific statements about that area and as the basis for interpretation of it. In practice, such methods have limitations, not least in their unreliability in detecting slight structural evidence like stake-holes; while on the whole they are fairly reliable in indicating medium to large features, a negative result cannot therefore be taken at face value. Nor are they much use on highly stratified sites except to show that something is there since they will not readily distinguish between features of different dates or layers. Again, though recognising their uses in certain circumstances, I personally have a sneaking feeling that, with all the sophistication of their gadgetry, essentially they relate to a conceptual stage in the development of archaeology which has passed. Excavation is about information, not things, and it is therefore about the blank area as well as the 50 m. deep well or the large stone building. If a site is to be excavated anyway, why base the excavation on such a highly selective data base as that provided by geophysics? Although the sampling represented by a scientifically unguided excavation will also be highly biased, at least one knows the origin of that bias.

One paragraph must suffice about sampling itself, unfairly but enough to make the main point. It is simply to stress the important influence of the mathematical sciences on archaeology, despite (or perhaps because of?) the lack of numerate archaeologists. The influence is seen now right across the range of archaeological activity in the pressure to count, to quantify, to order, to give mathematical value to cultural expression and the ways in which it is investigated.[20] In this context, excavation and field survey become sampling procedures and as such theoretically controlled and interpretable on a numerical basis. Here we are indeed a long way from the intuitive, personalised, 'I feel this is a good place to dig' style of archaeology; but fortunately there is room for both, though the latter is bound to seem more archaic in face of the omniverous precision increasingly demanded by the computer. Though in America statistical bases for both survey and excavation programme designs are common,[21] rigorous sampling by numbers is not yet influential practice in Europe though already whole excavation recording systems have been based on the needs of a subsequent computer programme. Nevertheless, a statistical base for both survey and excavation landscape sampling seems to me a reasonable way of testing claims about the quantity of

---

[20] Most recently, and clearly, expounded in J.E. Doran and F.R. Hodson, *Mathematics and Computers in Archaeology* (1975).
[21] E.g. in M.B. Schiffer and J.H. House, *The Cache River Archaeological Project* (1975), esp. chap. 5.

IV.1 Butser Ancient Farm Project, Hampshire: (a) a 1975 experiment in building a round house on the basis of a ground plan of post-holes only recorded in excavations at Baulksbury hill-fort, Hants. A year's life has subsequently shown design faults in the most conjectural part of this 'hardware model', the roof over the porch, and that part of the experiment will start again with a different structure. This well illustrates the difference between reconstruction for research and display. Meanwhile, a completely different structure, a sheep-pen, has been built on exactly the same ground plan; (b) Ploughing with an 'ancient' ard and sowing winter wheat in one of the 'Celtic' fields on which a series of long-term experiments are being conducted. March, 1976.

cultural material, the extent of the cultural resource base, in the British countryside. So far the nearest approach to quantification of this dimension are the crude averages, variously arrived at and differently expressed, of 1 site per $\frac{1}{4}$ square mile and 1 site per kilometre of newly-built motorway in lowland England.[22]

Experiment in archaeology

Popularly, science and experiment go together, and perhaps archaeology's apparent reluctance to experiment is one reason for its lack of scientific status. Nevertheless, within and on the fringes of archaeology, there is in fact a long history of small-scale experiment of a sort, though it is only recently that experiment rigorous enough to meet scientific criteria has come to be practised more commonly. Excavation itself has been described as an unrepeatable field experiment, an understandable concept but self-contradictory in that an experiment should by definition be repeatable. In that sense, archaeology never can be scientific since every site is unique, each excavation is unique and much of the available material is unique. It is only with mass-production that the individual qualities of material disappear. This is an important factor in archaeological experiment for it emphasises the need for strictly-defined objectives in experimental work and specifically whether the aim is reconstruction or to produce a copy or whether it is an experiment in producing a reconstruction. The first is not really experimental, since it is relatively easy to build a reproduction of an Iron Age house or part of Hadrian's Wall using modern materials and techniques: the finished product may look all right but erecting it thus and subsequently studying its decay through time are quite invalid experimentally. If, on the other hand, the house is erected using materials and techniques available to contemporary society, observation of its building and decay have an experimental value regardless of the appearance of the finished product. The experiment can be continued by varying carefully controlled elements in the construction and observing their effect, if any, on such qualities as stability, durability and appearance (Pl. IV.1a). As in culture change itself, time is of the essence in much archaeological experimentation from the firing of 'old' pottery kilns to studies of degradation on experimental earthworks (Pl. IV.2).[23]

Field experiment, and much 'indoor' or laboratory experiment, provide 'a trial, a test, a means of guiding a theory or an idea ... experimental archaeology provides a way, one way, of examining archaeological thoughts about human behaviour in the past ... it represents no more and no less than a channelling of intelligent curiosity towards an explanation of human behaviour in

[22] P. A. Rahtz, *Rescue Archaeology* (1974), 32, 128.
[23] J. Coles, *Archaeology by Experiment* (1973). *See* also P. J. Reynolds, 'Experimental Archaeology and the Butser Ancient Farm Project', *Rescue News* 11 (1976), 7–8.

IV.2 Overton Down experimental earthwork, Wiltshire: (a) General view of the bank and ditch in July 1976, 16 years after construction. The top of the bank was originally up to the bottom of the black bars on the central upright posts, the ditch was completely clean and there was of course no vegetation except on the berm between bank and ditch; (b) Section through the silts in the ditch after 16 years, showing the variable grading of the chalk 'tip-lines'. All the material has come off the side of the ditch, mainly through frost-shattering of the exposed chalk subsoil.

essentially practical terms'.[24] It is the physical, 'hardware' method of testing an hypothesis, an alternative to the 'mental model' testing we shall discuss in the next chapter. But experimental archaeology can rarely produce definite answers or proof; what it can provide are indications, perhaps preferred indications, of how processes could have been carried out. By providing negatives, it can help narrow the probability-band within which certain procedures took place; and with luck, the unexpected during the experimental procedures themselves can throw light on previously unasked questions. The revelation of the real amount of grain required to fill an Iron Age storage pit during recent farming experiments in Wessex is a classic example of the spin-off value of experiment.[25] Another great merit of experimental work, particularly in the field, is at the personal level almost regardless of academic results. Particularly as more and more archaeologists themselves come from urban backgrounds, and as archaeology itself develops its theoretical bases, field experiment brings the individual face to face and hand to hand with the raw materials and, to some extent, with the problems faced by increasingly alien earlier men grappling with the practical realities of non-urban subsistence economies, crafts and non-mechanical technologies. Much of this is conceptually as well as practically a long way from the experience of consuming, suburban man today (Pl. IV.1b).

It may seem inapposite to end a chapter on scientific archaeology, albeit a highly selective one, on such an anthropogenic, almost humanistic note; but scientific as much as any other sort of archaeology is constrained by the quality of both the input and the interpretation and both of those depend on the quality of archaeologists, not of science or even of archaeology.

[24] J. Coles, *op. cit.* note 23, 13.
[25] *Antiquity* 41 (1967), 214-5.

Bibliography

Antiquity 41 (1967) 214-5; 45 (1971) 275-82; 48 (1974) 261-4, 265-72; 49 (1975) 219-26, 252-72; 50 (1976) 61-3
F. Boaz, *Race, Language and Culture* (1940)
D. Brothwell and E. Higgs, *Science in Archaeology* (1969)
J. Coles, *Archaeology by Experiment* (1973)
G. Daniel, *150 Years of Archaeology* (1975)
S.J. de Laet, *Archaeology and its Problems* (1957)
G. Dimbleby, *Plants and Archaeology* (1967)
J.E. Doran and F.R. Hodson, *Mathematics and Computers in Archaeology* (1975)
E.A. Dowman, *Conservation in Field Archaeology* (1970)
J.G. Evans, *The Environment of Early Man in the British Isles* (1975)

J. G. Evans *et al.*, (eds.), *The Effect of Man on the Landscape: the Highland Zone* (1975)

R. Jessup, *Curiosities of British Archaeology* (1961)

Journal of Archaeological Science (1974–)

D. Leigh (ed.), *First Aid for Finds* (1972)

S. Limbrey, *Soil Science and Archaeology* (1975)

J.W. Michels, *Dating Methods in Archaeology* (1973)

L. Morgan, *Ancient Society* (1877)

W. Pennington, *The History of British Vegetation* (1974)

H.J. Plenderleith, *The Conservation of Antiquities and Works of Art* (1956)

Proc. Prehist. Soc. 30 (1964) 111–33; 38 (1972) 235–75, 389–407

P.A. Rahtz, *Rescue Archaeology* (1974)

C. Renfrew, *Before Civilization* (1973)

J. Renfrew, *Palaeoethnobotany* (1973)

P.J. Reynolds, 'Experimental Archaeology and the Butser Ancient Farm Project', *Rescue News* 11 (1976) 7–8

M.B. Schiffer and J.H. House, *The Cache River Archaeological Project* (1975)

Somerset Levels Papers I (1975) 54–5

Studies in Archaeological Science (1972–)

G. Thomson (ed.), *Recent Advances in Conservation* (1963)

M.S. Tite, *Methods of Physical Examination in Archaeology* (1973)

U.N.E.S.C.O., *The Conservation of Cultural Property* (1968)

T. Watkins (ed.), *Radiocarbon: Calibration and Prehistory* (1975)

Sir Mortimer Wheeler, *Still Digging* (1955)

G.R. Willey and J.A. Sabloff, *A History of American Archaeology* (1974)

5

THEORETICAL ARCHAEOLOGY

'Hypothesis is a tool which can cause trouble if not used properly'
W. I. B. Beveridge, *The Art of Scientific Investigation* (1950)

Although seeming to be so practical a subject, in a sense all archaeology is theoretical. Even at the very crude level at which it used to operate, that is of being primarily concerned to find things, it was theoretical in the sense that a, probably unconscious, hypothesis that something was buried here rather than there was proposed and was tested by digging a hole at 'here'. Hence the title of this chapter: although my concern now is mainly to discuss the interpretation of archaeological data, it is as well to stress that the theoretical constructs involved in interpretation are not a new feature at that stage of the archaeological process. Theory is involved from the very beginning.

Basically theory-making, or 'model-building' as we are now encouraged to call it, involves putting together an idea to cover some observed information. The expression of the idea can take different forms—a written argument, a diagram, a physical model,—or, as is often the case in the early stages of the archaeological process, it may not be expressed at all because it is self-evident, unnecessary or unconscious. One of the achievements of the so-called 'new' archaeology of the last decade or so (p. 136) has been to increase awareness of the theoretical basis implicit in routine archaeological methodology and to rationalise in conceptual terms the steps by which that methodology is executed. The parrot-cry 'Examine your pre-conceptions' which daily rang over one of my recent excavations, although originating as a slightly sick reaction to the bombast of some modern publications, is actually not a bad summary guide-line to theory in archaeological practice.

The 'meaning' of evidence

What, if anything, does archaeological evidence mean? How can we use it to construct knowledge about the past? Any piece of archaeological evidence, or a collection of pieces, does not in itself mean anything at all: interpretatively, it is inert. It only acquires meaning through the medium of the human mind which brings to it in various degrees, scholarship, experience, expertise, imagination, subjectivity, biases, ignorance and plausibility. It therefore follows that while archaeological evidence cannot lie, neither can it of itself reveal the truth. It is only we who can say the evidence is misleading (for whatever reason) or is proof of a past reality—though quite how we judge is difficult to assess in the absence of evidence other than the archaeological. It is, however, the informed balance of probabilities, or of improbabilities perhaps in the case of archaeology, that is the meat of scholarship; though, again perhaps particularly in the case of archaeology, there is sometimes a perilously thin line between judicious academic balancing and assertive, 'unacceptable' juggling.

Archaeological evidence then does not 'mean' anything: archaeologists, and others, give it meaning, often of a widely differing kind. Just look at the 'meanings' Stonehenge has had for different generations and indeed still has for different interests today: in all this variety, Stonehenge itself has not changed as a piece of inert archaeological evidence, though of course our reliable information about it has accumulated over the years. People have tended to find in it what they were looking for: primitive Britons, blood-thirsty Druids, religious mystery, scientific precision and socio-political investment. A recent cartoon suggestion that it was the remnants of a prehistoric motorway interchange flippantly makes my point: the cartoon offers a 'meaning' within a framework which simply did not exist for earlier interpretations. We touched on some of these points in Chapter 1 so let us take another example of a 'model' of rather wider significance, linking it to the discussion of dating in the last chapter.

Time and change through time are, as we said there, two of the essential strands in archaeology. What is required therefore, if the results of archaeological research are to be expressible, is some form of generalising model, a wide-ranging interpretation, to explain our information in comprehensible terms. From this desire to explain rather than merely collect archaeological material arose, initially in the first half of the nineteenth century, the Three Age System of Stone, Bronze and Iron for western European prehistory, subsequently elaborated into the Old, Middle and New Stone Ages (Palaeolithic, Mesolithic, Neolithic), the Bronze Age and the Iron Age (cf. fig. 4.4). Basically this view of the past has lasted until the present and a century of repetition and use has tended to give it the status of an immutable, self-evident truth; but in fact it is no more nor less valid than that view of English history which saw our island past cabin'd, cribbed and confined by regnal dates. Indeed, the latter type of model was the model for the former—history with dated, horizontal lines across it; and the 'Ages' way of looking at the past is no more than a model. It is an interpretation, not a fact. It is a view of the past, naturally evolving from what archaeology exclusively studied last century, based on technological development alone; but it has no inner validity, no essential Truth, other than that deriving from its own criteria. Yet it worked intellectually and for practical purposes in arranging museum material, and presumably it appealed unconsciously to a period of technological development and increasing material prosperity. Now it is falling out of use, at least among model-conscious archaeologists, and is being replaced by other views of the past: an economic model, a social model and, tentatively but surely, a chronological model deriving from the 'absolute' dating techniques already discussed (p. 113). The 'Iron Age' never existed in the last millennium BC; but the thousand years before the birth of Christ did, and during them iron was increasingly used in western Europe. Lots of other things actually happened too, but as far as we are concerned they all can only take place in our minds.

Model-building

However objective the methods and intentions of those who interpret the evidence, we in retrospect can detect the probably unavoidable element of subjectivity deriving from the temper of the time at which the interpretation takes place. One of the most influential books making people aware of these biases was Butterfield's *The Whig Interpretation of History* (1931) which exposed the unstated premises, e.g. that democracy is a 'good thing', underlying the writing of much English history. Piggott, following Butterfield and Beveridge's *The Art of Scientific Investigation* (1950), made explicit the idea of the existence of conscious or unconscious mental frameworks in archaeological thought and practice and firmly established the use of the word 'model' to describe this idea in archaeological writing. He summarised what he meant in *Approach to Archaeology*, p. 3: '(The historian must) try to put together, from all the available sources, something which will be consistent with the evidence he uses, and account for all the phenomena he has observed as convincingly as possible . . . the scientist investigating natural phenomena makes a number of strictly controlled observations . . . looks for the underlying connections between them, and then tries to devise some hypothesis or theory which will account for the observed phenomena in the most satisfactory manner. In scientific language, he will construct a *model*, a mental creation expressing the relationships and arrangements—perhaps in a mathematical formula—which will best account for all the observations he has made. The model will be a 'true' one in so far as it does satisfactorily account for the phenomena, but you can have more than one model at a time, all 'true', and the devising of a new model does not mean that all the others have to be scrapped, though some may have to be abandoned or drastically modified in the light of new thought' (fig. 5.1).

The quotation adequately describes the process of *conscious* model-building which can be applied to archaeological evidence which already exists ('observations . . . made by other scientists'), which we set out to acquire by research, or which, like fame, we have thrust upon us; but it is important to distinguish such deliberate and conscious model-building from the received and perhaps unconscious model-building which, for most scholars, exists in their intellectual equipment simply because they are products of

133

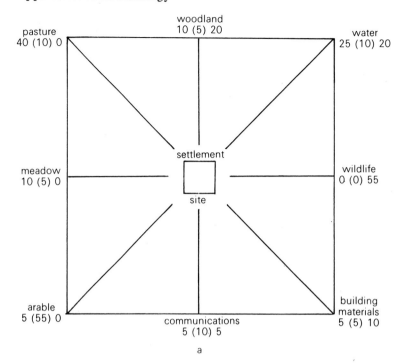

pasture
40 (10) 0

woodland
10 (5) 20

water
25 (10) 20

meadow
10 (5) 0

settlement
site

wildlife
0 (0) 55

arable
5 (55) 0

communications
5 (10) 5

building
materials
5 (5) 10

a

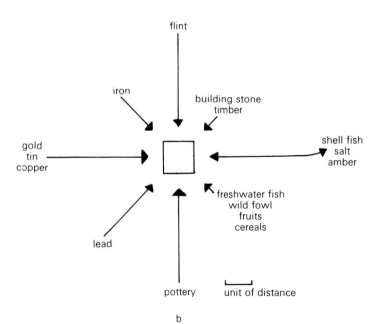

flint

iron

building stone
timber

gold
tin
copper

shell fish
salt
amber

freshwater fish
wild fowl
fruits
cereals

lead

pottery

unit of distance

b

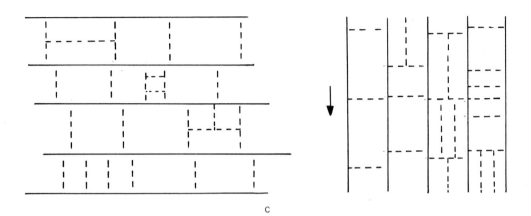

c

5.1 Three simple examples of interpretation of archaeological evidence, or 'conscious model-building', expressed as linear models illustrating spatial relationships:

(a) identifies a number of factors contributing to the economic viability of a settlement. Each of these factors is given a percentage weighting of 'importance' for three different economies, respectively pastoral, arable and hunter/gathering i.e. they are variables depending on the exploitive strategies of the settlements' occupants. Thus, theoretically, potential arable land is of no significance as such to a hunter/gatherer economy but of major importance in a cereal-growing economy; and the reverse is true of the locally-available wild-life resources. The model does not of course attempt to answer the question 'why?' or to judge whether available resources determine the economy followed.

(b) is somewhat similar but instead of representing the exploitation of resources as a variable through time it introduces distance at a particular point in time as the variable. It shows the distance from which the various resources represented by archaeological evidence had to travel to arrive on the settlement. Nothing is said or implied about how or why this 'trade' occurred: the model is static, merely showing that the economy required the input of resources acquired locally, from an intermediate zone, and from a distance. It is, however, a graphic supplement or even an alternative to a written list of 'finds', their identification and source. Two variables, direction and economic significance, could be added to the model without overcomplicating it by making the arrows come into the settlement from the appropriate direction and by expressing the resource's economic significance by a weighting device such as a percentage figure or an appropriate thickness of line.

(c) is quite different though still a linear model: it suggests how (prehistoric British) field systems could have evolved by the clearance of long, parallel swathes (solid lines), either across or up-and-down slopes, which were subsequently infilled with a variable but symmetrical pattern of small plots (broken lines). At the time this idea was proposed, it offered an alternative to the accepted view that such field systems developed by the irregular addition of more and more small fields around the edges of the existing system.

their own time and place. We are probably now much more aware of this factor in our thought processes than were previous generations, not least because archaeology is now old enough to have its own history in which we can study such mental constraints and influences against a social and intellectual background; but as a factor in our use of archaeological evidence, the meaning we give to it, the fashion of the times remains potent as, ironically, the cult of objectivity in the 'new' archaeology of our own day in fact demonstrates. I recently discussed, for example, a thesis on settlement archaeology suggested by a would-be post-graduate student in terms, received and largely unquestioned as valid by him, which would have been conceptually impossible ten years ago and could well be as dead as a dodo ten years hence. Despite his pretensions, the unstated assumptions behind his objectives were as biased and just as much a product of his time as were those informing the 'meaning' given to the evidence interpreted by, for example, Phelps in his *History and Antiquities of Somersetshire* (1836).

The question of conscious and unconscious model-building is so basic to the view of the past promoted by research and received by the world that it is worthwhile just quoting for comparison, without detailed comment, two statements arising from similar work but in different places and at different times. Phelps' survey of an English county, quite good of its type and for its period, reads on its title page as per fig. 5.2. To the unconscious models informing his approach as implied by that title—and a thesis could be written on that alone,—he adds specific objectives in the dedication to (and again what social comment) King William the Fourth: 'Deeply impressed with a grateful sense of your Majesty's gracious condescension, in permitting me to dedicate to your Majesty, my humble attempt to illustrate the History and Antiquities of an interesting portion of your Majesty's Dominion . . . (I hope) that it may be deemed, in some degree, worthy of the distinguished patronage conferred, as well as interesting and instructive to the general reader, and useful to the inhabitants of the important county . . .' Servile though this may seem, we can identify a number of assumptions and objectives, not the least of which is a hope that the work will be 'useful'.

Now compare that with, at random but fairly typical, the title and page 1 of Zubrow's *Population, Contact, and Climate in the New Mexican Pueblos* (1974): '. . . human populations . . . are not only facilitated by culture in adapting to their environment . . . the study of these adaptations is complicated by the addition of the cultural variable. A totally synthetic theory of culture . . . is operationally difficult to apply to the analysis of interdependent factors with which ecology must deal. . . . the analytical approach of human ecology must isolate variables from the systems of culture and ecology, and study them independently and in relation to each other. Thus the analysis in this study is not concerned with culture as an undifferentiated totality, but with aspects of culture as they are involved with the process of adaptation.' Which author is being the more 'objective'? Who, consciously or otherwise, is more dependent on models?

The archaeologist, like the scientist, must obviously be aware of the general conceptual framework within which he is thinking and working; and he ought to

THE

HISTORY AND ANTIQUITIES

OF

SOMERSETSHIRE;

BEING

A GENERAL AND PAROCHIAL SURVEY OF THAT INTERESTING COUNTY.

TO WHICH IS PREFIXED

AN HISTORICAL INTRODUCTION,

WITH

A BRIEF VIEW OF ECCLESIASTICAL HISTORY;

AND AN ACCOUNT OF

𝔗𝔥𝔢 𝔇𝔯𝔲𝔦𝔡𝔦𝔠𝔞𝔩, 𝔅𝔢𝔩𝔤𝔦𝔠-𝔅𝔯𝔦𝔱𝔦𝔰𝔥, 𝔕𝔬𝔪𝔞𝔫, 𝔖𝔞𝔵𝔬𝔫, 𝔇𝔞𝔫𝔦𝔰𝔥, 𝔞𝔫𝔡 𝔑𝔬𝔯𝔪𝔞𝔫 𝔄𝔫𝔱𝔦𝔮𝔲𝔦𝔱𝔦𝔢𝔰,

NOW EXTANT.

ILLUSTRATED WITH

MAPS, PLANS, ENGRAVINGS, AND VIGNETTES,

FROM ORIGINAL DRAWINGS, BY J. AND J. C. BUCKLER, P. CROCKER, Esqrs.

AND OTHERS.

___

IN FOUR VOLUMES.

VOL. I.

___

BY THE REV. W. PHELPS, A.B. F.S.A.

VICAR OF MEARE AND BICKNOLLER,

FORMERLY OF BALLIOL COLLEGE, OXFORD, AND AUTHOR OF " CALENDARIUM BOTANICUM, &c.

___

LONDON:

PRINTED FOR THE AUTHOR,

BY J. B. NICHOLS AND SON, 25, PARLIAMENT STREET.

___

1836.

5.2 An 'unconscious model': the title page of a typical nineteenth century county archaeology.

specify that model when offering an interpretation of his archaeological data. As was implied earlier (p. 133), the archaeologist is a creature of his own time and, to a lesser or greater extent, the view of the past that he offers reflects the concepts and misconceptions, even the intellectual and social needs, of his own time. Archaeology, like other scholarship, does not exist *in vacuo*. It relates to the intellectual climate of the times, and this influences and can indeed characterise underlying theory, practice, 'results' and the interpretation offered. This appears quite clearly in archaeology's own history: a concern with the technology of ancient implements reflects an interest of later Victorian England; the invasion basis of later British prehistory offered during the first half of this century is a natural reflection of insular reaction to involvement in, and indeed threat from, two continental wars; and similarly current interpretation of the past in terms of economic and social systems reflects present-day concerns.

Methodologically these shifts in common interest are reflected in the way, for example, that excavations are carried out and indeed what it is that is excavated. This was part of Pitt-Rivers' greatness: he started excavating settlements to find out how people had lived instead of just digging into barrows to find objects and burials. The excavation of a superficially undistinguished street in medieval Winchester, a city with fairly obvious and fine ancient monuments like a cathedral, a castle and city walls, would have been conceptually impossible a generation ago; similarly the stripping of large areas inside hill-forts instead of concentrating only on the surrounding ramparts and gateways reflects, however unconsciously, a shift in social and intellectual interest from the military concerns up to the 1950s to the civilian concerns thereafter.[1] There is a conceptual world of difference between the objectives and execution of the excavations at Hod Hill and South Cadbury Castle, two hill-forts only 27 kms. apart, investigated within a decade of each other (1951–58 and 1966–71 respectively).[2] Faced with writing up a hill-fort excavation myself (Cadbury Congresbury), one which has produced a quantity of non-local material, I cannot help thinking that forty years ago an excavator would have 'naturally' and indeed gladly presented it as positively crawling with invaders or at least foreigners; whereas now we dither about with socio-economic-religious models and frankly have very little positive idea of what it is that we have so far 'found'. Our ultra-cautious attempts to interpret our, as it happens, very carefully observed and recorded phenomena reflect, whether we like it or not, not merely an element of disillusion with the technological limitations of excavation itself but also the loss of a unifying *credo* in our own contemporary society (*cf.* fig. 5.3).

Accepting then that there is no ultimate, finite truth to be revealed by archaeological evidence, that all interpretation of it is relative, what is it that we can reasonably do with it? A very great deal is the short answer, provided that the word 'reasonably' is always in

---

[1] The Winchester excavations were described in a series of interim reports in *Antiq. J.* from 1964 to 1975.
[2] L. Alcock, *By South Cadbury is that Camelot* (1972); J.W. Brailsford, *Hod Hill I* (1962); Sir Ian Richmond, *Hod Hill II* (1968).

the forefront of our minds and that the inferential limitations of the evidence are fully recognised throughout. In many ways, the treatment of archaeological evidence for interpretative purposes is very similar in principle to the treatment of any other type of evidence, though obviously the techniques of examining the evidence are in many cases specialist ones. We have already discussed the nature of archaeological evidence itself (p. 82), emphasising that the evidential product of archaeological activity is first and foremost information; and we have noted that the information comes in many forms. But all the 'finds' from potsherds to post-holes to coprolites, however bulky, constitute only a fraction of the *information* available in and retrieved from the excavation. There are two other major information products, though both could be subsumed under the general heading of 'the record'.

The archaeological record

In addition to the 'things', there are also all the contexts of those things. Normally, the layers making up the matrix of a site are not totally removed from a site, though individual components such as a pit or a grave, with all their contents may be removed *en bloc* for later dissection in a laboratory; but information represented by these layers, which is just as valid and perhaps more significant than that of the contained objects, must also in effect be removed from the site. Hence the substitute removal by way of section drawings, just as plans represent a substitute removal of information available in the horizontal dimension. The plans and sections together constitute a substitute three-dimensional record of reality as observed. They, with photographs and whatever other video or audio record has been made of the observed phenomena, are just as much part of the archaeological evidence as the things also removed from the site.

The other major information product is the data-store, usually called the finds register, in which is recorded numerically and verbally what is essentially a series of relationships. In practice, the positions of movable objects, samples etc., are measured and often described, usually three-dimensionally to record 'where' they were found; but the repetition of the process time and time again is really building up, together with the graphic record, information about relationships in time and space some of which may not be perceived at the time of excavation. My point here is that, granted the information-goal of excavation, the total excavation product is as much, if not more, the paperwork as the artefact, and all of it is archaeological evidence. As one American fieldworker put it to me, apropos field survey rather than excavation, 'We collect pencil marks, not finds'.

And of course the same is true in non-excavational field archaeology. Each site, or perhaps we should say all the artificial components of the landscape, exists as archaeological evidence; but unless each one of those components is going to be personally checked every time it is used evidentially, the record of that component is also archaeological evidence. Whether one accepts this or not in principle, in practice it often has to be so for the site or feature can come to be destroyed by a combination of circumstances including excavation. The record then, whether it be air photograph, carefully contoured plan, quick sketch plan or notebook, is a form of archaeological data which has to be taken into account when it comes to interpreting the evidence. The point is stressed because so often archaeology is defined as being concerned only with material evidence: we have already seen that it is also very much concerned with environmental evidence and to that we must add that, certainly in practice, it is much concerned with archaeologists' evidence. Nor is this theoretical hair-splitting: so much of what was the surviving cultural evidence has now been destroyed or lost since first recorded that, in my experience anyway, much time has to be spent in dealing with what is in effect documentary evidence, a field in which the rules of diplomatic apply just as much as for the historian carrying out his normal documentary research. This applies too, of course, to the use of conventional documentary sources for research purposes in landscape archaeology (p. 38), though I appreciate that many archaeologists would not consider such evidence as within their purview. Leaving that aside, however, the definition of archaeology as the study of the material remains of the past is, by virtue of the nature of the archaeological record itself, unacceptably circumscribed.

Relationships and perception (fig. 5.3)

One example will help illustrate the point. It concerns the matter of relationships, and in this case those not perceived during excavation. In certain circumstances, it is now routine practice to record by exact measurements the three-dimensional position of every object found on an excavation. Clearly the data logged can soon amount to many thousands of units, so much so that a computer is necessary to store, never mind order, them. So stored, the position of any one object can be recalled automatically, which is the prime object, but further the spatial relationships between any selection of objects and between them and any other selection of features on the site can also be retrieved. In the case I am thinking of, ordering of the data after the excavation showed correlations in site distribution of groups of some types of artefact and some of the structures e.g. sherds of pottery types A and B and of glass type D not only occurred in the same three areas together but also avoided Building X; whereas pottery type C, as well as occurring in those three areas with A, B and D, also occurred in Building X which was the sole context of stone objects i, ii and iii. What these relationships 'mean' does not matter at this stage. My point is that those relationships were established only through the documentary record of the site and, having been established, they are as much a 'find', a 'fact', a part of the archaeological evidence from the excavation as the bits and pieces, the 'surviving cultural remains', more obviously 'discovered' during its course. Clearly, the physical and intellectual constraints of perception are in practice one of the limitations of the use of archaeological evidence for interpretation; but though obviously we cannot use it if we cannot perceive it, the technical difficulty of its being invisible to us denies neither its existence nor its validity as evidence.

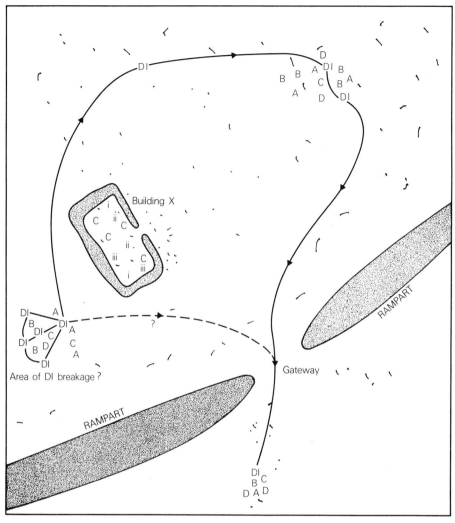

ABCD   selected types of artefact   i, ii, iii   another selected type of artefact

DI   parts of the same object of type D   ⌐:⌐!   other artefacts

5.3 A model illustrating the association of some selected 'finds' and their relationships to certain artefactual and structural elements isolated from the record of an excavation. Graphic explanations are suggested for the breakage point of one particular object (D1) and the path followed by its resultant sherds in an attempt to interpret a spatial pattern or distribution existing as a 'fact' on the site and in the excavation record but not perceived at the time of excavation. Implications of this patterning could be that Building X was standing when D1 was broken, that it is representing a particular human activity even if we cannot identify it, and that C has a close relationship with a function specific to Building X and the stone objects there. Even without the 'walk' suggested for D1 glass sherds, however, the model is an interpretation, not a statement, because it depends on the selection of certain data from a 'background noise' of many thousands of such data (represented by the scatter of undifferentiated dots).

Approaches to Archaeology

'Meaningful' questions

When we look at our assembled archaeological evidence then—the 'hardware', the paperwork, the raw results of all the analyses mentioned in Chapter 4,—and ask the question 'What does it mean?', we are clearly in a more complex situation than either ourselves or the bystanders' innocent 'Have you found anything interesting?' might have appreciated (p. 73). Granted, however, that interpretation is an act of conceptual creation and not merely one of reporting a self-evident truth, the problem is not so much of perceiving a meaning as of choosing one or more from several meanings; for evidence is almost always ambiguous i.e. capable of being interpreted in more than one way. The interpretation favoured will to a large extent depend on the questions asked and they should be framed at the start of research, not when the evidence has finally been assembled. We have already touched on this point (p. 74): it is no good our asking questions now, deriving from our current interest in palaeo-environment, of the evidence produced from the nineteenth century barrow-diggers because it is simply not in the record. It was in the barrows, but it was not looked for and so was not retrieved because the questions being asked of those barrows at that time did not include environmental ones. On the other hand, in some cases, particularly with field survey records, it is possible now to look back at old plans and ask new questions of them with hope of an answer, for sometimes information was recorded without necessarily having been understood. It is possible to do the same with some excavation records as Hawkes, Ashbee, Webster and Bradley have successfully demonstrated.[3] A potential for such re-interpretation should ideally always be in the record but it is not always achieved and re-interpretation is seldom attempted.

Ideographic and nomothetic

We have already suggested that the evidence obtained reflects the questions asked, that the data base reflects the research design (p. 91). So biases in the information are present when the interpreter comes to review his assembled evidence. There are two fundamental points here. First, what has just been said would be true if interpretation took place only at the end of a project. In fact, it should be taking place, daily, while work is in progress and new data is being assembled. It is no good continuing to ask questions about Mesolithic flint-knapping techniques if the site chosen for excavation is turning out to be a medieval castle—to give an extreme and crude example. You either stop, or alter the objectives (*cf.* p. 61). Second, it can be strongly argued that, rather than merely going out to survey an area or excavate a site, such actions should be executed within a conscious and stated research design so that not only the investigator,

[3] C.F.C. Hawkes and S. Piggott, 'Romans, Britons and Saxons round Salisbury and in Cranborne Chase', *Archaeol. J.* 104 (1947), 27–81; P. Ashbee, *The Earthen Long Barrow in Britain* (1970); G. Webster, 'The future of villa studies', in A.L.F. Rivet (ed.), *The Roman Villa in Britain* (1969), 217–49; R. Bradley, 'Maumbury Rings, Dorchester: the excavations of 1908–1913', *Archaeologia* 105 (1976), 1–97.

but others wanting to use his evidence, can judge it objectively in the light of the known bias. Here we are touching one of the theoretical divides in archaeology, particularly in relation to interpretation: do we proceed on an ideographic basis, being academically honest and as objective as we can but basically relying on intuition, inspiration and experience to produce results and a plausible interpretation covering the particular phenomena we have observed? Or do we proceed nomothetically or scientifically, that is by making our models specific and the testing of them the objective with interpretation directed towards the explanation of our data primarily in terms of whether or not they illustrate general laws? This is rather more than the difference between, on the one hand, simply going out, seeing what turns up and then trying to explain it and, on the other, having a theory and then looking for evidence to support or undermine it; for the difference also involves the nature of the end product, that is essentially whether it is seen as interesting in its own right, a law unto itself, or whether it is judged as 'an example of general relationships described by an established general law' (fig. 5.4).[4]

This may seem obscure but it is important and my explanation is as pure-driven snow compared to the mid-Atlantic jargon in which much of this debate has been conducted.[5] To see what is meant we need only look at British archaeology, most of which has been, largely unconsciously, carried out on an ideographic basis. The historical orientation of insular archaeology is the main reason for this: it has been much concerned with description—what is it? what happened? how was it built? how did it happen?—deriving from an empirical approach to problems of chronology and explanation often expressed as an end product in the form of a quasi-historical narrative. There has been little attempt, rightly or wrongly for I am making no judgement here, to interpret the evidence in terms of a general law and even less to try and identify any such laws. The nearest attempt, though surely the author would deny the charge of being a processualist, was Fox's *Personality of Britain* (1932). A work of solid scholarship and imaginative insight, *Personality* precisely tried to identify some general considerations affecting human behaviour in these islands, considerations against which old and new evidence could be assessed. Could new evidence be explained, for example, by Fox's Highland/Lowland Zone hypothesis? Was that hypothesis itself confirmed or weakened by new evidence? In the usual pragmatic British way, a lot of evidence has in fact subsequently been gathered which has a bearing on this and the twenty-four other Propositions in *Personality*; but there has been no deliberate programme of rigorous testing of the main hypothesis, even though it has become deeply embedded almost as a fact of life in British archaeological thought. At the time, it was an intelligent, knowledgeable and plausible explanation of a mass of observed data which has

---

[4] P.J. Watson *et al.*, *Explanation in Archaeology: an explicitly scientific approach* (1971), viii. The book is acutely reviewed in *Antiquity* 46 (1972), 237–9.

[5] *Cf.* L.R. Binford, *An Archaeological Perspective* (1972); D. Clarke, *Analytical Archaeology* (1968); and *Antiquity* 47 (1973), 6–18, 93–5, 158–60.

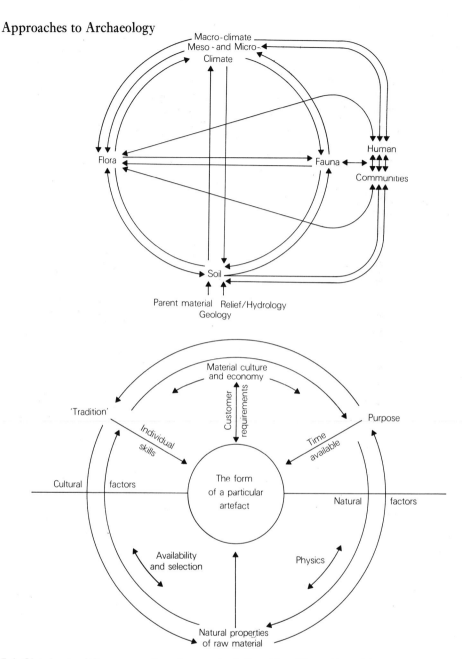

5.4 Circular models as examples of general relationships. They attempt to express a complex series of interactions between what are thought to be critical factors in two very different processes, respectively culture as part of a palaeo-ecosystem and the production of a single artefact. These diagrams, in putting forward hypotheses which can be tested, are also contributing to the establishment of 'general law' i.e. if tested many times and found to 'work', these models could be confirmed, in the light of existing knowledge, as being 'true' ones in so far as they satisfactorily account for the observed phenomena (p. 133).

subsequently been used to explain cultural, economic and social phenomena in the British archaeological record; but the 'law' itself has not seriously been proved or disproved in a strict scientific sense, as work has continued largely on its particularizing way e.g. 'That is what happened here'.

Those who urge the need to recognise general laws and to use them in scientific explanation might pause to consider whether such laws exist, let alone how they can be identified and defined, in as far as past human behaviour or its expression as cultural evidence is concerned. Personally, so far I have found it very difficult to see patterns in the past, and such generalisations as seem 'true' usually prove so general as to be (a) common sense and (b) not very helpful in explaining my particular problems. But then of course, being by nature and training a pragmatist from a historical background, doubtless my methodology and motivation are all wrong. I take comfort from a helpful book already quoted: '... it is possible that some part of the dispute does not really concern the relations of nomothetic to ideographic goals, but reflects what various archaeologists have been trained to do, are good at doing, and like to do ... the only possible separation between generalizing and particularizing processes in the acquisition of knowledge is one of emphasis, for they necessarily operate interdependently'.[6]

Predictive models

The limitations of archaeological evidence are not then simply inherent: there are limitations in the ways employed to use it. But of course part of the attraction of, perhaps even need for, archaeological theory is those limitations in the evidence itself. A piece of pottery can fairly easily be identified as such and so will the shape of the pot from which it came, but it will not immediately tell you how it was made, when or where it was made and where its clay came from though it may have such information locked up inside it and technically retrievable; but no technique yet known will tell you why it was made, why it was made in a particular way, who made it and whether or not he/she was a happy person. Yet answers to such questions are commonly available to the historian, though answers to the first questions, which archaeology can tackle, are frequently not forthcoming from documentary evidence, particularly about common-or-garden things like pottery or lowly people like potters. It is often said of archaeological evidence that, in descending order of competence or certainty, it can attempt to answer the questions what? how? when? why? and who? It is not very good at the last two questions and hence, on the one hand, the need for explanation theory and, on the other, the anonymity of prehistory. A theory cannot be proved by evidence appearing to fit into the explanation it offers, though increasing numbers of such fits obviously strengthen the theory, perhaps at the expense of others. The theory may in

[6] *Op. cit.* note 4, 170.

fact become sufficiently strong for it to become a 'predictive model', that is able to predict what will be found with what (p. 110), where sites should occur and what their nature will be. If, for example, we say 'Roman villas in western England frequently occur in river valleys, and were characteristically rebuilt in the late-third century, often with elaborate mosaics', we may in the first place be risking a generalisation on the basis of a great deal of evidence but we are really not so much making a 'true' statement of fact as creating a predictive model to the effect that new discoveries of Roman villas will tend to conform to the three criteria mentioned. If on the other hand, and inspired by the same evidence, we say 'Roman villas in western England utilised water power and were taken over in the late third century by dispossessed Gallic refugees with capital and a love for Classical decor', we may be right but we have added a considerable layer of interpretation to the first statement which will consequently now be that much more difficult to 'prove' or 'disprove'. It is therefore that much less valuable because by making it more general, it is less closely related to the hard, archaeological evidence. It is not really a predictive model nor much use as a general law for the time and place, not least because it raises the question of how you recognise archaeologically 'Gallic refugees with capital and a taste for Classical decor'.[7]

These examples may seem but a nuance of interpretation. They represent, however, the difference between what is strictly archaeologically acceptable and what is not, at least without a great deal of qualification and a specific admission that the second statement is merely a suggestion or working hypothesis. Even so, it is not easy to test. This sort of difference in interpretation seems to be one of the most difficult to put over to beginners in archaeology and to non-archaeologists. 'Be bold', 'let your imagination rip', 'surely the explanation is obvious' we are exhorted as we stuffily re-examine our data base and cautiously offer a crumb of interpretation from the altar of scholarship. My sympathies are entirely with the enthusiasts and the journalists who 'want to know, in simple terms and briefly, what it all means'; but while it may appear to be the archaeologist who is unwilling to oblige in those terms (and keep a clear conscience), more realistically it is the evidence which is often to blame.

The concept of culture

With regard to the anonymity of prehistory, with which admittedly it is difficult to identify, the archaeologist is faced with a real problem. One much-used way round it is to assume that a seemingly cohesive group of archaeological material in fact correlates with a racial or social group of people. Hence the 'Beaker people', 'the Mound-builders', 'the Megalith builders' and so on. That is a natural, simple and highly

[7] This example was unconsciously inspired by K. Branigan's paper 'Villas in the West Country' in K. Branigan and P.J. Fowler (eds.), *The Roman West Country* (1976), 120–41 but it obviously does not imply that my co–editor either wrote these words or 'interpreted' the evidence as fictitiously quoted.

questionable step to take. In recent decades, one of the most useful and most-used concepts has been that of the Culture whereby an unknown but assumed group of people are conceived on the basis of the recurrence of associated cultural traits as exhibited by archaeological evidence; such groups can, carelessly but quickly, become identified as historically existing entities. Hence the Wessex Culture, the Woodland Culture, the Cortaillod Culture and many, many more. The concept is very similar to that of a *genre* in artistic parlance where it can be defined as books, plays, films and so on that can be grouped according to elements they have in common, including conventions that are shared.

While the archaeological use of Culture may have begun as a form of identification for groups of material, it came to have a dynamic social meaning whereby the history of groups of people could be traced through time and across the landscape. The Bandceramik Culture is a notable example, moving from the Black to the North Sea, and characterised by economic and social traits as much as by its portable artefacts. The concept of culture also came to serve as an explanatory model: 'The excavation revealed a burial of the Wessex Culture', full stop, enough said. Manifestations of culture-related traits i.e. parts of the whole cultural assemblage, can indicate movement of people, trade, exchange, contact, influence—it depends how you interpret them. The exercise of the concept depends on recognising patterns—of recurring artefact-types, of recurring associations, of coherent distributions in space. And behind it lie the assumptions not only that common cultural traits represent some form of social grouping, but also that that fraction of the total cultural expression which survives and is recoverable as archaeological evidence also represents the same or a similar socially-cohesive and once-existing group of people or communities. Although cultures have by definition been conceptualised from the synthesis of existing information, they tend also to be predictive models. If they are unable to forecast, they cannot be soundly based as archaeological entities; but whether those entities really do represent groups of people in the past in a meaningful contemporary sense is another matter.

Distribution maps (figs. 1.1; 2.1; 2.5; 2.6; 3.5; 5.1; 5.5; 6.2; 6.5)

Culture, and many other facets of interpretation, are frequently expressed by distribution maps, one of the archaeologists' most useful tools (borrowed from the Natural Sciences of course).[8] We have already touched on its use in an excavation situation where, beginning as a form of record and expression of where material was found, it became a tool for interpretation (p. 141). The same principles apply in its use in wider contexts from local to world distributions. Basically, the plotting of

[8] As demonstrated by C. Fox, *The Archaeology of the Cambridge Region* (1923) and *The Personality of Britain* (1932), and most recently discussed by L.V. Grinsell in F. Lynch and C. Burgess (eds.), *Prehistoric Man in Wales and the West* (1972), 5–18.

5.5 Two different ways of expressing 'trade' from archaeological evidence:

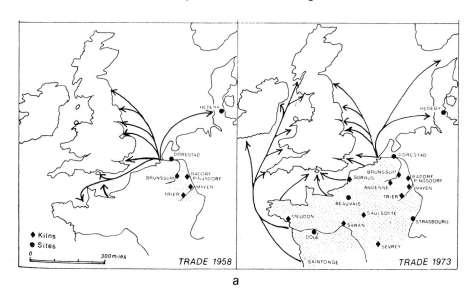

a

(a) the traditional way, using arrows from the sources to the destinations (or rather the recorded places of artefact discovery, which need not necessarily be where the 'export' was intended to go to or indeed where it initially arrived). In this particular case of early medieval pottery (broadly fifth–eleventh centuries AD) from N.W. Europe found in the British Isles and Ireland, the two maps show not only a pattern of activity at the time but also how the pattern of modern archaeological research affects our 'image of the past': the left hand map is an 'objective' statement of what was known in 1958, though in fact it accurately reflects a major research effort on the topic by German scholars in the Rhineland and the seminal, individual research of a handful of English scholars based on Oxford and Cambridge. A decade of new work, marked in particular by the appearance of 'research' in France by French scholars, by major urban excavations and by the development of an interest around the Irish Sea, provides a much fuller and indeed fundamentally different picture by 1973. Even so, however, the right hand map begs a lot of questions e.g. What is meant by 'trade'? Does pottery accurately or even adequately represent 'trade'? What about non-European imports at the time?

(b) is also concerned with 'trade' and pottery, in this case that made at a known kiln site in Savernake Forest, near the Roman town of *Cunetio* at Mildenhall, Wiltshire; but it is a more sophisticated type of distribution map trying to show not only a source/terminal relationship but also quantified relationships to other wares, to negative evidence and to a mathematically-deduced prediction. The original caption was: 'The distribution of Savernake ware. The widths of the bars and the sizes of the circles indicate the ratio of Savernake ware to other coarse pottery. *Bars:* assemblages of more than 30 coarse ware sherds, and coming from the first and

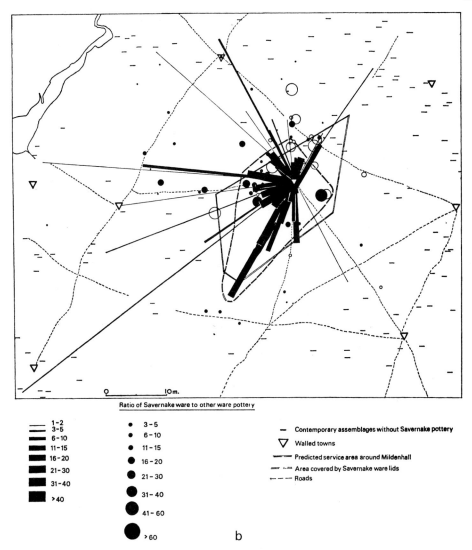

Ratio of Savernake ware to other ware pottery

1-2	● 3-5	— Contemporary assemblages without Savernake pottery
3-5	● 6-10	▽ Walled towns
6-10	● 11-15	Predicted service area around Mildenhall
11-15	● 16-20	Area covered by Savernake ware lids
16-20	● 21-30	Roads
21-30	● 31-40	
31-40	● 41-60	
>40	● >60	

b

second centuries A D. *Filled circles:* assemblages of more than 30 coarse ware sherds, but representing more than the first and second centuries A D. *Open circles:* assemblages of less than 30 coarse ware sherds'. The method is impeccable, the demonstration graphic and indeed dramatic: do either or both, while reflecting an enormous amount of collective and personal research, adequately account for: the inevitable subjective element in identifying 'Savernake ware' (the source of which is a poorly executed and incompletely published excavation); the assumption that the *quantity* of sherds (not complete pots) is a valid criterion; the highly variable nature of both the assemblages examined and of the methods by which they were acquired; relevant material inadvertently omitted? i.e. whatever the sophistication of the methods and the model, can the 'result' be qualitatively any better than the quality of the input? *Cf.* (a) opposite.

149

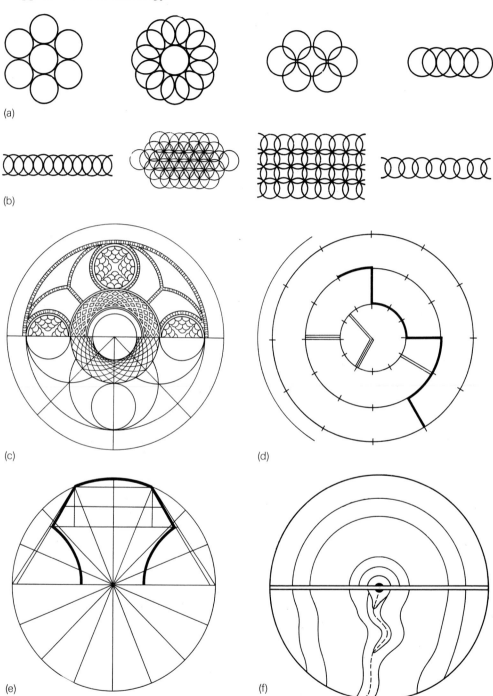

(a)

(b)

(c)

(d)

(e)

(f)

archaeological data on a cartographic base shows where evidence has occurred. The spatial relationships thus demonstrated may, however, themselves be a cultural expression to be observed, described and interpreted just as a stone axe can be so treated. The cartographic tool can of course also be manipulated in various ways to test hypotheses about distribution: significant features of the base can be altered, for example, to give a distribution an apparent 'meaning', accepting that this is an interpretation of the evidence, not a statement of 'truth'. It is not particularly helpful, for instance, to plot strip lynchets against a background of high ground when by definition the type only occurs on slopes (they should really be plotted against ecclesiastical parishes to bring out the significance of their distribution). Or the material plotted can be manipulated by selection, to introduce the temporal dimension for example by using sites or objects of common date, or by plotting diverse material on the same map to explore or demonstrate supposed spatial relationships, perhaps for the purpose of explaining cultural change or trade (fig. 5.5). In all these expressions, it can be readily seen that a distribution map is essentially a two-dimensional model, the expression of an hypothesis to be tested and refined and re-interpreted. It is not surprising therefore that the conscious archaeological model-building of recent years has turned to the distribution map and, learning from the techniques and theories of the 'new' geography, given it new life and new uses. Cartographic model-building, as in

5.6 'Aspects of reality a long time ago' as exemplified by a widely diverse use of that favourite device in demonstration and explanation, the circle:
(a) models of settlement expansion (radial, intermediate and linear).
(b) four designs abstracted from examples of Early Celtic art to contrast the arrangement of patterns in rows in the East (outside left and right, respectively from the neck of a 'pilgrim flask' from Dürrnberg, near Salzburg, and from a cup found at Praha-Hloubelïn) and in more extensive complexes in the West (left and right centre, respectively the frieze on a flagon fragment from Eigenbilzen, Limburg, and the scheme of openwork decoration on a piece from Somme-Bionne, Marne).
(c) the scheme of the composition on the Cuperly disc, Marne, all the original motifs of which are also based on compass-drawn lines.
(d) A hypothetical economic cycle model (with the lettering and shading removed) proposed for the Glastonbury 'lake village', showing three concentric zones of agrarian exploitation, infield, outfield, and wasteland. A quarter of the outfield (middle band, 12 o'clock till 3) and half of the waste (outer band, 11 o'clock till 5) are envisaged as flooded for 3 and 6 months of the year respectively.
(e) a reconstruction (without the scale) of the basis of the design of the hilt-plate of a bronze, ceremonial sword from Jutphaas, near Utrecht.
(f) another settlement model, in this case showing an idealised theoretical land-use system of (from the centre, top half) settlement, horticulture, sylviculture, intensive arable rotation, arable with long ley, three field arable, and pasture; with (bottom half) a theoretical demonstration of how the theoretical ideal might be distorted in reality by, for example, a navigable river (dashed line).

locational analysis and site catchment analysis to mention but two theoretical constructs, affords not only a different way of ordering existing archaeological data but also, as with all good models, provides a predictive function to help guide new research programmes. The main danger seems to be that the elegance of the models might well inhibit original thought and positively prohibit the intrusion of reality. It really does appear to be important to remember that the neat map laced by a fretwork of Thiessen polygons is an interpretation, the visual expression of an idea which, even if it 'works', can serve only to help explain in our terms unconscious aspects of reality a long time ago (fig. 5.6).[9]

There is in fact no one answer, nor will there ever be; and theories about the past, whether soundly-based on archaeological evidence or not, will continue to abound. We may follow the interpretation of a sound scholar or find our intellectual appreciation of the past illumined in the repetition of the observation—hypothesis—test—result—assessment process. 'We speak from Facts not Theory' confidently asserted Sir Richard Colt Hoare[10] at the dawn of the Classificatory-Descriptive Period of British Archaeology.[11] For all the conscious striving to be Scientific in our Explanatory Period, to judge from some of its products whiffs of the Speculative drift faintly o'er Academia once more. Whatever the Theory, in the last resort quality of interpretation depends on the quality of the evidence and, as I have said before, ultimately that depends on the quality of the archaeologist.

[9] P. Haggett, *Locational Analysis in Human Geography* (1965, 2nd ed. 1976), reviewing which Professor C. Renfrew emphasised 'that we have all been working on problems which have already been solved' (*Antiquity* 43 (1969), 74). Amongst many others, *see also* R. J. Chorley and P. Haggett, *Models in Geography* (1967), R.J. Chisholm, *Rural Settlement and Land Use: an essay in location* (1962, 2nd ed. 1968), W.C. Found, *A Theoretical Approach to Rural Land-Use Patterns* (1971), and D.L. Clarke (ed.), *Models in Archaeology* (1972). For archaeological applications in practice, *see* R.M. Newcomb, 'Geographical Location Analysis and Iron Age Settlement in West Penwith', *Cornish Archaeol.* 7 (1968), 5–14; the papers respectively by B. W. Cunliffe and A. H. A. Hogg in D. Hill and M. Jesson (eds.), *The Iron Age and its Hill-forts* (1971), 53–69, and 105–25; R.W.K. Reid, 'Facts and figures from fieldwork', *Proc. Soc. Antiq. Scot.* 104 (1971–2), 268–82; C.A. Smith, 'A morphological analysis of late prehistoric and Romano-British settlements in north west Wales', *Proc. Prehist. Soc.* 40 (1974), 157–69.
[10] R.C. Hoare, *The Ancient History of South Wiltshire* (1812), Introduction.
[11] Borrowing the phrase from G.R. Willey and J.A. Sabloff, *A History of American Archaeology* (1974), chap. 3. 'Explanatory' and 'Speculative' periods are from the same source.

Bibliography

L. Alcock, *By South Cadbury is that Camelot* (1972)
Antiq. J. (1964–75), Winchester excavations
Antiquity 43 (1969) 74; 46 (1972) 237–9; 47 (1973) 6–18, 93–9, 158–60
P. Ashbee, *The Earthen Long Barrow in Britain* (1970)
L.R. Binford, *An Archaeological Perspective* (1972)

R. Bradley 'Maumbury Rings, Dorchester: the excavations of 1908–1913', *Archaeologia* 105 (1976) 1–97

J. W. Brailsford, *Hod Hill I* (1962)

K. Branigan, 'Villas in the West Country' (120–41 in K. Branigan and P. J. Fowler, *op. cit.*)

K. Branigan and P. J. Fowler (eds.), *The Roman West Country* (1976)

R. J. Chisholm, *Rural Settlements and Land Use: an essay in location* (1962, 1968)

R. J. Chorley and P. Haggett, *Models in Geography* (1967)

D. Clarke, *Analytical Archaeology* (1968)

D. L. Clarke (ed.), *Models in Archaeology* (1972)

B. W. Cunliffe (53–69 in D. Hill and M. Jesson, *op. cit.*)

W. C. Found, *A Theoretical Approach to Rural Land-Use Patterns* (1971)

C. Fox, *The Archaeology of the Cambridge Region* (1923); *The Personality of Britain* (1932)

L. V. Grinsell (5–18 in F. Lynch and C. Burgess, *op. cit.*)

P. Haggett, *Locational Analysis in Human Geography* (1965, 1976)

C. F. C. Hawkes and S. Piggott, 'Romans, Britons and Saxons round Salisbury and in Cranborne Chase', *Archaeol. J.* 104 (1947) 27–81

D. Hill and M. Jesson (eds.), *The Iron Age and its Hill-forts* (1971)

R. C. Hoare, *The Ancient History of South Wiltshire* (1812), Introduction

A. H. A. Hogg (105–25 in D. Hill and M. Jesson *op. cit.*)

F. Lynch and C. Burgess (eds.), *Prehistoric Man in Wales and the West* (1972)

R. M. Newcomb, 'Geographical Location Analysis and Iron Age Settlement Pattern in West Penwith', *Cornish Archaeol.* 7 (1968) 5–14

R. W. K. Reid, 'Facts and figures from fieldwork', *Proc. Soc. Antiq. Scot.* 104 (1971–2) 268–82

Sir Ian Richmond, *Hod Hill II* (1968)

A. L. F. Rivet (ed.), *The Roman Villa in Britain* (1969)

C. A. Smith, 'A morphological analysis of late prehistoric and Romano-British settlements in north west Wales', *Proc. Prehist. Soc.* 40 (1974) 157–69

P. J. Watson *et al., Explanation in Archaeology: an explicitly scientific approach* (1971)

G. Webster, 'The future of villa studies' (217–49 in A. L. F. Rivet *op. cit.*)

G. R. Willey and J. A. Sabloff, *A History of American Archaeology* (1974) chapter 3

6
PRESENT ARCHAEOLOGY

'Who controls the past controls the future: who controls the present controls the past'
George Orwell, *1984* (1949)

Much has been written about the nature of archaeology and archaeological theory, about how to do archaeology and about the results, actual or supposed, of archaeological activity. Very little discussion is readily available, at least in popular form, about what archaeology is actually doing and how and why it is doing it.[1] In this last chapter therefore I will discuss at least some aspects of the current archaeological scene. Clearly my view is biased by my own experience and inevitably this account must be to some extent autobiographical; but, unless my experience is completely unrepresentative, a personal element should not be totally invalid on that account alone. I write with particular reference to Britain, though I hope, and indeed know, that some of my general points are not entirely inapplicable elsewhere. How then, in the mid-1970s, are the approaches to archaeology working out in practice? Who is doing the approaching, how and with what result?

---

[1] Sir Mortimer Wheeler's *Still Digging* (1955) is one of the few recent autobiographies by an archaeologist, *cf*. O. G. S. Crawford, *Said and Done* (1955), Sir Leonard Woolley, *As I seem to Remember* (1962). A sensitive personal statement is C. Nylander, *The Deep Well: archaeology and the life of the past* (1969, Pelican 1971). G. Clark, *Archaeology and Society* (1939, 1947, 1957) is an overt attempt to describe 'what archaeology is doing and why and how it is doing it', and recent books describing modern work in the field are, for example, R. Bruce-Mitford (ed.), *Recent Archaeological Excavations in Europe* (1975), P. J. Fowler (ed.), *Recent Work in Rural Archaeology* (1975) and P. A. Rahtz (ed.), *Rescue Archaeology* (1974). *Antiquity, Archaeology, American Antiquity* and *Archéologie* provide serious, 'popular' coverage several times a year; *Rescue News* campaigns and has contained some excellent up-to-the-minute, indeed anticipatory, material; *Current Archaeology*, currently nearly a year behindhand, sadly allows its aggressively quaint editorial views to colour its reporting of the archaeological scene.

154

Archaeologists

As previously discussed, let us begin with those two common misconceptions about, respectively, archaeology and archaeologists. The first is that archaeology equals excavation and that archaeologists therefore spend most of their time excavating. Neither the supposition nor the deduction is correct, though probably no amount of saying so will alter the popular fallacy. Sir Mortimer Wheeler, the only archaeologist most people have heard of, characteristically exploited this situation with the title of his autobiography *Still Digging* (1955). The misconception nevertheless is still so often the contact point in conversation with non-archaeological colleague and stranger alike: 'And where are you digging now?' The truthful answer, 'Nowhere', in 10 months of the year seems to be taken almost as an admission that one is not doing one's job properly. Even though there are now 'full-time diggers' (p. 168), in general most archaeologists spend by far the major part of their time in work other than digging.

That generalisation should really be qualified by a chronological factor for, by and large, excavating is a young man's work; yet the second misconception, thankfully now being successfully eroded, is that an archaeologist is, rather like God, an old man with a grey beard. Though there are some outstanding exceptions, most digging archaeologists seem to come in from the cold after about the age of 40, perhaps by choice but probably because they are weighed down with seniority, consequential adminstrative or other non-research responsibilities and by unpublished excavations. Most archaeologists in the field now, in Britain anyway, are in their 20s and 30s, and overall it certainly seems generally true that the bulk of an archaeologist's outdoor research is done in the first 15–20 years of his working life. So if you expect to meet an archaeologist on site, expect to meet a young person, with a beard if male, and not an old man. And incidentally, your archaeologist is almost as likely to be female as male, whether actually digging or supervising, whether in museum, laboratory or lecture hall.

If archaeologists only dig for less than half their working lives, and only spend a fraction of their time digging then, it is reasonable to ask what they do for the rest of the time. There are two answers, one concerning the nature of archaeological activity—especially excavation,—and the other concerning the structure of archaeological organisation with especial reference to the archaeological employers. Most truly archaeological activity i.e. creative research, like other research, can be broken down into phases of preparation, action, analysis, assessment and publication. If one is being systematic, they must take place in this order though of course phases can and do overlap in time e.g. analysis and assessment take place during the action. Converted into terms of excavation, phase 1 covers the identification of the problem, the drawing up of what American archaeologists aptly call a research design i.e. a systematic programme of investigation related to specific goals to be achieved within defined temporal and financial parameters, the raising of financial and other resources including staff, and all sorts of practical matters like access to the site, accommodation and commissariat—military analogies are difficult to avoid but in any case a considerable and time-consuming managerial task has to be successfully accomplished before any productive work begins. Phase 2 is the actual excavation. Phases 3 and 4 should begin during the excavation and will continue afterwards, each overlapping in time with the other. Phase 3 involves sorting out all the finds, samples and records, subjecting them to appropriate verbal, numerical, and scientific analysis—in other words, all the hard, unromatic 'backroom' graft which gives the mass of data 'meaning' (p. 131).

Phase 4 is probably the most difficult to accomplish satisfactorily not least because there is very little in the way of technique to fall back on here and also because, however much corporate endeavour has been involved up to this stage, here the situation sooner or later resolves itself into the silent room containing a lone person, a stack of data, a pen and a pad of blank sheets of paper. Those blank sheets of paper are probably the most fearsome sight in archaeology, so much so that many an archaeologist has not been able to face them. Remorselessly, however, let us move on to phase 5 which, if the previous four have been successfully achieved, should not be quite so difficult, that is preparing the academic report that is to be published and the total excavation product that is to become the permanent archive of the whole exercise. This phase will include the eventual secure deposition of that archive and dealing with the practical matters of publishing which may include popular booklets, exhibitions and T.V. and other audio-visual presentations as well as correcting proofs of the academic report (fig. 6.1).

I have to belabour the fact that, as should be perfectly clear, the act of excavation is but one part of a five-phase process. That in itself is answer to the question 'What do archaeologists do when they are not digging?'—'The other four-fifths of their job'. And in fact a time ratio of about 1:4 or 1:5 seems approximately right, that is from the director's point of view. On average, but perhaps minimally, a month's excavation creates 4–5 months' full-time work for the director and his immediate staff. Or to put it

6.1 (a and b) show the conventional way of organising an archaeological excavation team on a hierarchical basis and the much more management-conscious way practised recently on an urban excavation in Manchester. A cynic might say that (a) emphasises the importance of people, (b) of the system itself, but management, in the professional sense of the word, is a growing characteristic of not only excavations but the whole archaeological process. We see this in (c), again from Manchester, demonstrating a 'system of overall excavation strategy'. To the person interested solely in digging, it might be of some interest to see the place of the on-site work within its much wider context, even within a model confined to excavation; for the scholar solely interested in the research results it might be a helpful reminder of the other perfectly legitimate and perhaps equally or even more important objectives of the exercise. For some, the really interesting facet might well be that a research goal, generally to add to the sum of human knowledge or specifically to answer preconceived questions, is not itemised in the 'output' block.

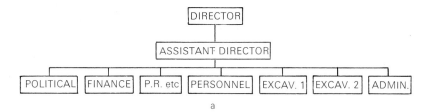

a

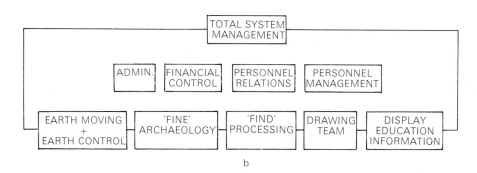

b

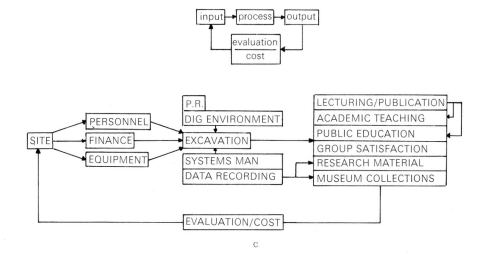

c

another way in percentage terms, the five stages of the excavation process respectively absorb about 10, 15, 30, 25 and 20 per cent of the total effort involved (though the 15% excavation part may well absorb 75% of the costs). For the site-workers, of course, the crew or team members with no academic or technical follow-up responsibilities, these figures do not apply: they can simply move on to the next site, or go back to work from their holiday, perhaps thinking how wonderful archaeology (=excavation) is. Perhaps if people only too eager to start an excavation themselves realised that, if they are to meet their consequential obligations, for every day they spend digging they are committing a week or so of their own time to the resultant work (assuming they have the competence to do it), then they might think twice before voluntarily taking on the responsibility. Out of the certain hundreds and probably several thousand unpublished excavations in Britain in the last 50 years, it is a justifiable guess that a high proportion of them have not surfaced because of an initial failure to appreciate this fact of archaeological life. 'Still digging?' 'No, sir, I'm trying to give it up.'

Archaeological employers

There are actually very few full-time digging posts at director level in archaeology, though many archaeologists now holding the various professional posts in archaeology first made their mark by directing excavations, often their own. Who then are the employers of archaeologists? They vary from country to country but basically they consist of central and local government, museums, universities and independent organisations. In the United States, for example, the universities and museums are the biggest employers but now the Federal agencies, like the National Parks Service, and State Governments are increasingly looking for archaeological staff too. In Holland there is a State Archaeological Service, closely linked officially and personally with the universities which have archaeological departments or institutes. At Amsterdam, for instance, there is a University Biological-Archaeological Institute. In Norway, to take a Scandinavian example, there is a virtual monopoly of archaeological employment exercised by the four main museums with the universities. In Britain the situation is, predictably, far more complex, a pragmatic compound of principle, tradition, opportunism and chance, with employers relying very much on voluntary effort, professional and amateur, for an under-capitalised structure to function on faith, hope and not much charity. Some professional archaeologists free-lance, particularly at the site assistant level and in providing particular expert or specialist services e.g. in reporting on animal bone assemblages or drawing small finds for publication. At the price of efficiency, however, the British system has the merit of flexibility and plenty of scope for initiative.

The archaeological employers in Britain by no means embrace all archaeologists or all archaeological activity; but they now come from a fairly wide range of institutional activity. Until recently, however, they were but three, the State, the universities and the museums, some private, most Local Authority. The State required archaeologists to administer the Ancient Monuments Act and hence, from 1882, the Ancient Monuments Inspectorate, now in the Department of the Environment, grew up; it required archaeologists from 1908 to staff its Royal Commissions on Ancient and Historical Monuments, statutorily committed to record all over England, Scotland and Wales 'those monuments illustrative of contemporary history' (up to 1714 originally); and from 1920 (but not apparently after 1975) it required an Archaeology Officer to guide its traditional archaeological interests in a field of growing responsibility. Furthermore, archaeologists were needed to curate the national collections in the State museums. Nevertheless, as Crawford and Wheeler recall in their autobiographies, there were very few archaeological posts, with the State or any other institution, in the 1920s and 1930s: the big explosion has come subsequently, and particularly in the 1970s. It is interesting to note that, after each of the World Wars, archaeology took a decade and more before it developed in terms of full-time appointments. Though universities gradually created chairs and lectureships, it was not until the 1960s that, in the optimistic days of expansion in higher education, many of the existing ones, though virtually none of the new ones, joined the ranks of archaeological employers, some by creating new departments, more by adding an archaeological lectureship to existing departments of history or classics or adult education.

Museums have for long employed archaeologists as curators or keepers, or, perhaps more accurately, have employed curators with archaeological interests. More recently, some have been taking archaeologists on to their staffs to practice archaeology in the field rather than to curate their collections. Indeed, the argument has been advanced that the recent expansion in archaeological provision (p. 166) could and should have taken place under museum aegis;[2] that, with a few successful exceptions, this has not happened, in Britain anyway, in part reflects the ambiguities in the relationships between the museum world, 'academic' archaeology and archaeological practice.

Returning to what archaeologists do, it must be emphasised that in the great majority of these posts, the person appointed was not primarily being paid to practice archaeology, let alone to excavate. He was appointed to the Civil Service or the Commission Staff or the State Museums to carry out statutory duties, to provincial and local museums to curate their collections, and to universities to teach. This may seem hair-splitting, but such people, though required to have archaeological knowledge to carry out their tasks, were not employed as archaeologists to carry out full-time archaeological research. Particularly with regard to excavation, though the same also applies to other research, original work was an extra that had to be fitted in, and still does, on top of the duties of administration, teaching and so on that are the basics of the posts. It is not perhaps surprising then that, in the light of the time-figures given for excavation by *full-time* archaeologists (p. 156), academic achievement has tended to lag

[2] N. Thomas, 'Museums and Archaeology', *Archaeology in Britain 1975–76*, C.B.A. *Report no. 26* (1976), 44–55.

behind field activity, particularly in the matter of the publication of final reports. In general, with a few notable exceptions, little original archaeological scholarship has come out of provincial museums, and recently, with other developments in archaeology to which we shall now turn, university archaeologists have found themselves unable to cope with the level of required archaeological activity, certainly in the field, on top of increasing teaching and bureaucratic loads. Archaeology is by no means unique in this respect: it is a phase of development which other disciplines have experienced, particularly in the last 25 years, but to remember the fact is a useful counterbalance to the romantic, starry-eyed approach to archaeology. In practice, whatever the theory of archaeology, its successful practitioners have to be administrators, managers, teachers and committee-men, in other words men of this world as well as students of past ones.

Applied archaeology

Recently, however, the ranks of archaeological employers have been joined by new members, particularly in Britain, creating a different situation in terms of archaeological employment. The number of full-time jobs in British archaeology, for example, has roughly doubled to about 600 though most are at junior levels, unestablished and with little security. Some of these new posts, as we have mentioned, have been created in non-archaeological central government agencies or in other national bodies. The British Gas Board, for example, recently appointed a field archaeologist, and for some years New Town Development Corporations, like those at Milton Keynes, Peterborough and Northampton have maintained an archaeological presence. The National Trust has a full-time archaeologist on a short-term contract in Wessex. Local Authorities at County and District level have also started to employ archaeologists in addition to those they might already employ in their museums; such posts tend to be in Planning Departments. The common characteristic in these apparently heterogeneous appointments lies with the employer, usually a non-academic as well as a non-archaeological institution: they all require archaeological advice, not primarily to further research or scholarship but for managerial, and perhaps public relations, purposes. In other words, what we are seeing emerge is a demand for what we can call, not practical archaeology, but Applied Archaeology in exactly the same sense as we talk about Applied Geology and Applied Physics. There is apparently a recognisable need for the development of archaeological practice in a way very similar to that in architecture for example. On the one hand, there is architecture as it is taught based on its history, a body of theory and certain techniques and, on the other, the practice of architecture, often corporately expressed as an architectural practice, meeting the needs of clients in the real-life situation of the modern world. Comparison can also be made with Medicine where, on the one hand, we see the Medical Research Council and all that it stands for in terms of pure as well as question-orientated research and, on the other, the training and subsequent work of the G.P. Because of its history, the way it is taught and its employment structure, archaeology lacked its G.P.s until recently, and even now producing them and recognising their role both in archaeology and in the public service are processes engendering, fairly predictably, ostrich-like stances in parts of the archaeological establishment.

In Britain most of the new jobs, however, have been created by new bodies brought into being in large part for that purpose (as if there were not enough employing agencies in British archaeology already). These bodies are small, largely independent committees, most of them legally trusts or charities created as devices to receive State, local government and sometimes other funds and to carry out work in 'rescue archaeology' (p. 172). This is very much a British phenomenon since elsewhere, in the United States for example, the same need has in large part been met by grafting the appropriate organisational structure on to existing academic bodies. This has happened in some cases in Britain—for example in the north using Durham University and in the City of London using the former Guildhall and now the new London Museum,—but over many parts of the country there are now these new bodies, at regional, county, district and town level employing archaeological staff in numbers ranging from one to thirty or forty. Now the point for present purposes is that, unlike the other forms of archaeological employment we have discussed, here the employer engages his archaeologists to practise archaeology, a particular form of archaeology admittedly, but nevertheless the staff are not employed to curate or teach or administer and fit in such creative archaeological work as they may on top of that. In practice of course administration of these new organisations is necessary and individuals may choose to do some teaching for a university extra-mural department for example; but such is incidental to the prime reason for the creation of the posts which is to survey, to excavate and to publish archaeological data. Whether this conception is the proper one is a different matter.

Voluntary archaeologists

The foregoing must not be allowed, however, to give the false impression that archaeology is now solely carried out by full-time archaeologists. Numerically, and certainly in Britain, there are far more part-time archaeologists or, perhaps more correctly, voluntary or spare-time archaeologists i.e. people who gain their livelihood outside archaeology but spend up to a high proportion of their non-working time in archaeological activities. These can range from the relatively passive, such as attending an occasional lecture or field visit, through serious study like taking a course, to heavy commitment in which other facets of personal life, like a job or domestic concerns, become subservient to archaeology. The background to this lies in the history of archaeology, firmly based on the origins and development of learned societies at national, county and local level and, more recently, in the apparent success with which 'Archaeology has already become part of the public scene in Britain, largely thanks to the efforts of a number of brilliant popularizers'.[3] While this quotation is only a half-truth at best, nevertheless there is a public awareness of archaeology and the past which, for better or for worse, simply did not exist even when I began my career. In this climate of opinion, there has been an increase in the numbers of people joining, and indeed forming, archaeological societies and of 'amateurs' active in the field. Very few such participants have recently produced substantive claims to scholarship, despite the great tradition of amateur scholarship of the last few centuries. Furthermore, the criticism can be made that some so-called 'research' groups have been guilty of confusing excavation means with academic ends through the therapeutic clubability of physical, group activity. Nevertheless, the fact is that to a large extent the structure and executive capacity of British archaeology depends on the dedicated individual, the voluntary societies and the large public interest beyond. Collectively, the 'amateur' contribution is essential and the envy of many other countries; furthermore, with all its limitations, the true amateur approach has basic merits which archaeology cannot afford to lose. In virtually none of this is archaeology in any way peculiar: it shares these characteristics and problems with a whole range of social, academic and conservation activities carried along by the subscriptions of the many and the enthusiasm, hard work and expertise of the few who together make up the 'Voluntary Bodies' covering everything from the A.A. to the Zoological Society.

Archaeological destruction

Why has archaeology then been relatively so successful in increasing the number of its employers and employees? What does this involve in practice? And what are the longer-term implications for archaeology itself? These are questions basic to approaches to archaeology today, involving issues of principle and theory quite as fundamental as the scientific/humanistic, nomothetic/ideographic, 'new'/old, debate briefly discussed above (p. 142). It is probably no coincidence that both debates rage simultaneously, for in essence both arise from dissatisfaction produced by the way in which archaeology was, and still is in many respects, being conducted. How, and to what end? are the basic questions behind both controversies, each of which signally contributes to the doubts and optimism in the present dynamic state of archaeological theory and practice.

Let us restate and briefly answer these three questions in order. First, why the explosion? Basically because so much archaeological data, so much of the 'cultural resource base' to use the very appropriate Americanism, is being destroyed (p. 25). Second, what does this involve? Basically a larger, more efficient and in some respects different archaeological response (p. 166). And third, what are the implications? Basically changes in the attitudes of a discipline which is in business to study change yet

[3] *The Times*, 2 July 1976.

persists in obstinate introspection (p. 183). Nevertheless, even here in an area concerned with the very practical issue of archaeological destruction, we are not far from an earlier statement (p. 131) that 'in a sense, all archaeology is theoretical'.

The destruction of and damage to archaeological evidence is, again in a sense, as old as man himself; they are factors inevitable in the process of cultural change and are integral to the nature of archaeological evidence. If human societies did not cast out the old for the new, knock down their inheritance and cover over the resulting debris, there would be no cultural layers in the soil and on the landscape and no sequence of artefacts. So straightway archaeology is in a dilemma, a 'Catch 22' situation. It relies on change for its dynamic yet must rigorously divert or oppose current change which threatens to obliterate the source of that dynamic. Nevertheless, in strictly archaeological terms, it should not argue for preservation because something is old or 'historic' or pretty but because it is a unique expression of human activity at a certain place and time (ideographic), all the more significant if it illustrates a generality (nomothetic). In other words, its archaeological value is evidential not antiquarian, sentimental or aesthetic. The social value or archaeological evidence is something discussed later (p. 192).

There have of course been periods and episodes of great archaeological destruction in the past, illustrated by the Romans (Herod's rebuilding of many an ancient site, for example, removed a lot of evidence), by white settlers opening up the eastern and central American states, and in the mid-eighteenth and nineteenth centuries in England. But none of this was on the scale which we are witnessing in our own life-times. Quite apart from the now serious threat to the world's archaeological heritage posed by the deliberate plundering of treasure-hunters spurred by the money of philistines, inflation-hedging collectors and, sadly, status-seeking art-oriented museums,[4] it is the rate and scale of physical change itself in the modern world which has brought a new dimension, an archaeologically unacceptable dimension, to the traditional role of destruction in archaeology (fig. 6.2). In the past, though we have little idea of what has been lost because so much development was relatively small-scale and manual, quite a lot of archaeological finds were made and some anyway found their way to museums. While archaeology was primarily concerned with finds *per se* rather than with context, function and explanation, archaeology's needs were, in a sense, being met. But as an awareness of the significance of context and of the need to explain in a chronological and cultural framework developed, as excavation technique improved and began to demonstrate the existence of 'remains' other than stone structures, so it slowly came to be realised what damage was being done by the ploughing up of sites hitherto existing as earthworks, by the appearance of suburban man in the countryside

[4] K. Meyer, *The Plundered Past: the traffic in art treasures* (1973); J. Percival in *The Listener*, 11 Dec. 1975, 793-4.

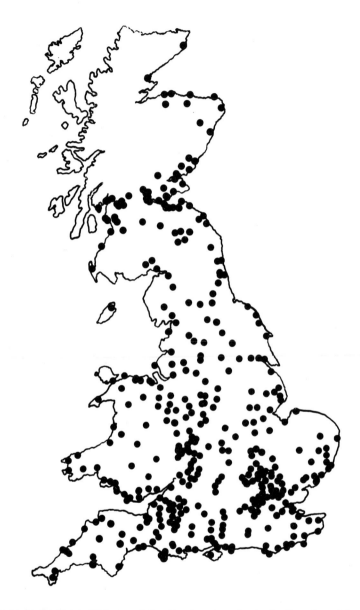

6.2 Historic towns in England, Wales and Scotland archaeologically threatened by modern development: the position in 1972 as published by the C.B.A. in a pioneer type of national archaeological survey. Clearly the situation was out of hand; though crises continue and losses remain heavy, a combination of concerted effort by many of the interests involved and of the effects of inflation have brought the situation, if not under control, then at least on to a more rational basis.

(the making of golf courses was of particular concern to Edwardian antiquaries),[5] and by the demands of an increasingly large and technologically-based society.

The depression of the 1930s gave much of archaeology's data base in the field a last decade or two of life but, from the 1940s onwards and particularly in the pseudo-prosperity of environmental exploitation in the 1960s, archaeological evidence suffered increasingly badly. The main adverse agents were those of 'normal' development: in the countryside, ploughing, forestry, mineral extraction especially of gravel, and all the constructions needed by an increasingly urbanised society—factories, housing estates, airports, motorways, roads, reservoirs, public utilities in, on and above ground, and of course the spaces for the exercise of one of the less happy of contemporary concepts, leisure; in the towns, redevelopment of the centres, development in the suburbs, with all the consequences in terms of disturbed ground. Most of this activity was not deliberately aimed at the destruction of archaeological evidence but it was inevitable that much should be destroyed during such activity and of course the destruction continues still and will continue to occur. It was the speed at which it had been occurring, the extent of its occurrence and, a new factor at least on the 1960s scale, the completeness of the destruction, which finally shook the archaeological world (or parts of it anyway) out of its traditional and quite proper concerns with scholarship, research and theory alone into new areas of moral concern, political agitation and self-questioning.[6] Particularly effective as it turned out were deliberate attempts to make the destruction of sites not merely issues of academic importance but also public issues; and belatedly archaeology tagged on to what, from different starting points had, by c. 1970, clearly become an awakening of environmental consciousness strong enough to have political implications.

Public archaeology

Most of the new jobs in archaeology, the great majority of which have been created in the last five years, stem from the increasing awareness among and the political pressures on the various powers-that-be. Clearly one must allow for a certain amount of informed understanding and goodwill amongst individuals within those powers but it would be a mistake to think that changes, legislative, financial and administrative, have occurred through institutional altruism or bureaucratic benevolence towards archaeology and its subject matter. On the whole, bureaucracy, which by definition has a vested interest in as smooth an operating procedure as possible, does not change unless it is knocked and knocked hard; and it only changes when the knocking reaches that point at which an easier alternative is offered by changing than by continuing existing procedures. This

[5] *See* the *Annual Reports* of the 'Earthworks Committee' of the Congress of Archaeological Societies in the early 1900s.
[6] C.R. McGimsey, *Public Archaeology* (1972); P.A. Rahtz (ed.), *Rescue Archaeology (1974)*.

is what may be read between the lines of official statements such as 'the Department has re-ordered its priorities within approved programmes . . . to make increased funds available . . .'[7]

For a Chapter about present-day archaeology in a book on approaches to archaeology, the approaches to the subject of those who hold the purse-strings and the approach of archaeology to them are extremely relevant to how and what archaeology is able to do. Time may well show that the major archaeological change, and I would hope conceptual advance, of the last decade has been not so much the impact of applied science nor the advent of the 'new' archaeology but the emergence of archaeology as a socially-involved and socially-responsible field of activity *in addition to* its normal and essential academic obligations. In other words, with a bit of luck, some 100 years after its British 'father', Pitt-Rivers, showed it how to walk and nearly 50 years after the Australian Childe began to show it what to walk towards, it might begin to leave adolescence behind.

The position of archaeology then in 1976 has changed in comparison to what it was as recently as 1966; and that change, certainly in America and Britain, has been brought about by the destruction of and threats to archaeological evidence and the reactions of archaeologists, their employers and other bodies to this situation. My second question concerned the practical effect these changes are having on archaeology. In crude terms, it means more: more money, more jobs, presumably more archaeology; it also is promoting the need for more standardisation, more training, more administration, more effective organisation and more thought about what archaeologists should be doing and where archaeology should be going. The big question is perhaps whether all this 'more' means better, and better for whom? —archaeology, archaeologists, the employers (many of whom are neither academic nor archaeological bodies), the interested public or the public at large, the present or the future?

Public money in archaeology

Let us deal with money first of all. The amount of money available for archaeological purposes is tiny compared with most other academic subjects and certainly compared with the sciences; but the amount has increased significantly in archaeology's terms over the last decade and again particularly in the last three or so years. Archaeologists in Britain, for example, used to handling £500 or £1000 for a 'Ministry dig' or £100 for a University department 'field week' up to *c.* 1970 now find themselves, individually or on committees, responsible for budgets in the £100,000 region (fig. 6.3). Similar but absolutely much greater increases have occurred in America. The real increases are of course affected by current inflation and the amounts available in the next few years could well be relatively smaller than in 1974–75. Practically all the increase, in the

---

[7] D.o.E. *Rescue Archaeology in England* (cyclostyled circular, June 1975), 1.

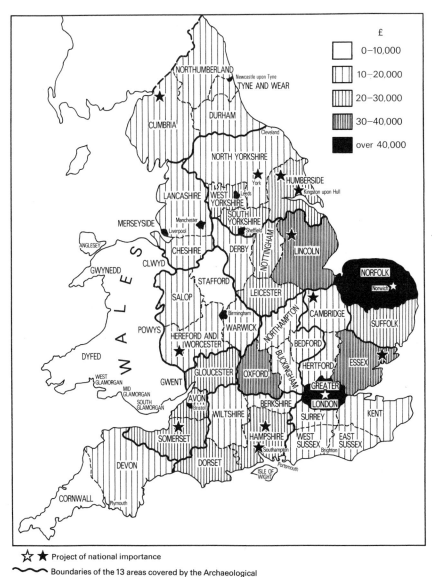

☆ ★ Project of national importance

〜〜〜 Boundaries of the 13 areas covered by the Archaeological
Advisory Committees for rescue archaeology 1976

6.3 Distribution map showing by county where central government's grants for rescue archaeology were spent in England in 1976–7. Grants from the same source to the 'projects of national importance' are not included in the county totals. Advice on the designation of such projects and on general policy is offered to the Secretary of State for the Environment by a national committee appointed by him; thirteen other committees, also appointed by him, advise on the academic priorities in the multi-county areas outlined on the map. The distribution of grants as much reflects their effectiveness and that of the various archaeological executive agencies in their areas (*cf.* fig. 6.5, b) in attracting favourable D.o.E. attention as the national incidence of archaeological destruction or research needs.

States and Europe, has come from governments and their agencies on a 'crisis' ticket, that is to cope with the archaeological consequences of modern society's voracious demands on its environment (p. 165). Certainly in Britain and America there has been an abrupt change from most archaeological fieldwork and excavation being carried out for avowedly research reasons to most of it being carried out for 'rescue' reasons — or at least being carried out with 'rescue' or 'salvage' money.

'Permanent diggers'

In Britain there began to be a related change, fairly abruptly terminated by inflation. As more money became available, particularly for rescue excavation, it became possible for a new group of archaeological helpers to emerge, the 'permanent diggers'. These were usually young people, mostly without archaeological ambition, earning a living by working continuously on excavations, moving from one to another the year round. Some developed into skilled technicians, greatly in demand, while from the director's point of view it began to be clear that, archaeologically-speaking, in circumstances where in particular time allowed, it was more efficient to work over a longer period with a small number of experienced assistants than, as is normal in Britain, to have a short summer excavation with a large number of volunteers, many unskilled, doing the digging under the supervision of the experienced few. But it has quickly become clear over the last two years that, even with the increased money, it is difficult to find enough to maintain a full-time excavating team. What people had overlooked was the difference in cost to the employer between a person on a minimal day rate and a person being paid even a minimal annual salary with the unavoidable overheads. With wage rates rising rapidly and inflation eroding the value of the government grants simultaneously, the potentially valuable establishment of permanent, full-time excavation teams has been largely stifled, and the unrealistic fears being expressed that the amateur and the volunteer were going to be squeezed out of major excavations have been proved groundless. For the time being anyway, it seems that the professionally-run, summer volunteer excavation will continue to be a feature of the British scene, if only for economic reasons.

'Voluntary diggers'

Unrelated to money considerations, of course, the issue of 'Who helps on digs?' has been present for a long time in archaeology. Pitt-Rivers employed in effect a full-time excavation team and the late Sir Ian Richmond always employed a few local workmen rather than volunteers on his excavations. Wheeler in the 1930s was really the first to tap the growing public interest in archaeology as a source of cheap or free labour, partly for economic reasons, and that was the tradition in which my generation grew up. Interestingly, it was noticeable how in 1975–76 it was again relatively easy to find volunteers, looking for a cheap holiday presumably, after some years in which increasing prosperity, and one suspects, a perhaps increasing awareness of a somewhat less than unqualified welcome from the growing number of 'professional' diggers, had tended to lessen the supply. So in one respect it has already been found that more money has not meant more archaeology.

Voluntary archaeological societies

For many involved in the voluntary societies, a fear exists that the current changes might mean no archaeology at all for them personally or for their organisations. Though in part the fear arises from the confusion, once again, of archaeology with excavation, it is justified but only in the sense that very few societies will be able to continue doing by 1980 what they were happily jogging along doing in 1970. The need to change does not of course mean there is no role to play, nor is it exceptional for societies to change the emphases in their functions. The fear of apparent redundancy, expressed by criticisms of the 'professionals', of new organisational structures, of national schemes for training and recognition in archaeology, indeed of many of the symptoms of change itself, — the fear is really of the need to change, to adapt to new circumstances. All the same, influence and certainly primacy has to a large extent passed from the voluntary bodies to professional organisations, though it is as well to remember that it is almost only in Britain that it was ever otherwise. It is doubtful now whether many societies could justifiably mount a large, first-rate excavation from their own resources, and the same is true of University Departments too; and, with a growing awareness of the implications of the act of excavation, it is a measure of the responsible attitude in local societies that many, now deliberately not excavating, should be perplexed as to their *raison d'etre*. But surely somewhere amongst the range of activities now covered by the umbrella of archaeology there is enough to occupy and satisfy as many societies and individuals as may wish to be involved. A problem is that involvement has to be—and admittedly this is, for some literally, the break-point,—on archaeology's own terms as it tries to adapt to the last quarter of the twentieth century. It needs help, it needs voluntary helpers in particular and not least those with non-archaeological skills—in management, public relations, accountancy, secretarial work, illustration and so on—and of course it needs help in the field. One can only hope that the help offered and given is accepted in relation to the needs of the later twentieth century and not to the, perhaps more enjoyable, more extrovert and certainly simpler, approaches to archaeology before 1970.

Publication (fig. 6.4)

One axiomatic feature of that period was that publication, particularly of excavations, was the essential objective of field research. This was and is a matter closely bound up with the voluntary societies since most of British archaeology's results are published through their learned journals. Indeed it is no exaggeration to say that the production of

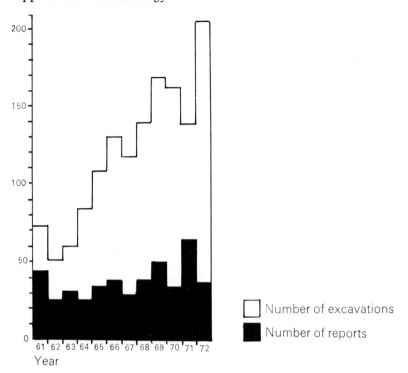

6.4 Histogram of State-financed archaeological excavations and published reports in Britain during the period 1961–72. 1433 excavations are listed as having been carried out in those twelve years while 450 reports, many interim and some very brief, were published. Of 56 'Ministry' excavations in 1964, only 22 had been published by 1972. During the 1960s, while lipservice was paid to the axiom that publication was the academic objective of excavation, few resources were devoted to that end, the assumption being that writing-up was an unpaid activity carried out by an individual in his spare time.

these journals, year by year and characteristically county by county, has been over the last century and more the single most significant contribution to British archaeology from the amateur side. These volumes are literally irreplaceable; yet now, many of the publishing societies are seeing their role diminishing even in this field. They find themselves being squeezed by inflationary publishing costs as excavation reports in particular are becoming bigger, more difficult to edit and less intelligible to the majority of their interested but lay subscribing members. Furthermore, new commercial and perhaps subsidised publication outlets elsewhere can cream off major items of local interest to a greater extent than hitherto, again leading to a local fear that the typical county *Proceedings* is being offered only the second rate or the relatively unimportant. And this is happening. As one of Britain's most prolific archaeological report-writers and editors percipiently remarked: 'Paradoxically the more important the site, the less detail can be published because of length and expense; a single trench can be adequately published while extensive excavations of sites covering several hectares are increasingly difficult to place'. Rahtz went on to summarise 'three grades of archaeological reportage . . . (a) the conclusions, hypotheses, syntheses and interesting finds; (b) the exposition of the evidence; (c) the detail of the stratification, features, finds and scientific reports on which (a) and (b) are based'; and concluded 'It is a paradox that the difficulties of publication apply more to the *evidence* which is unique and unrepeatable, than to the *interpretation* and *discussion* which could be done at any time'.[8]

In the face of these difficulties and, it must be said, in default of regular, major, academic publication outlets through State-subsidised media in Britain such as are enjoyed by archaeologists in, for example, Scandinavia, Holland, West Germany, America and Eastern Europe, the axiom of publication has now been modified. Since it now appears that it has been more honoured in the breach than the observance over the last 25 years anyway (p. 170), perhaps little practical change will result; but certainly the report of a Department of the Environment sub-committee which looked at the problems of publication is conceptually important.[9] 'Publication in printed form of all details of a large modern excavation is no longer practical, and it is necessary to redefine acceptable practice.' After identifying four levels of records arising from excavation, the report recommends that, '*provided certain conditions are fulfilled*, refined publication at Level IV should be the objective in future . . . for archaeological excavations in general. The conditions, which are essential, are:

(i) that all the original records of the excavation, properly organized and curated, are housed in readily accessible form in a permanent archive,
(ii) that data at what we have described as Level III are readily available on request.

This presupposes an archive with duplication and, if possible, computer print-out facilities and equally demands from the excavator a high standard of preparation of Level III data, equal to that required for publication itself.' Level III is defined as 'Full illustration and description of all structural and stratigraphical relationships. Classified finds-lists and finds-drawings, and all specialist analyses'; while Level IV is 'Synthesized description with supporting data. Selected finds and specialist reports relevant to synthesis'.

The implications of this recommendation, such a radical break from the British tradition that it is a cardinal principle that archaeologists should publish their work in

[8] P. A. Rahtz in L. V. Grinsell *et al.*, *The Preparation of Archaeological Reports* (2nd ed., 1974), 19.
[9] D.o.E. *Principles of Publication in Rescue Archaeology* (October, 1975).

full in a permanent form,[10] are very considerable, not only for the publishing societies but also for archaeologists and archaeology, and for museums. The last are enjoined in the same report not only to undertake the custody of Level I-III records as a condition of obtaining custody of the finds but also that custody of the excavation records involves a duty to make available Level III data on request at cost price. Though the logic of all this is irrefutable, the whole scenario seems to bear little relationship to the real world of present-day archaeology, lacking cohesive organisation, adequate resources and internal self-discipline but with a huge backlog of unassimilated material and a, still, largely amateur background. Furthermore, some of the deductions are questionable since not all the background data are seen to be correct; and no consideration is given to the thought that Local Record Offices, which are equipped for the job, rather than museums should be the repository of all the original documentary material resulting from an excavation. It will nevertheless be interesting to see how near archaeology comes to meeting these principles in practice in the rest of this century. I would have thought a more realistic way of tackling the undoubted crisis in publication would be to restrict very considerably the number of new excavations supported by public funds by putting extra effort into their avoidance rather than into machinery with which to cope with their consequences. By accepting the premise that archaeology's 'main sources of new raw material' is excavation and by making rescue archaeology synonymous with rescue excavation throughout, the Report avoids some significant issues and developments on the current scene concerning not only publication but also what is actually happening in British 'rescue' archaeology. Nevertheless, it is a very important document and one hopes, a harbinger of the better-quality advice beginning to emanate from central government in this field.

Archaeological organisation and rescue archaeology (fig. 6.5)

Moving on to some of the other practical effects of the changes in the last few years, in many ways archaeology must present a sorry, or at least a gauche, sight to the outsider; for in many respects, the increased money (and in America in 1974, a change in the law putting statutory responsibilities on the developer with regard to the cultural resource base), came too suddenly. So much effort was put into bringing about the change that there had been little thought or preparation for coping with the consequences. As a result, archaeology in England especially is organisationally fragmented while belated attempts are made to start, even to think about, matters which are fairly basic to the new order and which, in a well-run organisation, would have been sorted out in advance. Practical matters like training archaeologists for the new roles which they are now expected to perform in the public service, non-degree accreditation, career structures—these, and a range of other matters inevitably arising when staff are taken

[10] Stated in almost exactly these words by P. Rahtz, *op. cit.* note 8, 18.

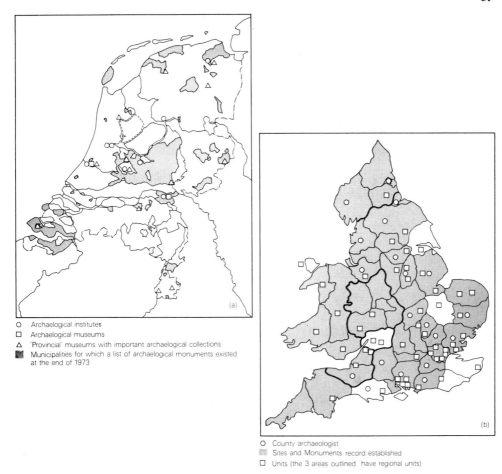

○ Archaelogical institutes
□ Archaelogical museums
△ 'Provincial' museums with important archaelogical collections
▨ Municipalities for which a list of archaelogical monuments existed
   at the end of 1973

(a)

(b)

○ County archaeologist
▨ Sites and Monuments record established
□ Units (the 3 areas outlined have regional units)

6.5 While not completely comparable, these two maps of Holland and England/Wales give some idea of the extent and distribution of local, professional, archaeological executive resources in two of the most 'archaeologically advanced' countries in the world, particularly in relation to rescue archaeology (major caveats must be the differences in the roles of the universities, the museums and local voluntary societies in the two countries). The equivalent of the Dutch archaeological institutes does not really exist in Britain except at London University though, given time, one or two of the 'Units' in England or Wales might perhaps develop in that direction. Their basis in counties rather than regions (with three exceptions) is not in their favour in this respect, however, for a county is too small an area for long-term academic institutional worthwhileness, whatever its convenience for political and Local Authority administrative purposes. Some of the 'Units' shown here are only of one or two people and have no security. More permanent should be the County Archaeologists, some now with their own staffs; the spread of these across the map—there would have been one symbol ten years ago— represents one of the most remarkable of British archaeology's recent developments. The growth of systematic, Local Authority-based archaeological records, though many are in their infancy, is also a recent phenomenon, distributionally now impressive, and this phenomenon probably can be fairly compared with the Dutch situation.

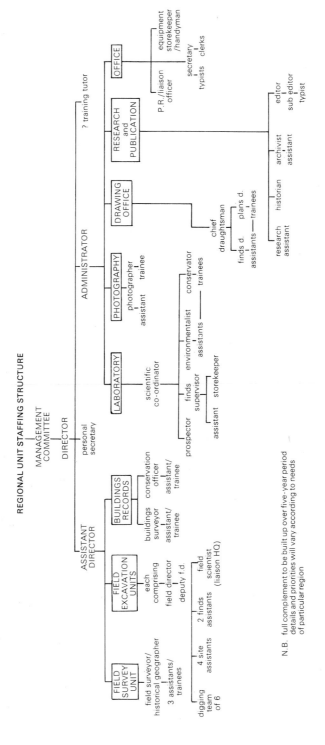

REGIONAL UNIT STAFFING STRUCTURE

MANAGEMENT COMMITTEE

DIRECTOR

personal secretary

ASSISTANT DIRECTOR

ADMINISTRATOR

? training tutor

FIELD SURVEY UNIT

field surveyor/ historical geographer

3 assistants/ trainees

digging team of 6

4 site assistants

2 finds assistants

FIELD EXCAVATION UNITS

each comprising

field director

deputy f.d.

field scientist (liaison HQ)

BUILDINGS RECORDS

buildings surveyor

assistant/ trainee

conservation officer

assistant/ trainee

LABORATORY

scientific co-ordinator

prospector

finds supervisor

assistant storekeeper

environmentalist

assistants

conservator

trainees

PHOTOGRAPHY

photographer

assistant

trainee

DRAWING OFFICE

chief draughtsman

finds d. assistants

plans d. trainees

RESEARCH and PUBLICATION

research assistant

historian

archivist assistant

editor

sub editor

typist

OFFICE

P.R./liaison officer

secretary

typists

clerks

equipment storekeeper /handyman

N.B. full complement to be built up over five-year period details and priorities will vary according to needs of particular region

174

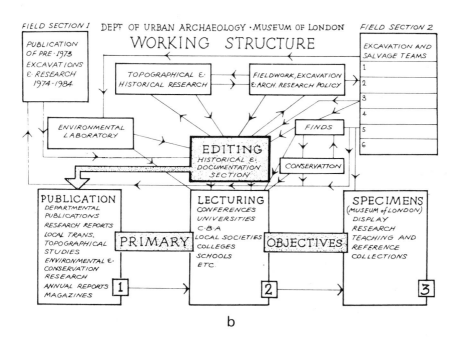

b

6.6 Dream and reality: (a) shows the sort of regional archaeological organisation envisaged in England in 1972–3 at the time when central government funds for rescue archaeology suddenly increased. A dozen or so such organisations were thought necessary and possible and, despite the 'rescue' tag, the intention was to set up in effect a series of research institutes rather on Dutch lines. The result is displayed on fig. 6.4, a large number of small units of questionable academic and cost-effectiveness. (b) is a flow chart demonstrating a co-ordinated working structure with multifarious operations and specific objectives as drawn up (1976) by the chief executive of one of the largest of the new archaeological organisations to emerge from the 1972–3 situation, ironically perhaps, in view of the hopes then, confined to one of the smallest local authority areas in the country, the City of London, and largely committed to a field programme of urban excavation alone.

on by employers, have largely been left to chance, improvisation and individual initiative and hard work. No principles, no practical guide-lines, except an indication that 'regional arrangements' were to be encouraged, were intitially promulgated from the Government Department issuing the money but unwilling to shoulder the consequential, and legally quite frightening, responsibilities. A regionally-based executive organisation would in fact have had the support of most archaeologists but the idea was stillborn and what many feel was a marvellous opportunity to restructure important sections of British archaeology was lost, not to return in my time, in the summer of 1973 in a muddle of non-archaeological politics, indecisiveness and incompetence (fig. 6.5). Two years later, the continuing poverty of thought about first principles, and the lack of appreciation of the realities of even the limited field of 'rescue archaeology', were devastatingly revealed in a long-awaited DoE circular which was sent to Local Authorities.

Its first words are:

> '1. Archaeology is the study of the physical evidence—structures and artefacts, both visible and buried—of the history of mankind. In Britain selected monuments and archaeological sites have long been protected and preserved under the Ancient Monuments Acts. But preservation is not always possible, and sometimes may not be essential since excavation to discover and record the evidence concealed beneath the ground may be sufficient. The particular purpose of *rescue archaeology* is the speedy investigation of the evidence contained by sites which are shortly to be destroyed, archaeologically speaking, by urban re-development, new roads, mineral extraction and various other forms of development.'[11]

Though tempted to write that there is no answer to such a misleading statement,[12] one or two points about it are worth comment as we move on to my third question (p. 162) about the longer-term implications of the changes for archaeology. Since some archaeologists deplore the fact that the 'rescue' tail now wags the archaeological dog, we ought to look a little more closely at this curious appendage because a lot depends on what is meant by 'rescue archaeology'. I have just quoted the official definition but will not waste time on it since its elementary confusion of rescue archaeology with salvage excavation is so obvious. Excavations consciously to 'rescue' information from sites threatened with destruction were first undertaken by the Government during the 1940s, though clearly there had been a lot of salvage work before that (p. 163).[13] Such

[11] *Op. cit.* note 7, 1.
[12] Though one is provided from within the Department itself by the Chief Inspector of Ancient Monuments and Historic Buildings in 'Rescue Archaeology', Appendix 2 to the *Twenty-second Annual Report* of the Ancient Monuments Board for England (June 1976). *Cf. Rescue News* 10 (1975), 11–12 and *Antiquity* 199/200 (1976), 230–2.
[13] Ministry of Works, *War and Archaeology in Britain* (1949).

excavations continued, slowly increasing in number but not in proportion to the increase in destruction in the 1950s and 1960s;[14] and, while in America the 1950s saw the development of long-term 'salvage' programmes, attempting to bring academic good out of what appeared at the time to be practical necessity, by and large reactions in Britain remained *ad hoc* and single-site-oriented.[15] The exceptions to this generalisation were significant, however, for it was out of such planned, long-term 'rescue' programmes as those on deserted medieval villages, henge monuments (both largely emanating from the DoE itself) and Winchester that a new consciousness of what rescue archaeology, as distinct from smash and grab digs, could and should be began to emerge.[16] About the same time, from the mid-1960s onwards, but particularly with the development of the Council for British Archaeology's role vis-a-vis Town Planners and County Councils,[17] and subsequently with the formation of a 'popular' action organisation in 1971 called RESCUE (it was actually extremely unpopular in some quarters), it fairly quickly came to be realised that the problem was being tackled in the wrong way (fig. 6.6).[18] Instead of dashing around trying to stop the increasing number of holes in a leaky bucket, the thing to do was to change the bucket or, better still, put the water somewhere else. The emergence of archaeology as a factor in the Planning process, first for its own sake and then as a positive contributor to informed Planning decisions and land-management in the public interest, has been and remains one of the more satisfactory developments that I have seen. The development has a very long way to go yet, but it has already had a considerable effect.[19]

[14] R.C.H.M., *A Matter of Time* (1960); *Monuments threatened or destroyed* (1963); *Report of the Committee of Enquiry into the Arrangements for the Protection of Field Monuments* (Cmnd. 3904, 1969). Activities and attitudes are generally reflected in the *Annual Reports* of the Ancient Monuments Board and the C.B.A.

[15] *Cf.* for example, some of the American projects on river basin/reservoir areas with the annual, one-by-one barrow excavations (mostly unpublished) financed by the Ministry of Works in Wessex.

[16] M. Beresford and J.G. Hurst (eds.), *Deserted Medieval Villages* (1971); G.J. Wainwright and I.H. Longworth, *Durrington Walls: Excavations 1966–68* (Soc. Antiqs. Research Rpt. 29, 1971), with a general view of the 'henge programme' summarised by G.J. Wainwright in P.J. Fowler (ed.), *Recent Work in Rural Archaeology* (1975), 57–71; for Winchester, interim reports *Antiq. J.* (1964–75, final reports in M. Biddle (ed.), *Winchester Studies* I—(1976–).

[17] C. Heighway, *The Erosion of History* (1972).

[18] *Current Archaeol.* 23 (1970), 343–5 gives an already dated but contemporary view immediately before the foundation of Rescue. The situation as perceived and possible developments from it were discussed by several authors in P.J. Fowler (ed.), *Archaeology and the Landscape* (1972). *See also* Rescue/C.B.A., *Archaeology and Government* (1974); and note 16 above.

[19] The real test in England will be during 1977 when it should become apparent whether or not County Councils are making more than a formal nod in the direction of 'the historic environment' in the preparation of their statutory Structure Plans. Meanwhile, it is difficult to give publication references for successful archaeology/Planning co-ordination because it best occurs *within* County Councils and other bodies with archaeologists on their staff and therefore with little publicity, but an early and excellent example of the *genre* was the Consultative Draft of the Aspect Report *The Historical Environment* (1973) prepared and circulated by Bedfordshire County Council when reviewing its County Development Plan. Documents along similar lines have been prepared or are being prepared in other counties e.g. Essex, Wiltshire, Somerset.

Approaches to Archaeology

Tomorrow maybe too late.
Rescue

6.7 The poster produced by RESCUE soon after its inception in 1971. This deliberate, visual dramatisation—'You *must* include Stonehenge to get across to the public',—of the destruction of archaeological sites was certainly effective, despite the shudder of distaste in certain quarters and the unintentional ambiguity of the picture itself. Some people misinterpreted it, thinking that the bulldozer had swooped in and *rescued* Stonehenge from some unspecified threat, and consequently gave it a meaning—'Rescue! Hurray!'—exactly the opposite to the one intended. The design nevertheless became the logotype of RESCUE, symbolising much that was wrong and much of the archaeological motivation around 1970. It is already inappropriate since it no longer represents the vanguard of archaeological practice or concern, even within the 'rescue' field itself.

The Historic Environment

Outside the new, major, urban 'rescue archaeology' units such as those in the Cities of London and York, for example, a high proportion of the effort of the new archaeological organisations created in the wake of rescue archaeology's political success is going into field survey, not excavation. This is reflected in the growing list, from 1974 onwards, of their publications, surveying gravels, towns, whole regions.[20] The best of them represent a step forward from the 'implications of development' surveys of the previous decade because they not only deal with the principles of what we can legitimately call, again borrowing from across the Atlantic, 'conservation archaeology' rather than with specific threats, but they also present a basic academic statement of the archaeology and its potential in the topic or area they cover. In fact, some go further because what they are really identifying, wholly or in part, and consciously grading into a hierarchy of conservation merit, is what in another piece of jargon we can call 'the historic environment'. Conceptually, this is most significant because in it we see one of the ways in which archaeologists are breaking away from survey as merely the preliminary to excavation, from excavation as the be-all and end-all, from a single-site orientation, and from a backward-looking stance to a present in which they are in effect trying to identify that part of our cultural heritage in the landscape which could, if society so wishes, survive into the twenty-first century.[21] In other words, largely through the work of archaeological practitioners, we have moved very quickly from a desperate position in which we were literally scraping pieces of the past off the bulldozer blade, through one where we were allowed to survey and excavate within defined parameters of space and time on specific developments, to one in which archaeological data is being collected and assessed generally, not merely to make archaeological decisions, not merely the better to inform Planning decisions, but crucially to contribute towards better-informed land-management programmes of a long-term nature.

Following the initial break-through into the consciousness of some land-managing interests, the sympathy and interest of their professional staffs has greatly facilitated the

[20] The policy decision behind this is set in its 'official' context in D.o.E., *Archaeological Excavations, 1975* (1976), 2–3. Examples of the product are, for a whole region, P.A.G. Clark and P.F. Gosling, *Archaeology in the North* (1976); for the towns in a county, R. Leech, *Small Medieval Towns in Avon* (1975), K. Rodwell (ed.), *Historic Towns in Oxfordshire* (1975), M. Hughes, *The Small Towns of Hampshire* (1976) and J. Haslam, *Wiltshire Towns* (1976). Similar surveys are in preparation for other counties e.g. Cornwall, Devon, Dorset, Somerset, Gloucestershire and Berkshire. The countryside is more difficult to come to grips with and among the few quotable references so far are those in Chap. 2, note 11, plus C. Gingell, *Archaeology in the Wiltshire Countryside* (1976).

[21] The pioneer book is T. Rowley and M. Breakell (eds.), *Planning and the Historic Environment* (1975). Parallel with the development of the idea of managing archaeology as a resource comes the argument that archaeologists must manage themselves and their other executive resources. The influences are strongly transatlantic: for belated English reactions *see*, for the former, P. J. Fowler and A. Ellison, 'Archaeology on Exmoor: its nature, assessment and management', *Exmoor Review* 18, 1977, 78–84 and, for the latter, B. Hobley, 'The Need for Modern Management in Archaeology', *Rescue News* 11 (1976), 5–6.

development of archaeology's interests in their concerns. One is thinking here, for example, of major land-managing interests like the National Trust, the Nature Conservancy Council, the Forestry Commission, the War Department, the Countryside Commission, the Duchy of Cornwall and Local Authorities. While much of the progress here has come through the employment of professional archaeologists by the Local Authorities and the new archaeological Units, an interesting side-effect has been the need for authoritative, independent advice. As a result archaeological consultancy on a professional but personal level has begun to grow on similar lines to, for example, geological and engineering consultancy. The C.B.A. has tried to 'help those requiring archaeological advice by compiling lists of appropriate people' for developers and those responsible for the care of churches; and there are now at least two, albeit small, archaeological consultancy companies. For a compound of reasons, however, archaeology's professional practitioners in these fields are not yet professionally organised in Britain, whereas in America a scheme of professional accreditation is now being implemented.

Although it may appear from this that the development of archaeology as a land-management factor represents a professional monopoly, curiously and happily the same factor has produced reactions in the amateur sector too. Some reactions are, sadly, sour—'We've had a county archaeologist for a year and he hasn't done an excavation yet' is typical,—but they stem from misunderstanding of a professional's role in this field. He is not there to do old style archaeology but to do something different, something which archaeology simply did not attempt before. One man on his own, however, cannot simultaneously tackle the brief for this type of post, characteristically phrased as:

> To establish and develop a Sites & Structure Record for Loamshire
> To liaise with Planners and Developers on archaeological matters
> To advise the Council as appropriate on its statutory obligation in matters relevant to Ancient Monuments & Historic Buildings
> To develop the Council's Archaeological Service

VI.1 '... to try and cut out such situations before they develop': salvage excavation and recording along a waterpipe trench outside Uleybury hill-fort, Glos., in July 1976, here cutting through a Roman temple. A throwback to the bad old days of 1960s-style rescue archaeology, this episode could have been avoided if archaeology had been a factor considered at the planning stage. By the time knowledge of the plan surfaced in archaeological circles (by accident as it happened), it was too late to alter the line of the necessary trench which went through a scheduled hill-fort and a roman settlement outside. Given the circumstances, everyone concerned was most helpful and the archaeological consequences were coped with successfully but at considerable cost and inconvenience.

> To co-ordinate Rescue Archaeology
> To develop the existing links between the Council, the Inspectorate of Ancient Monuments, the C.B.A. and the voluntary and academic interests working in Loamshire

The basis of the post is the county Record or Index of Sites, Monuments and Structures, probably non-existent to begin with, and it is here that the volunteer and local society can help (fig. 6.4). The single professional can never hope to cover, let alone known in detail, the whole of his area, so he must rely on others to build up the basic record which, quite apart from its academic significance, is primarily going to be used as a source of information and assessment in everything from Structure Plans to individual Planning applications. Even without a County or other full-time archaeologist, some local societies have seen the need for putting their existing information together in a systematic way so that others can use it and for carrying out further systematic survey. The 'parish checklist' of one kind or another is now a growing form of amateur activity and, in returning to the roots of the English archaeological tradition, represents probably the most worthwhile role that the local society can perform in the field today, for itself, for its locality and for archaeology.[22]

The particular purpose of rescue archaeology is not, then, 'the speedy investigation of the evidence contained by sites shortly to be destroyed'. It has a particular responsibility to identify and record the cultural resources in the landscape, and to communicate the information to planners, to other land-managers and land-users, and to the public. In practice this means, for example, not merely sitting back and waiting until the next pipeline cuts through the next Roman settlement, which is then 'salvaged' with whoops of masochistic joy in a blaze of publicity, but in taking deliberate and conscious action to try to cut out such situations before they develop (Pl. VI.1). To do this means, *inter alia*, trying to educate a wide range of non-archaeological, often professional, interests. Archaeology needs to do that anyway, but what it needs above all in Britain is adequate legislation similar to that in America, most European countries and many of the newly-emergent countries. It is needed not just to provide static preservation or to inhibit archaeological activity with red tape but to give the field evidence its rightful status, and to provide the subject with the necessary base for educating other land-using interests in their responsibilities towards the cultural heritage.[23]

[22] The rationale is developed in P. J. Fowler (ed.), *Archaeology and the Landscape* (1972), chaps. 3 and 4. The results of such activity are represented in recent times by the classic V. Russell, *West Penwith Survey* (1971) and current issues of, for example, *Cornish Archaeol.*, *Proc. Devon Archaeol. Soc.*, *Somerset Archaeol. Natur. Hist.* and *Bull. Bristol Archaeol. Rsch. Gp.*

[23] As is happening in America. The most recent official English legislative proposals are in the 'Walsh Report' (Cmnd. 3904), *op. cit.* note 14, now in part overtaken by events. Further legislation has been prepared by the D. o. E. and more is pressed by the C.B.A. but, even if all were agreed, it seems almost impossible to find Parliamentary time to introduce new proposals.

VI.2 '. . . such episodes represent failure': quarrying of the interior of the largest hill-fort in England on Ham Hill, Somerset, in 1975, an episode resulting from legal loop-holes, unawareness and non-communication between the various public bodies involved. The archaeological (and other) consequences of a decision to build a nearby by-pass which required hardcore could have been brought to light long before the crunch if an American type environmental impact statement had been commissioned before or when the decision was taken. As it was, given that a totally avoidable situation had arisen, the good-will of the several parties involved, stimulated by considerable public pressure and media coverage, sorted out the problems at one site meeting.

Education and the media

To educate and communicate is indeed one of the major problems now facing not just rescue archaeology but the whole discipline. While archaeology's audience was but a few *cognoscenti*, the problems did not exist and the subject was self-justifying; but now the audience is of millions and its appetite is voracious. Yet it is at this time that archaeology has lost the simple, extrovert character which enabled it unselfconsciously to be good 'copy' and popular 'show-biz'; it has lost confidence and become introverted, it has changed its objectives and methods from the discovery of 'lost civilizations' and the drama of desperate eleventh-hour digging, and it is tending to wrap itself up in protective, verbal gobbledygook. Even rescue archaeology is not truly exciting any more in media terms for there is little journalistic mileage in a Sites and Structures Record or a parish checklist. And when a Roman villa does unexpectedly turn up, or a coin-hoard is salvaged from beneath a bull-dozer, the realistic archaeological practitioner knows in his heart of hearts that such episodes represent failure (Pl. VI.2). 'We are trying to take the drama out of rescue archaeology' I said in a recent public lecture, and you could hear the interest silently switch off.

There is then a dichotomy between 'good' archaeology and the public expectation of the archaeological product; yet never has archaeology so needed public support. It is, however, important to distinguish between archaeology as 'news' and archaeology as a topic for popular but informed consideration. For the latter, archaeology can be straightforward as well as sophisticated depending on the needs of the occasion,

VI.3 'countless . . . lectures on sites . . .' A professional archaeologist acting as a part-time University Extra-Mural tutor expounds to a group of adults on a residential weekend course the significance, not of the ecclesiastical architecture, but of the position of the church in relation to the topography of the Saxon 'burg' of Langport, Somerset. 1976.

without being false to itself; it is more difficult to retain integrity in the former. The dichotomy is really between, on the one hand, the television cliché of the trowelling row of pretty young girls kneeling towards the camera or the newspaper headline BIG DIG BONES UP ON 'FRED' and, on the other, the presentation of modern archaeology as a responsible, changing and significant contribution to society. The latter can be achieved, as some newspapers and some television and radio productions demonstrate from time to time, but this line is not exciting in the way that the mass media seem to expect archaeology to be. Furthermore, presumably in part because at the intellectual level archaeology has now shifted its focus, archaeologists themselves seem to find it more difficult to project either themselves or their interest with quite the conviction or simplicity of the earlier days of popular archaeology. This is understandable, however regrettable in public relations terms, but somehow archaeology and the media have to develop a new understanding based on archaeology as it is rather than how it was ('Where is today's Sir Mortimer?' is a question I have been asked). Yet, paradoxically, there is already more exposure and presentation of archaeology for the public than has ever previously existed, not only through radio, T.V. and the press but in countless displays, exhibitions and lectures on sites, in museums, libraries and other gathering places (Pl. VI.3). The demand is presumably there otherwise publicly-supported organisations like the B.B.C., universities and museums would not devote their self-justifying resources in this way, and commercial organisations, like publishers, would not risk their money on it. At the same time, more people than ever before are visiting archaeological monuments, putting pressure on the custodians of this public part of the cultural heritage not only in practical terms of crowd control but also in more subtle ways concerning what people expect and what they should be provided with. Hence the growing awareness of 'Interpretation', not in the academic sense in which the word has hitherto been used here but with the meaning of acceptable presentation to an educational end. American experience, particularly in the National Parks Service, is influential here and can be seen at work in those Visitor or Interpretative Centres already active in Britain.[24] It should cause little surprise to archaeologists to find that once again Pitt-Rivers had wise things to say on this subject too, 85 years ago: 'The outing is in itself an important accessory in a visit to a country museum. A pretty country, a pleasant drive in their country carts, an attractive pleasure ground, a good band, a menagerie of birds and animals, and, lastly, a museum, are the means . . . which I am justified in recommending to those who wish to draw the people out of the towns into the country . . . .'[25]

Most archaeological sites are presented to the public in totally inadequate terms by such criteria, modern or nearly a century old, and while it is clearly not desirable to turn even all the 'public' sites into junketing places, the field of Interpretation could well

[24] Countryside Commission, *Guide to Countryside Interpretation, parts 1 and 2* (1975).
[25] Lieut.-General Pitt Rivers, *Excavations in Bokerly and Wansdyke, Dorset and Wilts 1888–1891*, III (1892), Appendix D, 307.

represent the area for some of the most significant developments in archaeology as a serious but popular study in the next decade and more.

Particularly is this so as archaeology becomes increasingly used as a subject in schools, not perhaps so much in its own right but as part of environmental and field studies. Indeed, a great deal more thought and effort has to be put into archaeology-as-education generally, since again new and different demands are being made on it compared to the not very distant days when educationally and academically it sufficed for it to attend almost exclusively to the needs of future archaeologists at University level. In all this of course archaeology is merely growing up, and these symptoms of the process are shared in many respects with other fields of scholarship which, having 'gone public', continue to require an academic base. 'Natural History' is the obvious parallel.

Treasure-hunting and the 'lunatic fringe'

There are, however, two activities in which present-day archaeology, as a rational method of investigating the past for the benefit of contemporary and future society, is particularly vulnerable to harm. Both undermine its conceptual or intellectual base and one, treasure-hunting, is also a serious threat to its material base. The quest for treasure in the sense of intrinsically valuable objects is of course a long-standing tradition in which institutions and individuals, museums and antiquaries as well as collectors, have participated; but it has not been a major activity on British soil over the last century although the Crown, by perpetuating Treasure Trove, a medieval provision for its own financial benefit, has been ready to reward at market value those who declare finds of gold and silver. This typically insular anachronistic compromise worked at least to the satisfaction of the British Museum while most such finds of gold and silver were made *accidentally*; but since c. 1970, archaeology has found itself in a totally different situation following the commercial promotion in Britain from America of the idea of treasure-hunting as a fun-hobby for the family and a regular source of income for the dedicated 'professional'. The promotion, appealing to the ERNIE or football pools vision of the sudden (and unearned) cash jackpot, was made possible by the development of transistorized metal detectors, electronic gadgets which in a different guise are familiar to every airline passenger. Metal detectors in themselves are socially useful and unobjectionable; the use of any one or a number of differing detecting devices is, and has been for three decades, a normal procedure in archaeological site investigation.[26] What is new, or at least a pernicious rehash of an old idea, is the encouragement for financial profit, by the manufacturers, sales organisations and the individual, of the concept and practice of treasure-hunting; both must be totally unacceptable to

---

[26] R.J.C. Atkinson, *Field Archaeology* (1946), with a section on resistivity surveying added in the 2nd ed. (1953), 31–9; *see also* Section VII: 'Prospecting' in D. Brothwell and E. Higgs (eds.), *Science in Archaeology* (2nd ed. 1969), and M.J. Aitken, *Physics and Archaeology* (2nd ed. 1974).

archaeology. The concept is dangerous to archaeology, which by definition is not profit-motivated but which can so easily seem to have profited from treasure-hunting in the past; the practice is injurious because of the physical damage it occasions to archaeological sites and material, because of the secrecy it encourages, the cash value it places on normal as well as exceptional archaeological finds, and the anti-archaeological publicity it engenders. All the media, television, radio and newspapers (including 'respectable' ones), have been guilty of archaeological—and I would say social,—irresponsibility in their attitudes towards treasure-hunting in the last few years: in that the promotion and practice of treasure-hunting seeks to exploit a communal heritage for personal gain, it must be anti-social as well as academically unacceptable.

The well-organised treasure-hunting lobby of course say that their followers do not damage archaeological sites and counter the production of tangible proof, as at Blaise Castle, Stokeleigh, Uleybury and Ham Hill, to mention but four scheduled hillforts alone within thirty miles of where I write, by saying that the predators are not true treasure-hunters. I suppose that means they are irresponsible treasure-hunters. But in any case, the claim of non-interference is nonsense because, while the practice involves the digging of little holes all over the place to remove metal objects, how can any one judge whether or not a site has been damaged?—you cannot assess a house by looking through a keyhole. Even though a lot of messing about with metal detectors is innocent, in the sense that wilful or malicious damage is not intended, the effect is the same: a context is lost, potentially a site is damaged, some information has gone forever. As far as the objects are concerned, undoubtedly many never surface for academic appraisal and, though some appear in salerooms, the rest pass into private collections or are exported. When objects are reported, museums are in a particularly awkward situation and their roles have been in some cases ambiguous if not distinctly dubious. Is it better to accept, probably pay for, an unprovenanced object or collection, with no questions asked, for the sake of the object but knowing such a course could well be party to theft, is almost certainly conniving at archaeological damage and will probably encourage further depredations in the field; or is it better to refuse, knowing that the material will probably find a buyer elsewhere and could well be lost to public availability? The dilemma is real and acute though archaeologically, since the objective is information not objects, there is really no doubt that the second course is the only option. Fortunately, some of the more responsible museums are openly announcing their adherence to such an accessions policy: context not aesthetics or cash is slowly becoming at least a princeling if not yet king.

Archaeology itself is virtually defenceless against the idea and practice of treasure-hunting. In Britain anyway, part of its tradition has been to make freely available the locations of sites and finds: its information base is readily accessible on Ordnance Survey maps, on museum labels and in countless well-intentioned books and other publications. Furthermore, now that its as yet unrecorded material is known to be in effect ubiquitous (p. 51), any digging anywhere has an academic potential. It is too late to shut the stable door for the horse, quite properly, was allowed out centuries ago. But it is precisely this availability of information which is being exploited by treasure-hunters, and here lies the archaeological dilemma: excepting the chance find, the sources, indoor research and field methods necessary for successful treasure-hunting are virtually identical with those for successful archaeological field research. The only, but significant, differences are in motivation and the end product: self-profit v. intellectual curiosity; cash v. a contribution to knowledge. While, therefore, attempts have been and are being made to thwart treasure-hunters by scattering metallic waste over sites, by mounting twenty-four-hour guards over excavations, by not publishing particularly sensitive information, by deliberately not mentioning certain finds in lectures and by various other tedious and academically dangerous subterfuges, the conflict is essentially one of radically different approaches to the past and must be fought as such. In that the desperately-required new legislation necessary at least to inhibit the activities of cultural looters will be an expression of society's wishes and not just what archaeologists know to be needed, then the battle to be won is strategically a philosophical one and tactically a political one. It may seem a minor issue but basically it raises the questions of who the past is for and how it is to be treated. Is it there to be exploited at will and at the whim of the individual for private gain, or is it there to be used carefully in the interests of society as a whole? In other words, in the last resort legitimate archaeology will not prevail, although it undoubtedly has a case by its own criteria, by arguing that treasure-hunting is *academically* unacceptable; it must present, and win, the argument that treasure-hunting is *socially* unacceptable.[27]

Unfortunately, no such case can be presented, at least with conviction, against the other recent development which is solely an intellectual threat to legitimate archaeology. This is the romantic, speculative approach to the past, based on selective use of evidence, imagination and a populist appeal to the past's mysterious aspects. Though there has recently been a veritable flood of such obscurantist publications, it would still be possible to dismiss them as merely a modern manifestation of the attraction of archaeology to an ever-present lunatic fringe were it not for the fact that the trend has developed from being just popular to become, in certain quarters, a cult. The cult of the mysterious through pseudo-study of megaliths and stone circles, ancient art, Celts and Druids, folk-lore, folk-tradition and place-names, often linked together by old straight tracks and ley-lines, is easy enough to sneer at from a superior academic point of view but, whether or not it presents a 'true' picture of the past, it presents a plausible picture to the layman and apparently an increasingly attractive model of the past to the disillusioned, anarchic element in the outlook of modern society. Certainly it appeals strongly to many students. In those senses, it has to be taken seriously by legitimate archaeology, the position of which it is seriously eroding.

---

[27] For the obvious reason that I do not wish to provide free publicity for anti-archaeological interests, this section has no references.

It is a challenge which archaeologists have not accepted, largely on the principle apparently that if you ignore or are sufficiently rude about something, it will go away. But there are now probably more people, generally interested in or actual students of the past, whose appreciation of the past has been initiated by, or whose understanding is influenced by, the persuasive writings of 'the mysterious past' school of romanticism than there are adherents of an archaeological approach based on reason, learning and academic judgement. 'What is the reason for reason?' asks the enquiring but cynical young mind, faced with the inconclusiveness and apparent irrelevance of much current archaeological scholarship on the one hand and, on the other, the vision of a past when men walked in harmony with Nature, possessed powers since blunted by industrialisation, capitalism and urban living, were guided by forces we can no longer perceive and, *in extremis*, solved problems and initiated change with the help *deorum ex machinis* (the space sort). It is a very attractive picture to many in the modern world, and publishers in particular, some with otherwise respectable archaeological lists, have not been slow to exploit the bandwagon. And how is the layman, even if he so wished, to choose between 'good' and 'bad' archaeology when the pseudo, often looking more attractive anyway, nestles cheek by jowl with the genuine on the shelves in the archaeology section of reputable booksellers? Just as treasure-hunting quite seriously presents society with an alternative to archaeology in its treatment of and attitude towards material culture, so does the cult of mystery with all its attractions to the modern mind present an alternative interpretation of that material culture which is easier, more confident and in many ways more plausible than the hard-won fragments of archaeological scholarship. If a function is adduced for archaeology (p. 192), and yet an alternative, unarchaeological approach to the past is more successful in producing what society wants, then archaeologists should indeed be worried.[28]

Archaeology and the 'cultural resource base'

Despite, or perhaps more urgently because of, the strains imposed on the subject and its practitioners as a result of becoming 'popular', archaeology nevertheless has a basic, general responsibility, like other branches of learning, to the academic interests of its field of study as well as to the society of which those practitioners are but the informed members in this particular field. In both respects, archaeology has to think very hard about its own attitude towards its source material. The discipline of archaeology does indeed require a continuous flow of new information: that is its life-blood by which it shapes our changing appreciations of the past. But the assumption that new data must come mainly, or can come only, from excavation is an assumption to be questioned. For long it has been a commonplace that excavation of necessity destroys as it proceeds: it is a non-repeatable exercise on a unique combination of circumstances, and hence the

[28] *Op. cit.* note 27.

189

emphasis, so strong in archaeology until recently, that excavations must be published in full. But just as other development exploits our natural resources, and indeed our cultural ones too, so archaeology in relying so heavily on excavation is also exploiting that cultural resource. Furthermore, it is a finite resource. We may be creating the archaeology of our own times and discovering that of the nineteenth century, but we cannot add one jot to what is already there, on, in and under the ground. We can discover, as has indeed happened, that more exists than we knew of, and it is of course accepted that our knowledge is relative; but the evidence, the data, the cultural resource, call it what you will, is finite in quantity and, like the world's mineral resources, is being depleted. In some cases, parts of that resource are already exploited to extinction, they are worked out: you could not, for example, go to see surviving on the ground an example of a 'Little Woodbury', one of the best-known types of late prehistoric settlement site in southern England. The fact that air photography is revealing hitherto unknown types of site is another indication of what has been flattened and, in some degree anyway, lost; and unlike wild-life or flora, since man's cultural heritage is in itself inert, for all our cleverness we cannot breed back lost species of site.

With so much being destroyed anyway, one would have thought it possible to construct academically viable research programmes by the exploitation of sites with limited futures. This is of course precisely what American-style 'contract' archaeologists and some British rescue archaeologists are trying to do, once they have built the archaeological dimension into land-management programmes. There is little future in trying to deal with every salvage opportunity after it has arisen and archaeology must develop the maturity and strength to say 'no'. Equally, it must develop the status which begins by getting the facts right so as to be able to say 'no, not under any circumstances' to development proposals for certain representative as well as outstanding parts of the historic environment. That 'no' must be for archaeological exploiters in the guise of research excavators and site-conservation experts as much as for the public utilities and the commercial developers. We quoted a passage above (p. 120) asserting the rights of other scientific interests in archaeological sites and we would extend the principle further. Archaeologists have tended to assume that, because they 'know about such matters', sites belong to them. They do not. They belong to the

VI.4 '. . . communally they will need a past . . . a sort of social reference point . . .': Tourists and holidaymakers in August, 1976, at the *Cutty Sark*, part of the nautical complex available to the public at Greenwich, downstream from London. Public access to and interest in maritime history, particularly appropriate in Britain's case, has developed simultaneously with the provision of land-based 'Interpretation' and is reflected academically by the growth of 'nautical' archaeology as a serious discipline. Facilities like the *Cutty Sark* seem to meet a public need; equally, the public's money is needed to preserve and maintain such 'living history'.

present as its heritage and potentially to the future as its heritage from us. What our successors make of it is up to them and is neither our responsibility nor really our concern; but part of our responsibility is to see that they are at least able to exercise an option on their heritage. They may not want it, they may destroy the lot; but unless we are to postulate a radical change in the nature of being human, we must assume that, in some way, communally they will need a past. The cultural heritage which archaeology seeks to find, examine and explain provides a sort of social reference point, a form of communal memory, a group identity (Pl. VI.4). People need to know where they are and to feel that they belong, in time, in place and with their fellow human beings.[29]

This book has been as much concerned with the approaches of archaeology to the past and the present, as with the approaches of the past and the present to archaeology. Despite studying the past, we cannot scientifically predict the future; but it is part of the human condition which prompts curiosity about the time dimension, just as it does with space, to try to find out and, at worst, to guess. If the study of man-made things has a purpose, surely it can be realised through its contemporary society, now and in future, rather than through a fossilized past. Archaeology is indeed not about things but people, and the quick as much as the dead.

[29] For me, this is the underlying message of George Orwell's *Nineteen Eighty-Four* (1949), perhaps the most cogent and sustained argument in print for the need of a past.

Bibliography

M. J. Aitken, *Physics and Archaeology* (1974)
American Antiquity
Antiq. J. (1964–75)
Antiquity 199/200 (1976) 230–2
Archaeology
Archéologie
R. J. C. Aitkinson, *Field Archaeology* (1946, 1953)
M. Beresford and J.G. Hurst (eds.), *Deserted Medieval Villages* (1971)
M. Biddle (ed.), *Winchester Studies* I- (1976–)
D. Brothwell and E. Higgs (eds.), *Science in Archaeology* (1969)
R. Bruce-Mitford, *Recent Archaeological Excavations in Europe* (1975)
Bull. Bristol Archaeol. Rsch. Gp.
G. Clark, *Archaeology and Society* (1939, 1947, 1957)
P. A. G. Clark and P. F. Gosling, *Archaeology in the North* (1976)
Congress of Archaeological Societies, *Annual Reports* of 'Earthwork Committee' (early 1900s)
Cornish Archaeol.

Countryside Commission, *Guide to Countryside Interpretation, parts 1 and 2* (1975)

O.G.S. Crawford, *Said and Done* (1955)

Current Archaeology 23 (1970) 343–5

D. o. E., *Archaeological Excavations 1975* (1976); *Principles of Publication in Rescue Archaeology* (1975); *Rescue Archaeology in England* (1975) 1

P.J. Fowler (ed.), *Archaeology and the Landscape* (1972); *Recent Work in Rural Archaeology* (1975); and A. Ellison, 'Archaeology on Exmoor: its nature, assessment, and management', *Exmoor Review* 18 (1977) 78–84

C. Gingell, *Archaeology in the Wiltshire Countryside* (1976)

L.V. Grinsell *et al.*, *The Preparation of Archaeological Reports* (1974) (P.A. Rahtz 19)

J. Haslam, *Wiltshire Towns* (1976)

C. Heighway, *The Erosion of History* (1972)

B. Hobley, 'The Need for Modern Management in Archaeology', *Rescue News* 11 (1976) 5–6

M. Hughes, *The Small Towns of Hampshire* (1976)

R. Leech, *Small Medieval Towns in Avon* (1975)

C.R. McGimsey, *Public Archaeology* (1972)

K. Meyer, *The Plundered Past: the traffic in art treasures* (1973)

Ministry of Works, *War and Archaeology in Britain* (1949)

C. Nylander, *The Deep Well: Archaeology and the life of the past* (1969, 1971)

George Orwell, *Nineteen Eighty-Four* (1949)

Lieut. General Pitt-Rivers, *Excavations in Bokerly and Wansdyke, Dorset and Wiltshire 1888–1891* (1892)

Proc. Devon Archaeol. Soc.

P.A. Rahtz (ed.), *Rescue Archaeology* (1974)

R.C.H.M., *A Matter of Time* (1960); *Monuments threatened or destroyed* (1963)

Report of the Committee of Enquiry into the Arrangements for the Protection of Field Monuments (1969)

Rescue/C.B.A. *Archaeology and Government* (1974)

Rescue News; 10 (1975) 11–12

K. Rodwell (ed.), *Historic Towns in Oxfordshire* (1975)

V. Russell, *West Penwith Survey* (1971)

Somerset Archaeol. Natur. Hist.

G.J. Wainwright and I.H. Longworth, *Durrington Walls: Excavations 1966–68* (1971)

Sir Mortimer Wheeler, *Still Digging* (1955)

Sir Leonard Woolley, *As I seem to Remember* (1962)

FURTHER READING

For the serious student or teacher, the best advice is to acquire *British Archaeology: an introductory booklist* (1976) from the C.B.A., 7 Marylebone Road, London NW1 5HA, price 75p. In referring to the many publications in the footnotes, some care has been taken to quote recent books and other publications which should be reasonably easily obtainable, and to indicate some of those with good bibliographies and those which this writer finds particularly useful. That information is not repeated here; the following are a few *additional* recommended titles primarily for the beginner, the student or the lay person looking for a reliable opening into some aspects of the fairly extensive bibliographical field touched on in the preceding pages.

Chapter 1
G. Childe, *Man Makes Himself* (1936, 4th ed. 1965); *What Happened in History* (1942); *Social Evolution* (1951, 1963); *Piecing Together the Past* (1956)
G. Clark, *World Prehistory* (1969); *Aspects of Prehistory* (1970)
G. Clark and S. Piggott, *Prehistoric Societies* (1965)
G. Daniel, *The Idea of Prehistory* (1962, 1964); *The Origins and Growth of Archaeology* (1967)
T.S. Eliot, *Notes towards the Definition of Culture* (1948, 1962)
B.M. Fagan, *Introductory Readings in Archaeology* (1970); *In the Beginning: an Introduction to Archaeology* (1972)
P. Gardiner, *The Nature of Historical Explanation* (1952, 1968)
E.H. Gombrich, *In Search of Cultural History* (1969)
A. Marwick, *The Nature of History* (1970)
J.H. Plumb, *The Death of the Past* (1969)
F.T. Wainwright, *Archaeology and Place-Names and History* (1962)
J.N. Woodall, *An Introduction to Modern Archaeology* (1972)

Chapter 2
M. Aston and T. Rowley, *Landscape Archaeology: an introduction to fieldwork techniques on post-Roman landscapes* (1974)
H.C. Bowen, *Ancient Fields* (1961)
J. Forde-Johnston, *Hillforts of the Iron Age in England and Wales: a survey of the surface evidence* (1976)
W.G. Hoskins, *The Making of the English Landscape* (1955)
Ordnance Survey, *Map of Southern Britain in the Iron Age* (1967); *Map of Roman Britain* (1956); *Britain in the Dark Ages* (1966); *Britain before the Norman Conquest* (1973)
O. Rackham, *Trees and Woodland in the British Landscape* (1976)
L.D. Stamp, *Applied Geography* (1960)
C. Taylor, *Fields in the English Landscape* (1975)
U.N.E.S.C.O., *Field Manual for Museums* (1970)
D.M. Wilson (ed.), *The Archaeology of Anglo-Saxon England* (1976)

Chapter 3
S. Hirst, *Recording an Excavation 1: The Written Record* (1976)
G.D.B. Jones, *Roman Manchester* (1974) (pp. 173–83, 'System Planning in Urban Archaeology')

Chapter 4
K.W. Butzer, *Environment and Archaeology* (1972)
J. Renfrew *et al.*, *First Aid for Seeds* (1976)
A. Rosenfeld, *The Inorganic Raw Materials of Antiquity* (1965)
S.A. Semenov, *Prehistoric Technology* (1964)

Chapter 5
W.I.B. Beveridge, *The Art of Scientific Investigation* (1950)
C.L. Redman (ed.), *Research and Theory in Current Archaeology* (1973)

Chapter 6
P.V. Addyman and R.K. Morris (eds.), *The Archaeological Study of Churches* (1976)
M. Biddle and D. Hudson, *The Future of London's Past: a survey of the archaeological implications of planning and development in the Nation's capital* (1973)
J. Bishop, *Opportunities for Archaeologists* (1976)
R.A. Buchanan, *Industrial Archaeology in Britain* (1972)
C.B.A., *Signposts for Archaeological Publication* (1976)
A. Thom, *Megalithic Sites in Britain* (1967)
U.N.E.S.C.O., *Underwater Archaeology: a nascent discipline* (1972)

ACKNOWLEDGEMENTS

Figures

Although most are new drawings, many are derived, in inspiration or content, from specific sources which it is a pleasure to acknowledge. The co-operation of the extant organisations and living individuals referenced is greatly appreciated.

1.1 A. L. F. Rivet and D. Allen in *Britannia* 1, 1970, figs. 2 and 1, respectively pp. 38 and 4.

1.2 Andrews' and Drury's *Map of Wiltshire* (1773) (reproduced in facsimile, *Wilts. Archaeol. Nat. Hist. Soc.* 1952).

1.3 W. Phelps, *The History and Antiquities of Somersetshire* (1836), Pl. V; O. G. S. Crawford and A. Keiller, *Wessex from the Air* (1928), fig. 34; G. Wainwright, *Trans. Bristol Gloucestershire Archaeol. Soc.* 86, 1967, fig. 2 opp. p. 43.

2.1 R.C.H.M., *Dorset* III, pt. 2 (1970), maps in end pocket.

2.2 Author.

2.3 O.G.S. Crawford, *Air Survey and Archaeology* (1924), Pl. IIIB.

2.4 Institute of Cornish Studies, Exeter University and Cornwall County Council.

2.5 a/c author; b/d C.C. Taylor, *Wilts. Archaeol. Natur. Hist. Mag.* 62. 1967, 82, 98, figs. 2, 7.

2.6 D.R. Wilson, *Antiquity* 49, 1975, 183, fig. 2; R. Cramp in D. M. Wilson (ed.), *The Archaeology of Anglo-Saxon England* (1976), 202, fig. 5.1.

3.1 P. A. Rahtz, *Excavations at St Mary's Church, Deerhurst, 1971–3* (C.B.A. Rsch. Rpt. 15, 1976), fig. 2. *See also Antiq. J.* 55, 1975, 352, fig. 2.

3.2 M. Biddle, *Antiq. J.* 55, 1975, opp. 320, fig. 16.

3.3 Author.

3.4 P. V. Addyman, *Antiq. J.* 54, 1974, 220, fig. 11.

3.5 W. A. van Es, *ROB*, 22, 1972, 121, 122, figs. 1 and (part of) 2.

3.6 Author.

3.7 P.J.R. Modderman, *Nederlandse Oudheden III*, 1970, Taf. 7.

4.1 Author.

4.2 R. M. Clark, *Antiquity* 49, 1975, 256, fig. 2.

4.3 W. Pennington in J. G. Evans *et al.* (eds.), *The Effect of Man on the Landscape: the Highland Zone* (C.B.A. Rsch. Rpt. 11, 1975), 77, fig. 3; P. J. Spencer, *op. cit.*, 101, fig. 4.

4.4 L. P. L. Koojimans, *ROB*, 20–1, 1970–1, 31, Table 1.

5.1 Author.

5.2 W. Phelps, *The History and Antiquities of Somersetshire* (1836).

5.2 Author, very much influenced by the work of P. A. Rahtz and other colleagues in the preparation for publication of the excavation report on Cadbury Congresbury, Avon (*forthcoming*).

5.4 J. A. Taylor in J. G. Evans *et al.*, *op. cit.* 4.3, 9, fig. 2; G. Ll. Isaac in D. L. Clarke (ed.), *Models in Archaeology* (1972), 177, fig. 4.1.

5.5 J. G. Hurst in D. M. Wilson (ed.), *op. cit.* 2.6, fig. 7.1, E, F; I. Hodder, *Wiltshire Archaeol. Natur. Hist. Mag.* 69, 1974, 74, fig. 5 (*also* in *World Archaeol.* 6, 2, 1974, 185, fig. 21).

5.6 A. Ellison and J. Harris in D. Clarke (ed.), *op. cit.* 5.4, fig. 24.27; O. H. Frey and F. Schwappach, *World Archaeol.* 4, 3, 1973, 348, fig. 19, and 351, fig. 22; D. L. Clarke in D.L. Clarke (ed.), *op. cit.* 5.4, fig. 21.10; J.J. Butler and H. Sarfatij, *ROB.*, 20–1, 1970–1, 306, fig. 4; ultimately J.H. von Thünen, *Der isolierte Staat in Beziehung auf Landwirtschaft und Nationalökonomie* (1826), trans. by P. Hall (ed.), *von Thunen's Isolated State* (1966).

6.1 B. E. L. Long in G. D. B. Jones, *Roman Manchester* (1974), 178–80, figs. 58, 57, 60.

6.2 C. Heighway, *The Erosion of History* (C.B.A. 1972), Map 1.

6.3 *Rescue News* 13, 1977, 1

6.4 P. V. Addyman, *Rescue News* 6, 1974, 1, fig. 1.

6.5 W. Van Es, *Rescue News* 8, 1974, 8–9, figs. 1, 2 (*cf.* also R.H.J. Klok, *ROB.* 22, 1972, 88, fig. 4); D.o.E., *Archaeological Excavations 1975* (1976), 164, fig.

6.6 1, and (for Wales) Dyfed Archaeol. Trust Ltd., *Report 1975–6* (1976), 6.

6.7 P. A. Rahtz, *Rescue News* 4, 1973, 3; B. Hobley, *Rescue News* 11, 1976, 6, fig. 3. RESCUE, *A Trust for British Archaeology* (1971).

Plates

All are from photographs taken by the author except:

II.3   O. G. S. Crawford, *Air Survey and Archaeology* (1924), Pl. III.

Acknowledgements

II.4	Professor J. K. S. St. Joseph, Director in Aerial Photography, University of Cambridge.
II.5–6	John White, West Air Photography, Weston-super-Mare, Avon.
III.1	J. Curle, *A Roman Frontier Post and its People* (1911), Pl. XI, 1; T. Zammit, *Archaeologia* 17, 1916, Pl. XV, fig. 3.
III.4	D.o.E., courtesy of Dr. G.J. Wainwright.

INDEX